marquee

THE STORY OF THE WORLD'S GREATEST MUSIC VENUE

ROBERT SELLERS
WITH NICK PENDLETON

First published in 2022.

Text © Robert Sellers 2022. Prologue © Nick Pendleton 2022

A CIP catalogue record for this book is available from the British Library.

ISBN 978-0-9935702-4-7

Edited by Andrew Humphreys
Proofread by Omer Ali
Book design and layout by Gadi Farfour
Cover by Gadi Farfour

www.paradiseroad.co.uk

Printed by TJ Books Limited, Padstow, Cornwall

'The reason I liked the Marquee was because it was scruffy and a hellhole, and your feet stuck to the floor, and that's exactly what a rock and roll club should be like.'
Lemmy

CONTENTS

PREVIOUS SPREAD: The Marquee stage set
up for a gig by Twelfth Night, in November 1983.

ACKNOWLEDGEMENTS

Special thanks must go to Harold and Barbara Pendleton. And to our editor Andrew Humphreys. We would also like to thank the following Marquee musicians, fans and staff members for sharing their memories and stories: Kingsley Abbott, Gaye Advert, Matt Aitken, Ian Anderson, Jon Anderson, Buttz Babysitter, Tom Bailey, Eddie Baird, Chris Barber, Jack Barrie, Dermot Bassett, Arturo Bassick, Raymond Bennett, Ed Bicknell, Ian Broudie, Bill Bruford, Garry Bushell, John W Callis, Phil Carson, Nick Cash, Zal Cleminson, John Coghlan, Mel Collins, Gail Colson, Laurie Coombs, Len Crawley, Jimmy Dickinson, Chris Difford, KK Downing, Timothy du Feu, Johnny Duhan, Graham 'Dumpy' Dunnell, John 'Eddie' Edwards, Peter Egan, Graham Fellows, Graham Field, Fish, Dana Gillespie, Alan Gorrie, Dennis Greaves, Ron Griffiths, Robert Hagger, Phil Harding, Pete Haynes, John Helliwell, Des Henly, Myra Hickey, Jon Hiseman, Mike Hugg, Nigel Hutchings, Lee Jackson, Brian James, Paul Jones, Simon Kirke, Steve 'Lips' Kudlow, Ray Laidlaw, Phil Lancaster, Dave Lawson, CP Lee, Carl Leighton-Pope, Graham Lewis, Leo Lyons, Manfred Mann, Barrie Masters, John Mayall, Robin Mayhew, Jim McCarty, Tom McGuinness, Klaus Meine, Dave Meniketti, Tony de Meur, Les Mitchell, Adam Mole, Michael Monroe, Gerald (GT) Moore, Tony Morrison, Pauline Murray, Steve Nardelli, Dale Nathan, Peter Nicholls, Roger Nickson, Simon Nicol, Andy Parker, Andy Powell, Don Powell, Uli Pritz, Colin Richardson, William Ritchie, Steve Rowland, Jim Sach, Joe Satriani, Jill Saward, Andy Scott, Keith Scott, Paul Shuttleworth, Ed Silvester, Dave Sinclair, Judge Smith, Dee Snider, Sal Solo, Spike, Spizz, Pete Staples, James Stevenson, Dennis Stratton, Trevor Tanner, Dick Taylor, Ian 'Bush' Telfer, Bruce Thomas, Ray Thomas, Mike Tobin, Bernie Torme, Simon Toulson-Clarke, Edward Tudor-Pole, Nick van Eede, Brian Walkley, Johnny Warman, Geno Washington, Pete Waterman, Stan Webb, Robb Weir, Chris Welch, Howard Werth, Simon White, Alan Whitehead, Steve Williams, Muff Winwood, Pete York and Bob Young.

The publisher would like to thank Peterjon Creswell, Mike Holmes and Peter Watts.

PROLOGUE

Bust my back on the Levy, broke my strings on the BBC
Found my chops on Eel Pie Island, paid my dues at the Marquee
Slagged off by the NME, *lost my stash, my virginity*
In this cockamamie business
'Cockamamie Business' by George Harrison

In appearance, the Marquee was nothing special. It was, for most of its life, a small venue on Wardour Street in Soho. There was little to see from the street, except a plate-glass front door. Inside, the main room looked like a bomb fall-out shelter. It could only legally accommodate about 600 people, although that limit was frequently broken. Most of the bands were barely known at the time they first appeared at the club. They had to contend with backstage facilities that would shame a village scout hall, and a performance space that could get so hot and starved of air that performers occasionally passed out. Initially, there was no booze either, because the club didn't have a licence. But it was the place every band wanted to play. A gig at the Marquee announced that a band had left the orbit of the suburban pub circuit and was on its way up. It was the place where agents, managers and journalists went to check out new talent: contracts could be signed before the stage was cleared and a memorable performance could land a band their first notices in the music weeklies. It was the gateway to the big time.

A gig at the Marquee was no guarantee of success in itself, but the list of artists that were launched from its cramped stage started with the Rolling Stones and ran through Manfred Mann, the Yardbirds, the Who, Pink Floyd, David Bowie, Jethro Tull, Yes and King Crimson, to Adam and the Ants, Dire Straits, U2 and Marillion. It was a roll call that served as an inspiration to every musician that passed through the doors of 90 Wardour Street. Such was the legend of the Marquee that when Paul Weller and Pete Townshend arranged to meet for the first time they wanted to be photographed together outside the club. The Stones, Bowie, the Sex Pistols and Wham! filmed there. There were probably more live albums recorded at the Marquee than any other venue. When

North American artists like Simon and Garfunkel, REM, Metallica, Bryan Adams and Guns N' Roses came to the UK they wanted to play the Marquee. As Mike Rutherford from Genesis said: 'You're often asked what you wanted to do when you left school. I remember thinking at the time that my goal was simple: to play at the Marquee.' Rutherford wasn't thinking of the building or the facilities; the Marquee was special because it was the right venue, at the right time, in the right place, run by the right people.

The right people started with my dad, Harold Pendleton. He launched the club in 1958, assisted by mum, Barbara. It started as a jazz club but when my parents sold the Marquee thirty years later, it was as a venue for rhythm & blues, psychedelia, rock, pub rock, prog rock, heavy metal, punk, new wave, indie, goth and more. Unlike say, the Cavern, the Marquee was never associated with any one band, or any single musical genre. No other club was ever home to so many tribes.

The Marquee also set itself apart through a strong brand identity. There was that wonderfully distinctive logo, which was launched relatively early in the club's history, and which quickly came to represent a stamp of quality. There were music fans who would visit the club almost regardless of who was on. They knew there was always the chance they'd be watching the superstars of tomorrow. 'The Marquee had that reputation of developing major acts,' says Jethro Tull's Ian Anderson. 'That in itself engendered a brand identity which was very powerful.'

The location, slap in the middle of Soho, added greatly to the appeal of the club for musicians and fans alike. Here was where the songwriters and agents of nearby Tin Pan Alley mixed with the TV and film executives of Wardour Street; where the ad men of Golden Square mingled with music biz talent spotters, pluggers and managers, along with the producers and technicians from nearby recording studios. Coffee shops, restaurants, bars and late-night clubs provided a life-support system to keep it all turning over, 24/7. Soho was one big enticing shop window and any band playing the Marquee knew they were performing for an audience studded with the promotors, journalists and fellow musicians who could help on them on their way. And there would be a guaranteed good night after the show.

Like most things in life, luck and timing were critical to dad and mum's success, but to my mind, my parents were skilled at making the best of the opportunities that came their way. In many cases those opportunities came about because there were a number of unglamourous but fundamental principles that helped steer them in the right direction.

The first of them is that the Marquee was born out of a passion for music. My dad left the money-making potential of the City to pursue his love of jazz. He had an idea that he could make a living from what was at the time an amateur pursuit, patronised by the rich or those bohemian enough not to care about money. He wasn't interested in making his fortune or in being famous – and he never achieved either, although his sound grasp of finances meant we were always comfortable and his streak of independence earned him some notoriety in the business. His motivation was to provide a platform for the musicians playing the music he loved and to share that music with the widest audience possible.

But dad was shrewd enough to see beyond his own passions. The Marquee was always focused on what was coming next. The club embraced every new genre and indeed helped create many of them, particularly in the mid 1960s when it seemed there was a new movement coming along every month. Not being defined by any one musical genre was key to the club's longevity.

From the beginning, the Marquee was also more than just a music venue. Its impact was enhanced, at the time it was launched, by being part of a wider group, the National Jazz Federation. Later, the Marquee would expand to include an artists agency, a management company, a recording studio, a production company, a supplier of sound and light services, and a festival. This meant that Marquee bands could benefit from far greater exposure and opportunities than the typical live music venue could offer.

The Marquee was run professionally. My dad, a keen but limited jazz drummer from Southport who trained as a chartered accountant, was an unlikely music entrepreneur. But a personality that inclined him to honesty, meticulousness and a view to the long-term, while also being open to risk and taking a punt on an intriguing idea, led to the creation of a successful and long-lasting multi-stranded enterprise that never felt corporate. While some clubs, festivals or promoters shone brightly and made a splash, all too often they blinked out of existence, typically leaving a shower of unpaid bills and angry creditors. The Marquee and its associated festival just kept going. They were known within the industry for being the most consistent and well-run musical showcases and the safest venues for fans. Dad liked to say, 'I don't want to be the biggest, just the best.'

The Marquee companies flourished by sharing responsibilities and encouraging innovation. Everyone found in my dad a willing backer and reliable partner. He supported Kit Lambert and Chris Stamp's ground-breaking promotion of the Who's residency at the club; funded Phillip Wood's construction of a recording studio; supported Giorgio Gomelsky in his temperamental management of the Rolling Stones and Yardbirds; allowed Charlie Watkins of WEM to debut the world's first 1kW outdoor sound system; gave the go-ahead to Keith Albarn (father of Damon) to design a new type of festival stage; partnered with Pat Chapman to set up Entec to revolutionise lighting design; backed DJ Gerry Collins to run the first London gay super club; hosted Stock, Aitken and Waterman at the Marquee Studios while they developed the 80s Hit Factory sound; and helped Peter Gabriel secure the future of his Womad festival. Dad was always open to a good pitch and operated like a one-man *Dragon's Den*.

When I reflect back on what I am most proud of about the Marquee, it's not any of the landmark gigs, or the innovations or collaborations. It is the fact that my dad was brave enough to follow his passion and was dedicated enough to learn the skills to make his dreams a reality. The fact he created a group of companies that positively impacted so many lives, and were instrumental in creating so many moments that so many people will never forget. That he met and married my mum, worked with her as an equal partner in business and life for over sixty years, and encouraged other family members to join them. And, among all of this – and the music business is a notably volatile environment – together they gave me such a loving and supportive home. That is a legacy to which everyone can aspire to, whatever it is we do.

Nick Pendleton

WELCOME TO THE JUNGLE

'It's good to be in fuckin' England, finally!' shouts Axl Rose as Guns N' Roses take to the stage and immediately kick into opening number 'Reckless Life'. It's Friday 19 June 1987 at the Marquee, and it's the band's first gig in Europe – almost their first gig outside of their home base of Los Angeles. A roar of applause greets the end of the first song and, before it dies down, Slash's fuzzy sheet-metal guitar kicks into 'Out Ta Get Me'. It's all looking good – until the first can of beer whistles by Rose's head.

Over the previous two years, GN'R had been working the West Coast rock scene, one among a host of flash bands with radical hair and a 1970s album collection. It was their manager Alan Niven's idea to fly the band to the UK in the hope of creating a media buzz that would give them some credibility back home. Niven knew about the Marquee, knew that it was where the Rolling Stones and the Sex Pistols had played – *Exile on Main Street* and *Never Mind the Bollocks* were GN'R favourites. He thought it wouldn't hurt to have his band linked with bands like those.

In advance of their transatlantic jaunt, the band's label, Geffen, had flown a bunch of UK music writers out to see GN'R live in LA, so when the band arrived in London there was already a buzz building. The five band members – Rose, Slash, Izzy Stradlin, Duff McKagan and Steven Adler – spent the week leading up to the gigs rehearsing at a rental studio, and otherwise hanging around Soho, shopping for clothes, getting drunk and picking up girls. The Marquee's manager, Ian 'Bush' Telfer, had been warned that the band's performances were so incendiary that on occasion they exploded into riots. 'They ended up being the nicest bunch of blokes,' says Bush. 'I had to tell Axl to stop calling me sir.'

Before the first show, Niven sat the band down for a pep talk. Listen, he said, they're going to look at you like a bunch of LA wankers. They're going to test you. They're going to yell at you. They're going to spit at you. And if you blink, you're dead. You give as much as you get.

Which may be why Axl Rose's response to that first thrown can is to scream, 'Hey! If you wanna keep throwing things, we're gonna fuckin' leave. Whaddaya think?' Another missile crashes into the drum kit.

'Hey!' Axl screams. 'Fuck you, pussy!' Clearly rattled, the band continues on with 'Anything Goes'. They perform eight of the twelve tracks on their soon to be released debut album, *Appetite for Destruction*. The missile throwing stops but there is plenty of heckling between songs. GN'R close out the show with Aerosmith's 'Mama Kin', introduced as a song they play 'better than the other fuckers'. As the band leaves the stage, Slash invites the crowd to a drink at the bar.

'They came off drained,' recalls Bush. 'I came backstage and Axl was collapsed on the floor of the dressing room and Slash was being sick in the sink. The crowd were baying for more, and I told them to get back on stage. They did another couple of numbers, came back off again and they couldn't even talk.' A journalist for the heavy rock fortnightly *Kerrang!* was not impressed. He thought the band had bottled it, rattled by some thrown beer cans.

The second Marquee show was three nights later, on 22 June. The support band that night was Little Angels, a rock outfit from Scarborough. Keyboard player Jimmy Dickinson remembers arriving early for the gig and catching Slash soundchecking on stage. 'He's literally got a cigarette in his gob, he's got his top hat on, he's stripped to the waist and he's playing his Les Paul down by his knees with his ear up against an enormous speaker going, "I can't hear my fucking guitar." I literally couldn't stay in the room because it was so loud. I was seventeen and it just blew my mind.' Dickinson watched the Guns N' Roses set from the bar. 'It was unbelievably exciting. There was something in the air, you could smell it, this electricity, and you just knew they were going to take over the world from that one tiny show.'

During their stay in the UK there were numerous reports of the destruction wrought, particularly on their accommodations, but the band seemed to have nothing but respect for the Marquee. 'Nothing untoward went on,' says Bush. 'They were only too happy to get a case of beer as a little present at the end of each night.' Their sole mark on the place was made on the night of their third and final gig, on 28 June, when the band added a scrawl on a dressing room wall that read 'Guns N' Roses, a way of life'. But there was already so much graffiti on the wall that the new addition was hardly noticeable.

Four months later, GN'R were back in London, walking off stage having performed to a packed Hammersmith Odeon, and well on their way to becoming the biggest rock band in the world. By early January of the following year, *Appetite for Destruction* had sold a quarter of a million copies in the US and would eventually reach No.1 on the *Billboard* chart. But, as band manager Alan Niven said, 'It was in Britain that we first generated a buzz'. Just another band blasted to stardom from the modestly sized launch pad of the Marquee stage.

Slash of Guns N' Roses interacts with fans at the Marquee in June 1997.

ARE YOU HERE, HAROLD?

Getting off the train at Euston Station, not knowing a thing about London, twenty-four-year-old Lancastrian Harold Pendleton caught the first bus that came along and told the conductor, 'Drop me off where the action is.' This turned out to be the top of Charing Cross Road. Walking down past the street's parade of bookshops, Harold came to a place with a notice in the window that read 'Jazz records'. 'I went inside and there was a chap in a mac going through a pile of 78s. I tapped him on the shoulder and said, "Excuse me, do you know where the London Jazz Club is?" He said, "Yes, I'm going there myself. You can come with me." It was Chris Barber.' The year was 1948.

Dixieland jazz was Harold's passion. He discovered it by chance thanks to an afternoon paddle off the coast of his hometown of Southport. He often went swimming with a friend called Frank Wilson, who happened to play trumpet in a traditional jazz outfit called the Dixielanders. One morning, Frank asked if Harold fancied coming to a gig of theirs on Southport pier. 'I really only went along because my mate was playing, and I was hooked immediately.' This was the early 1940s, well before the explosion of rock'n'roll, so, like a lot of teenagers of the time, Harold's musical tastes until that point were for barbershop quartets or dance bands. Jazz music was a revelation, totally different to anything he had heard before.

Born 17 June 1924, Harold was the first son of George and Ada – he was later joined by a brother, Bob. As a boy he helped out in the family confectioner's business. He was an avid reader and a good dancer, regularly visiting the nearby Blackpool Tower ballroom. Once he got the jazz bug he was keen to get his hands on as much of the music as he could, which wasn't easy with Britain at war with Germany. However, just a few miles away was Liverpool, terminus for the transatlantic supply convoys, and Harold would ask merchant navy seamen who came into the family shop to bring him back records from America.

After leaving school he qualified as a chartered accountant and, after securing a job in the City of London, he moved down to the capital. He and Chris Barber would sit around for hours listening to jazz records and going to concerts. 'It was the start of a lifelong friendship,' says Barber. One afternoon Chris surprised Harold by turning up at his house with a trombone. 'I've just bought this for five pounds,' he said.

'Are you going to hang it on the wall?' asked Harold

'No, I want to play jazz as well as listen to it,' replied Barber.

Barber's father wasn't convinced but he decided that if his son was going to, in his words, 'muck about with that rubbish', then he should at least do it properly, and so he sent him to the Guildhall School of Music to study trombone and double bass. 'I didn't see Chris during that period,' says Harold. 'I only saw him again when he'd finished and launched a jazz band. But we kept in touch.'

Harold found life in the City frustrating because all the best work was taken by those returning from the war. Some of the lessons he learned, however, about how things can go wrong in a business if finances run out of control, would prove useful in years to come. He resigned and took up a post as an accountant with a printing firm, where he lasted two years until a disagreement with his boss resulted in dismissal. 'It was a shock,' recalls Harold, 'the first and only time in my life I'd been sacked. I decided that this was no way to live, working for people who could sack me. I decided to work for myself.'

At this time there was no such thing as a professional in the field of jazz. Everyone was an amateur, working a day job and indulging their enthusiasm by night. Harold wanted to make a business of it. He'd been playing drums for an outfit called the Gallion Jazz Band and he knew he wasn't going to get anywhere as a musician. What he thought he could do was manage and promote bands.

In the meantime, life without a regular income was tough. On occasion he was reduced to joining the queue for hand-outs at a soup kitchen by Waterloo Bridge. His pride stopped him calling home for money. By chance, he ended up sharing lodgings with a bunch of musicians in Beckenham. 'They were called Doug Whitton's Jazz Band and they were really awful,' he recalls. He used to help carry the drummer's kit and occasionally deputise for him when he was late for gigs, but his main job was to find the band bookings. He landed them a gig at a club on the fringes of Soho, where they could play one night a week, as long as they were out by 11 o'clock. That was when the real business began, after the pubs closed and the drunken businessmen staggered in looking for girls and sex. A little later, Harold found a better space, in a basement at 44 Gerrard Street, in Chinatown. 'We called ourselves the Club Creole. We did very well there. I made a living and the band got paid.' It was at the Creole that Harold gave his friend Chris Barber and his band their first professional gigs, on Christmas Eve and New Year's Eve, 1952.

The National Federation of Jazz Organisations of Great Britain and Northern Ireland was the nearest thing the UK jazz scene had to an organising body. It was run by a committee of musicians, critics and club owners, and its president was the Marquess of Donegall, whose Chelsea jazz club was informally known as the Lords. Harold loved jazz but not bureaucracy, so he'd never bothered with the Federation until one day the critic James Asman asked him to attend its annual general meeting. 'I'll give you membership,' he said. 'Providing you vote for me.' There was going to be an election and Asman was worried he was going to lose his position as secretary, so he needed the support.

Harold ended up with two tickets and took along a friend, Brian Nichols. 'We arrived and up on this platform, looking like the Politburo, were all these well-known people in jazz like George Melly, Steve Race [a musician and broadcaster] and Sinclair Traill [jazz critic].' When the voting began, Harold dutifully backed Asman, who lost anyway. When it came to the vote for the role of treasurer Brian gave Harold a nudge: 'Why don't you put your name forward. You're an accountant.' Harold went along with the idea but lost out to the incumbent treasurer who then, to everyone's surprise, announced he didn't want to continue in the post and resigned on the spot. 'I suppose we'd better see who came second,' said the chairman. 'Harold Pendleton, with two votes. Are you here, Harold?' A bemused Harold stood up and, as he recalled, everybody looked at him wondering who the hell this was.

Over the next twelve months Harold had cause to regret his spur-of-the-moment decision. He discovered that the Federation was virtually paralysed by the arguing that went on between two stubbornly entrenched camps; on one side were supporters of traditional jazz (the traddies), who followed the gospel as laid down in New Orleans by the old-school likes of Kid Ory, King Oliver, Louis Armstrong and Sidney Bechet; on the other side were the modernists, who were devoted to the jazz that emerged later in Chicago, which was more free-form and venerated soloists. It was clear to Harold that this bunch were never going to get anything done. He found an ally in Steve Race and, between them, the pair managed to oust just about everyone else on the committee and replace them with more agreeable types. The last to be ousted was Race himself, leaving Harold unopposed as president. The first item on Harold's agenda was to deflate some of the pomposity afflicting the organisation. He started by shortening its name to the National Jazz Federation, or NJF. After that, his mission was simply to make jazz popular and expose it to the widest possible audience. One early success was a series of concerts that featured both traditional and modern jazz at the recently inaugurated Royal Festival Hall on London's South Bank. Here, the NJF scored a coup when one of its concerts was attended by a young HRH Princess Elizabeth; the *Melody Maker* headline read, 'Royalty Honours Jazz'.

Melody Maker was the leading music publication of the time. It covered jazz, but not exclusively, and Harold thought there was need for a more dedicated publication. On behalf of the NJF, Harold bought a printworks and used it to publish *Jazz News*, a weekly journal that ran successfully from 1956 until the mid 1960s (by which time it was called *Jazz Beat*). The friend whose vote helped Harold become NJF treasurer, Brian Nichols, became the journal's first editor.

By 1953, Harold had closed the Club Creole and launched another venue, on Greek Street, in Soho, which ran on Friday and Saturday nights and went by the name of the National Jazz Centre. Around this time, Harold became Chris Barber's manager. Barber had the first true trad jazz band in the UK. It spawned a host of imitators and nurtured all manner of talent – a prime example being Lonnie Donegan, who was a member of the Chris Barber Band when, in July 1954, he recorded 'Rock Island Line', the track that launched the UK skiffle craze, which ultimately gave birth to the Beatles, Bee Gees, Hollies and Shadows, and inspired members of the Rolling Stones, the Who and Led Zeppelin to pick up instruments. By 1957, Harold was organising around 200 concerts a year. Meanwhile, the Chris Barber Band had extended its popularity beyond the UK; over the next decade they would travel the world, including multiple tours of the United States and ground-breaking performances behind the Iron Curtain. The US trips, in particular, would give Barber and his musicians the chance to meet many of their American jazz heroes and, with the help of Harold and the NJF, bring some of them across the Atlantic to play for British audiences.

Harold and the NJF rented office space at 18 Carlisle Street, just off Soho Square. In the drive to put his expanding empire onto a more professional footing, Harold decided he needed a secretary. Ads were run and one of those who responded was twenty-year-old jazz fan Barbara Coombs. Graduate of a secretarial course at Kingston Polytechnic, Barbara had been a junior typist with the jewellers Mappin & Webb in Regent Street, before taking a more senior position with a company nearer her home in Richmond, southwest London. She was intrigued by the idea of working for the NJF and called the office: 'I understand you want a secretary.'

'When can you start?' asked Harold.

'Don't you think you should interview me first?'

Barbara was escorted to the interview by her mother, who didn't like the idea of her daughter travelling to Soho alone. While her mother waited in a coffee bar, Barbara went into what she remembers as a grubby building and followed directions up to the first-floor office. 'I opened the door and there were two dishevelled chaps standing there. This was Harold and Chris. Chris was sat in a chair and immediately went to sleep.' Harold remained awake and liked what he saw. He renewed his job offer. As well as the normal secretarial duties, she also found herself running the Chris Barber fan club and forging his signature on photographs when he was too busy to sign them himself.

Meanwhile, the National Jazz Centre proved short-lived. It was shut down following a police raid. The target was one of the other businesses in the building but the upshot remained that Harold lost his club. One afternoon a man called Peter Burman dropped by the office. 'I understand you're looking for another club,' he said. 'I know a ballroom that's being run as a jazz club, but it's about to close because it's not doing well.'

'How do you know?' asked Harold.

'I'm the one running it,' said Burman.

165 OXFORD STREET

Joe Harriott | Johnny Dankworth | Humphrey Lyttelton |
Wally Fawkes | Tubby Hayes | Ronnie Ross | Ronnie Scott
| Dudley Moore | Dexter Gordon | Anita O'Day

The ballroom was situated in the basement of the Academy cinema at 165 Oxford Street, which was about a five-minute walk west of the NJF offices. A landmark in London film history, the cinema opened as the Picture House in 1913 as a semi-permanent home for one of the first full-colour feature films, *The Miracle*. It became the Academy in 1931. Bomb damage closed the cinema briefly in 1940 and it reopened in 1944 under the management of Austrian émigré and filmmaker George Hoellering. He ran the place as an art-house cinema and it was a favourite haunt of serious film buffs, who turned up to see works by the likes of Ingmar Bergman, Satyajit Ray and Jean-Luc Godard. Defiantly independent, Hoellering occasionally courted trouble by screening foreign films that the censors had banned. The building's basement wasn't used by the cinema. Instead, in 1948, it was leased to the recently formed Institute of Contemporary Arts and used as the venue for its inaugural exhibition, which displayed works from the burgeoning Cubist movement alongside a selection of international artists, including Dalí, Kandinsky, Klee, Magritte and Picasso. Six years later, the basement was given a makeover, orchestrated by noted portrait photographer and theatrical set designer Angus McBean, and relaunched as a ballroom. Visitors descended a sweeping staircase to a beautiful checker-floored lobby, where there was a box office with a colourful carousel horse on top. The lobby led to a ballroom with a dazzling red-and-white striped colour scheme, complete with a striped ceiling canopy. When Harold saw it his first thought was that it wasn't going to work. 'It was too posh for a jazz club,' says Barbara. On the plus-side, it could hold about 600 people and had a sprung dance floor, plush banquette seating, a beautiful Steinway grand piano on the stage, an espresso coffee lounge and a decent sound system. There was something else Harold liked about it, too: the name. It had a nice ring to it – it was called the Marquee.

MARQUEE

This is THE
NATIONAL JAZZ FEDERATIONS

"JAZZ AT THE
MARQUEE"

SECRETARY: BRIAN HARVEY

★ Open every FRIDAY
SATURDAY and SUNDAY
7.30 to 11 p.m.

ASSOCIATE MEMBERSHIP OF THE NATIONAL JAZZ
FEDERATION IS OPEN TO ALL JAZZ ENTHUSIASTS.
APPLY IN WRITING TO THE MEMBERS' SECRETARY,
NATIONAL JAZZ FEDERATION, 37 SOHO SQUARE,
LONDON W.1.

you can join now!

The entrance to the basement at 165 Oxford
Street was round the corner on Poland Street.

Originally, Harold said he'd take just the Saturday but he was told he'd have to take Sunday as well. 'I had no clear plan what I was going to do, except that I was going to put on jazz,' he recalls. The Marquee was far from the first jazz club in the West End. A short distance away along Oxford Street was the Humphrey Lyttelton Club (later renamed the 100 Club) specialising in trad jazz, where Humph had sessions seven nights a week featuring the likes of Acker Bilk's Paramount Jazz Band, Wally Fawkes and His Troglodytes and Terry Lightfoot's Jazzmen. A little to the south, on Wardour Street, was the Flamingo, which featured modern jazz. The Marquee was halfway between the two so, befitting the location, Harold decided to feature both trad and modern. For the opening night, on Saturday 19 April 1958, he booked Jamaican-born alto saxophonist Joe Harriott and his piano-based quintet (sax, trumpet, piano, drums, bass). Harriott was part of a wave of Caribbean jazz musicians who arrived in Britain during the 1950s. He was a bebopper, who is now widely acknowledged as one of the worldwide pioneers of free jazz. Also on the bill that first night were the Vic Ash Quintet; Ash was an English saxophonist and clarinetist who accompanied Hoagy Carmichael and Cab Calloway on their UK tours. The following night was the turn of the Dill Jones Quintet and the Kenny Baker Half Dozen. The host and compere for both nights was Peter Burman.

There was a changing roster of artists for the first few months of the club's existence but by July the line-up settled down to Harriott playing every Saturday and Sunday with support from the likes of Ronnie Ross, Bruce Turner, Allan Ganley and the Michael Garrick Quartet. From November, Harriott was given Sundays off, replaced by a sixteen-piece Latin American dance band, Andre Rico's Cha-Chaleros – 'the band everyone is raving about,' claimed the Marquee's advertising. In summer 1959, Harold managed to pull off a major coup by luring top modern jazzer Johnny Dankworth and his orchestra from a rival club. 'This other club was run by a couple of guys who were only interested in making money,' recalls Harold. 'Musicians are also interested in money but they're even more interested in people who like their music.' Chris Barber was also added to the programme, playing a new mid-week Wednesday slot. The trombonist was a top draw since his band's recording of Sidney

Bechet's 'Petite Fleur', featuring a clarinet solo by Monty Sunshine, had spent twenty-four weeks in the UK national charts, making it to No.3 and selling over one million copies.

Before the year was out, Harold had also managed to land trumpeter Humphrey Lyttelton, who was handed a new Tuesday night slot. The club's advertising could now boast that the Marquee featured all the top 'Musicians of the Year – Dankworth, Ross, Lyttelton, Barber, Harriott and [Tubby] Hayes.' Dankworth was given licence to curate his Sunday nights; he performed most weeks with his orchestra, sometimes with singer Cleo Laine – his wife since 1958 – and featured regular support from Dudley Moore, who fronted his own trio, as well as special guests.

The club got so busy that friends were drafted in to give Harold and Barbara some time off. Their relationship had now blossomed into a personal one. The catalyst was the George Lewis Band, who Harold had brought over from New Orleans to tour the UK. 'The other tours Harold promoted I was never allowed to go on,' recalls Barbara. 'I had to stay behind to look after the office. But when it came to George Lewis, I put my foot down because I was a huge fan.' By the time the tour finished Harold and Barbara were an item. They married in 1960. Harold joked at the reception that now Barbara was his wife it saved him having to pay her the raise he'd promised. She probably deserved one: when normal work hours ended at the NJF's Carlisle Street offices, Barbara packed up a little box with a roll of tickets and a tin of loose change, and walked around the corner to open up the box office at the Marquee.

Chris Welch was a teenage editorial assistant at *The Scotsman* in Fleet Street, a jazz fan and an aspiring drummer (he would later make his name as a star writer at *Melody Maker*). He was also a regular at the Marquee. 'It was the most comfortable, the most sophisticated venue around,' says Welch. 'It had nice furnishings, mirrors, pleasant staff. I felt like I needed to dress up in a nice suit when I went there.' He remembers that all the club clientele were smartly dressed and included a lot of women; it was, he says, a very adult clientele, and they were all there for the music. The first band he saw at the club was Johnny Dankworth's Orchestra in January 1961 – 'I know I enjoyed it a lot because I wrote it in my diary.' He was back in February for the *Melody Maker* awards night, when the Dudley Moore

The Joe Harriott Quintet, who played at the launch of the Marquee on 19 April 1958.

Trio played. 'At the time, the Marquee didn't sell alcohol,' recalls Welch, 'which was good for me as I was drinking too much anyway. I also went to other clubs – one of my diary entries records a night at the Flamingo as "Fantastic but not 'alf as enjoyable as an evening at the Marquee!"'

Welch also caught American tenor sax player Dexter Gordon on 9 September 1962. 'It was wonderful to see a real American jazz musician in his prime playing brilliantly. The place was packed out because there were so few American musicians [playing in London].' Other Americans dropping by the Marquee around this time included Sister Rosetta Tharpe (original soul sister and godmother of rock'n'roll), saxophonist Zoot Sims, who made his name with Woody Herman's big band, saxophonist Lucky Thompson, who played alongside Dizzy Gillespie and Charlie Parker, and big band singer Anita O'Day. 'It was thanks to Harold that British fans could see the American stars in a club setting,' says Welch. 'It was like manna from heaven.'

In Febuary 1962, the Marquee launched Friday night sessions dedicated to trad jazz. It was an attempt to rebalance the programme, which until this point had one night of trad, on a Wednesday, to two of modern jazz (Saturday and Sunday). In May, the club added Thursday nights; these featured neither trad nor modern but another kind of music altogether, which within about two years would come close to wiping jazz off the Marquee programme altogether.

THE ROLLING STONES

Alexis Korner | Blues Incorporated | The Cyril Davies All-Stars | Long John Baldry | The Rolling Stones

In addition to being jazz fans, Chris Barber and Harold were both enthusiasts of the blues. As Barber often said, 'Jazz without the blues is nothing.' Almost as soon as they got their feet under the desk at the NJF, the pair began battling with the Musicians Union to bring American blues artists to Britain. The MU ruled that for every American musician that came over to play, a British musician had to go the other way. Despite the headaches this caused, in April 1958, the NJF had brought over two of America's foremost folk-blues singers, Sonny Terry and Brownie McGhee, to accompany Barber on a UK tour. Later that year, the NJF arranged for Muddy Waters, along with Chicago blues pianist Otis Spann, to tour the UK. To the shock of British audiences, Waters took to the stage with an electric guitar. At a gig at St Pancras town hall some of the audience walked out. 'Jimmy Asman, along with two or three others, left,' recalls Harold. 'In the interval I went across to the pub where Jimmy was and asked him why. He said, "I want to hear a guitar, not a fucking vacuum cleaner."'

Undeterred, Chris and Harold continued to bring over more American artists. Champion Jack Dupree visited Britain in 1959 and, in the following years, Big Bill Broonzy, Howlin' Wolf, Sister Rosetta Tharpe, Jesse Fuller and Memphis Slim, among others, all made the trip. From 1962, Harold partnered with German promoters Horst Lippmann and Fritz Rau to bring the American Folk Blues Festivals to the UK, which, in addition to the artists above, also included acts like John Lee Hooker, Lightning Hopkins, Willie Dixon, Buddy Guy, Sonny Boy Williamson, Big Mama Thornton and Sugar Pie DeSanto.

Barber championed the blues in his own recordings, releasing an album in 1961 called, *Chris Barber's Blues Book*, with vocals by his wife Ottilie Patterson, 'the world's only Irish blues singer'. Arguably his most significant contribution to the blues in Britain was his encouragement of a young guitarist named Alexis Korner. The son of a Jewish Austrian father and a Greek mother, Korner smoked black cigarettes and wore his hair shaggy and, according to Harold, was strange and wild: 'He looked like a Balkan terrorist'. For a time, Korner played with the Chris Barber Band, assaulting purists with his amplified guitar playing. But his passion was the blues, not jazz. Along with another enthusiast, the beefy, wailing harmonica player Cyril Davies, Korner formed the Barrelhouse & Blues Club, which originally met above the Round House pub at 85 Wardour Street. In the first few days of January 1962, *Jazz News* caught the scent of something new and exciting: 'The Marquee club last Wednesday night was the scene of great excitement when guitarist Alexis Korner combined with Barber band trumpeter Pat Halcox on piano and harmonica player Cyril Davies to play a set of rhythm-and-blues numbers.'

Around the same time, Korner and Davies formed their own band at the invitation of Acker Bilk, who was looking for a contrasting band to support him. They brought in Keith Scott on piano, Danny Craig on drums and Malcolm Cecil on bass and called themselves Blues Incorporated. There were early gigs in Colchester and Croydon then, starting 17 March 1962, Blues Incorporated set themselves up with a Saturday night residency out at the Ealing Club, a trad jazz venue below a tea shop at the remote western end of London Underground's Central line. The Saturday night sessions pulled in every serious blues enthusiast in the country – of which there were probably no more than a hundred at the time. Blues Incorporated was an anonymous name under which any musicians could play, and the line-up changed almost gig by gig, depending on who was available on the night. Occasional players included singers Long John Baldry and Art Wood (elder brother of Ronnie), saxophonist Dick Heckstall-Smith, bassists Andy Hoogenboom and Jack Bruce, and drummers Ginger Baker and Charlie Watts. After a few numbers, Korner would open up the stage to enthusiasts in the audience, which is how a young slide guitarist named Brian Jones first got to meet teenage singer Mick Jagger and his guitarist friend Keith Richard.

In early April, Alexis Korner and Cyril Davies began playing the interval slot for the Chris Barber Band on Wednesdays at the Marquee. They immediately became so popular that the crowd wouldn't let them go and this ate into the time allocated for Barber's second set. 'Can't you give them a slot of their own, Harold?' the trombonist suggested. Until now, the club was closed on Thursday because it was the night before payday and nobody came out, but Harold decided to give it a go with Blues Incorporated, starting 3 May. The Marquee's in-house newsletter gave them a big build up: 'Britain's only rhythm and blues group. If you want an evening of gutsy, swinging music that's different, come along.' Audiences were modest at first, 'but within about a month or so they were queuing at the door and people were having to be turned away,' recalls pianist Keith Scott. 'That move to the Marquee was a highly significant one, and not just for the Marquee. It was the real commercial beginnings of the British blues movement.'

Within a few weeks, London's *Evening News* was reporting on this new sound: 'This is rhythm and blues, old as the hills in America, but we're fast developing a taste for it here. It promises to be the most exciting thing since Bill Haley.' *Jazz News* gleefully reported that Thursday night audiences 'now reach almost 700 souls nearly every session... jiving, twisting, raving, just listening.' Korner noted that the crowds were more extrovert than those he'd experienced at other clubs, dancing on tables and shouting their appreciation. Ginger Baker wrote in his autobiography, *Hellraiser* (2009), 'Our gigs in the Marquee were like no other I had ever played before. There were so many people crowded in that the very walls seemed to be bulging. I had never seen such a crowd at a gig. They created an electric atmosphere.'

As at the Ealing Club, the audience included many eager young musicians, people like Portsmouth's Paul Pond (shortly to change his name to Paul Jones). 'I used to infest Alexis Korner's gigs with monotonous regularity. Alex deserved his reputation for immense generosity by calling a few of us up onto the stage. He would point and beckon and we'd be standing so close to each other all along the front of the stage that everybody would go, "Who was he calling?" I would jump up and sing a few songs.' It was after seeing Alexis Korner at the Marquee that Eric Clapton returned home to ask his grandparents to buy him an electric guitar. Hanging around after the gigs, Clapton often missed the last train home and ended up walking the streets of Soho until dawn when services started running again.

Manchester's John Mayall – soon to play his own part in the Marquee story – also credits Korner with being a godfather to the British blues movement. 'He encouraged a lot of young musicians who were just starting out. Everybody just sort of gravitated toward him as a father figure. He was a total gentleman, very friendly, totally into the music. He was a great guy.'

The success of the Marquee residency led to Blues Incorporated being offered a slot on the BBC's Thursday night *Jazz Club* radio show. There was a problem in that this clashed with their residency at the club. Korner asked the band's occasional vocalist, Long John Baldry, to fill in. The evening also required an interval act, so Korner suggested to Harold that he should give a chance to one of the promising young musicians who he frequently invited on stage to jam. This was Brian Jones, a middle-class grammar-schoolboy from Cheltenham. Musically gifted from an early age, Jones was obsessed with the blues and regularly hitchhiked to London at weekends to visit the Ealing Club and Marquee. By summer 1962, he'd relocated to the capital and was placing ads in *Jazz News* looking for fellow musicians to play with. When he got the call from Korner he rounded up a bunch of fellow blues-loving irregulars. The legend is that Jones then called *Jazz News* to announce his band's debut gig and when asked what the name of the band was he didn't have one so he quickly plucked something from the track-listing of a Muddy Waters' album he had with him, and the Rolling Stones were born. Except the listing that ran in *Jazz News* that week gives the main act as Long John Baldry's Kansas City Blue Boys with support from 'Mick Jagger and the Rolling Stones'. That did not come from Jones. No way would he have given his new band second billing to Mick Jagger.

On Thursday 12 July 1962, fortified by Scotches and brandies to calm their nerves, the Rolling Stones stepped onto the stage at the Marquee to play their first professional gig. The line-up was Mick Jagger on vocals, Keith Richards and Elmo Lewis (Brian Jones's stage name) on guitars, Dick Taylor on bass, Ian Stewart on piano and possibly a drummer, possibly not. Mick Avory, who later joined the Kinks, was supposed to be behind the kit that night but he never made the gig, and no one can recall who, if anyone, replaced him. According to the handwritten set list, among the numbers they performed were songs by their heroes Jimmy Reed, Elmore James, Chuck Berry and Fats Domino. Taylor remembers being more than a little terrified. 'It's probably the only time I've ever had real stage fright in my life.' For Taylor it didn't feel like he had just taken part in rock history.

Jazz News announces the first gig by the Rolling Stones, July 1962.

'There was no lightbulb moment, like, this band is going to be huge one day, it was more a matter of really having to concentrate on the music and do the best we could.' After sharing the thirty-guinea performance fee the band retired to a nearby pub where the mood was upbeat. They were joined by drummer Charlie Watts, who'd been in the audience. He thought the group had 'obvious appeal' and looked like stars in the making – although it would be a further six months before he could be finally persuaded to join them.

Harold, owner of the club where this landmark event took place, remembers nothing of the Rolling Stones' first-ever performance, possibly, he once told an interviewer, because he was at the pub. The Stones were the interval group, he explained, put on to fill up the time while the main band went to the pub – and Harold usually went with them.

By this time, news of the popularity of Blues Incorporated had reached the carpeted corridors of the record industry and Decca offered Korner & co a contract. The resulting LP was called *R&B at the Marquee*, which was misleading since the recording wasn't live and was made at Decca's studios in West Hampstead, in north London. Nevertheless, according to those who were there at the time, it comes very close to capturing the atmosphere generated by Korner, Davies and their musical cohorts – drummer Graham Burbridge (formerly of the Chris Barber Band), bassist Spike Heatley (veteran of the Johnny Dankworth Orchestra), pianist Keith Scott, and saxophonist Dick Heckstall-Smith – on a Thursday night down at the Marquee. Vocals on the album are shared by Long John Baldry and Cyril Davies. According to a notice in the 30 May issue of *Jazz News*, Mick Jagger was originally slated to sing on the session. It's an album that music presenter Bob Harris would call as important as James Brown's *Live at the Apollo*, marking, as it did, the arrival of R&B in the UK as 'an irresistible force'.

The irony was that within weeks of the album hitting the shops, in November 1962, Alexis Korner and Cyril Davies had parted ways. Davies felt that the group was moving away from the pure Chicago blues he loved. 'Their relationship was fractious,' remembers pianist Keith Scott. 'Alexis was ex public school, had quite a bohemian background, while Cyril was by trade a panel beater. He had a workshop in Harrow. His attitude to life was very working class, as opposed to Alexis, who was a bit more gentrified. They argued constantly. And in the case of Cyril, he sometimes threw things, any projectile that came to hand – harmonicas were quite a good weapon.'

Korner carried on without Davies, replacing him with the multi-talented Graham Bond (vocals, keyboards, saxophone). Blues Incorporated even stepped up to two nights a week at the Marquee, filling in on Monday nights, in addition to Thursdays, while the Dick Charlesworth City Gents were off touring. But as the year came to a close, the Flamingo club lured Korner away – 'Bribed,' says Harold. Korner said it was because he wanted to play for a more mature, late-night audience – the audience were sent on their way home at 10.30pm from the Marquee. Also, the Flamingo offered Korner three slots a week, including a Friday all-nighter. His last Marquee gig was New Year's Eve 1962, sharing the festive bill with his former employer, the Chris Barber Band.

In the meantime, Cyril Davies pulled together a new group. Proper blues musicians were still thin on the ground, so he appropriated a bunch of rock'n'rollers from Screaming Lord Sutch's backing group, the Savages, billing them as the 'All-Stars'. The new band played their first gigs around London in December then, when Korner moved to the Flamingo, Davies and the All-Stars took over Thursdays at the Marquee, starting 3 January 1963, igniting a rivalry between the two former band mates over who could attract the bigger audience. Davies was a far less genial band leader than his former comrade. 'He ran that band as if they were employees in his breaker's yard,' says Keith Scott, who'd stayed on as Davies' piano player. Also throwing in his lot with Davies was Long John Baldry, a charismatic singer who during the late 1950s had been a prominent figure in the Soho skiffle and folk scene. 'Baldry was incredibly tall,' recalls Scott, 'and he created a very dramatic stage persona for himself. He was a bit camp but he had a very good voice.' Backing vocals were supplied by four South African girls, billed as the Velvettes. They'd come over to England in 1961 as members of the all-black cast of the jazz musical *King Kong* – about the life of the boxer Ezekiel Dlamini – which had played all over South Africa with Hugh Masekela and Miriam Makeba. When the show closed, the girls stayed on in London. Davies may have looked like a particularly ill-tempered provincial bank manager, but with a storming band behind him, the louche charm of Baldry up front and four singing-dancing black girls, the All-Stars were a sensational act. Someone who used to hang around the Marquee at this time and play the occasional session with Davies, was a young art student named Jimmy Page: 'The All-Stars were a fantastic band', he recalled years later. 'The best blues band of the day.'

The departure of Alexis Korner from the Marquee turned out to be bad news for the Rolling Stones. Although they managed to land the interval slot with the All-Stars at the Marquee, Davies was never a fan and after just a handful of appearances he told them not to bother turning up again. Harold remembers coming out of the club and seeing the band loading their gear into a van. 'I said good night to them and they told me to fuck off.' For years the band was convinced Harold had a hand in their dismissal. Keith Richards accused Harold of holding a grudge against their band because of the threat R&B posed to his beloved jazz. The truth was, Harold had no prejudices when it came to music, as long as the band was decent and they brought in the punters.

MANFRED MANN

Blues by Six I Dave Hunt's R&B Band I Big Pete Deuchar's Country Blues I Manfred Mann I Graham Bond Quartet

As 1963 began, two out of the Marquee's six nights were dedicated to R&B. In ads in *Jazz News*, the club proclaimed itself as the 'London headquarters of R&B'. There was the Cyril Davies All-Stars on Thursdays and now resident on Mondays were Blues by Six. This latter outfit were led by Brian Knight, a guitarist who was part of the Ealing Club scene. Knight had sung in one of the bands Brian Jones put together but Knight was a devotee of Muddy Waters, while Jones favoured Chuck Berry, so the two parted ways. For a brief time, Charlie Watts was the drummer with Blues by Six until he finally plumped for the Rolling Stones in mid-January.

Regular support for the two headlining acts was provided by the Rolling Stones (until Davies sacked them), Dave Hunt's R&B Band and Big Pete Deuchar's Country Blues. Both Hunt and Deuchar's bands had been playing trad jazz until recently, but they'd quickly picked up on the new vibe and ditched the clarinets and trombones for electric guitar and bass (for a brief time, the guitarist in the Dave Hunt Band was a pre-Kinks Ray Davies). There was another new outfit, first namechecked in a January issue of *Jazz News*, and they were the Manny Manne Group. Their route to the Marquee began at a Butlin's holiday camp in Clacton-on-Sea, where drummer Mike Hugg was in a fix. His pick-up band had landed a summer-season gig and they were short one piano player. Eventually, Hugg managed to get hold of the phone number of a pianist he'd seen playing at the Bull's Head in Barnes, southwest London, and he persuaded him to come on board. This was Manfred Lubowitz, who had left his native South Africa in 1961 and found work in London teaching music theory and writing highly technical pieces on the mechanics of jazz for *Jazz News* under the pseudonym Manfred Manne (after jazz drummer Shelly Manne). Hugg and Mann clicked and after Clacton they returned to London and put together a jazz quartet. One night they went along to the Marquee to see Blues Incorporated. 'It was so invigorating and refreshing. I thought that this would be really exciting music for us to play,' recalls Hugg. The pair immediately reinvented themselves as an R&B outfit. They scared up a few gigs along the south coast of England and then landed a residency at the Roaring Twenties, a new club on Carnaby Street, where they played as the Manfred, or Manny, Manne Group. In March, they made their first Marquee appearance, playing the interval slot for Pete Deuchar, and appearing under the name the Mann-Hugg Blues Brothers. 'The only problem was Monday was a duff night,' recalls Mann – although he came to realise that any night at the Marquee was a good night when Graham Bond, who fronted his own R&B quartet, containing John McLaughlin (guitar), Ginger Baker (drums) and Jack Bruce (bass), called up with a proposition: 'I've got this great gig next Monday in the Midlands. Why don't we swap? It'll be a real chance for you to break into an area where you don't normally play.' Mann thought it seemed like a good idea. 'We got up to the Midlands and it was a dreadful gig. It was complete bullshit. He just was trying to steal our Marquee residency.' (The Graham Bond Quartet would play just the one gig at the Marquee, but Bond would later land a residency with his Organisation in 1965.)

Less than twelve months old, the R&B scene had already become competitive, and Mann and Hugg decided they needed a proper singer. Auditions were held at the Roaring Twenties and, from those who tried out, Paul Jones (the former Paul Pond, friend of Brian Jones) was selected. 'I was told afterwards,' says Jones, 'that out of the six people in the band two of them thought I was good, two thought I was bad and two thought

I would do until they found somebody else.' With a new front man, the band shortened its name to the Blues Brothers. The following month they changed it again, to Manfred Mann.

'At our very early gigs you could see from where you stood on the stage patches of the floor,' says Jones. 'But as time went by, we were playing to packed houses.' They also drew the attention of the record companies and were signed by EMI. Their first two singles flopped but packing up after a gig at the Marquee the group were introduced to the producer of ITV's hip new pop show *Ready Steady Go!*, who wondered if they would be interested in supplying a new theme tune. 'That was the easiest job we ever had,' says Jones. 'The guy said to us, "I want plenty of it to be instrumental and we must have a countdown." So, by the time he told us what rhythm it was in, how much vocal and how much instrumental there should be, and that there should be a countdown, he was well on the way to writing "5-4-3-2-1" himself. We just filled in the gaps.'

After making their debut appearance on the *Ready Steady Go!* stage on the Friday night, Manfred Mann were back at the Marquee the following Monday. As they were setting up someone ran in yelling that '5-4-3-2-1' was No.29 in the *New Musical Express* chart after only two days' sales. 'I remember screaming with excitement,' says Mann, 'because I realised that we had moved from being an obscure band to being on the national scene.'

By the time the single peaked at No.5, the band had welcomed another new member in guitarist Tom McGuinness, a friend of Paul Jones. With his band the Roosters (featuring a second guitarist in the form of Eric Clapton) McGuinness had opened for the Manfreds at two early Marquee gigs, only for the Roosters to walk away over a dispute about money. 'I remember Manfred saying we were mad and that there were bands that would kill to play that support slot. I'm sure he was right. We didn't have any game plan and broke up not long after.' Weeks after the collapse of the Roosters, McGuinness found himself in the Manfreds as their new bass player, even though he had never picked up the instrument before in his life. 'I figured, two strings less, how hard can it be?'

Manfred Mann continued with their Monday residency through 1963 and much of 1964. Bob Dylan showed up one night and then sang their praises, declaring the band 'real groovy'. After the single 'Do Wah Diddy

Diddy' went to No.1, touring commitments saw Marquee appearances reduced, and after 'Pretty Flamingo' hit No.1 in May 1966, they became rarer still. The Manfred's final appearance was in October 1971. By this time, the band in its various incarnations had appeared at the club ninety-four times – this would stretch to ninety-nine times if you include the five appearances by Manfred Mann's Earth Band from 1971–76. Beside some of the early jazz artists, no other group would rack up so many appearances at the club.

THE MARQUEE'S GARDEN PARTY

1st National Jazz Festival, Richmond 1961 | 2nd National Jazz Festival, Richmond 1962 | 3rd National Jazz and Blues Festival, Richmond 1963

Back in 1956, Harold had been asked by Lord Montagu of Beaulieu to stage a jazz festival in the grounds of his stately home on the edge of the New Forest in Hampshire. Montagu was keen to raise some much needed extra income and, being a jazz fan, he thought a festival might be one way of doing it. Harold was dubious. Open-air festivals were fine for America or on the Continent, but summer weekends in England had a tendency to end up wet. Despite his reservations, Harold was eventually persuaded to take on the challenge. As it happened, the Beaulieu Jazz Festival, the first open-air popular music event in the UK, turned out a success. Headlined by the Avon City Jazz Band, it drew about 600 people. Preparations began almost immediately for a second festival the following summer, but somewhere along the way Harold fell out with Montagu. One point of contention was that the festival had been a one-day event and Harold wanted to expand it to run over a weekend but Montagu thought he'd get a better return by keeping it to the one day and cramming in more people. 'A festival is more than just a band playing on a big stage. To me that's a concert,' says Harold. 'With a festival you have to encourage the punters to make a weekend of it.'

Montagu brought in a London agency to run the festival, which became an annual event and did, in fact, expand to fill a weekend. For the 1960 edition, the BBC turned up to televise the event. The producers asked if the audience could be penned back away from the stage so they wouldn't get in the way of the cameras, and Montagu obliged, stringing a rope across the field, guarded by two elderly gents. 'The concert started,' recalls Harold, who watched it all at home on television, 'and there was this huge empty space between the stage and the audience, who thought, bugger this, and ducked under the rope and moved forward.' This was the cue for a mass crowd surge that shunted those at the front up against and then onto the low-rise stage where Acker Bilk's band were performing. Some members of the audience scaled the lighting gantries, a banjo was smashed and the musicians fled. The BBC pulled the transmission. 'Just incompetence on all sides,' says Harold.

The next day's newspapers were full of the incident, which many were calling the 'Beaulieu Riot'. Jazz fans were condemned as hooligans and festivals condemned as dangerous affairs. Local councils across the country cancelled forthcoming jazz events. Come the next year, Montagu decided to go ahead and stage the festival again. This time there was a genuine ruckus as various strains of tribal youth showed up on the promise of trouble and made sure they got it. Jazz was getting itself a bad reputation.

As president of the NJF, Harold felt compelled to do something. What that might be came to him one sunny afternoon in the unlikely setting of the Richmond Royal Horse Show. Barbara's father, Lawrence Coombs, was the chief fire officer of Richmond. She was brought up in a flat above the fire station – which was where the Pendletons held their wedding reception. The station was a few streets from the local rugby club, and in hot weather the firemen would occasionally help out by directing their hoses over the pitches. In return, the Athletic Association, which looked after the grounds, was in the habit of giving complimentary tickets to the fire station for matches and other events, one of which was the horse show. It was a big deal – the Queen attended. Harold and Barbara went the year they married. 'Once you've seen two or three horses jump over a fence you've seen enough and I dozed off,' recalls Harold. 'But then I suddenly bolted awake with the thought, I can run a festival here!' He could show

Lord Montagu, the BBC and the national media how a festival should be run. He pitched the idea to the Athletic Association, whose response was, 'Absolutely not'.

Six months later Harold received a phone call: the association had changed its mind and he could use the grounds for his festival after all. 'I later discovered they were hoping that the jazz fans would riot and set fire to their old grandstand, which they wanted to get rid of. They were hoping they could get a new one built with the insurance money.'

Organised under the auspices of the National Jazz Federation, the first National Jazz Festival took place in Richmond over the weekend of 26–27 August 1961. Chris Barber and leader of the Modern Jazz Quartet John Lewis acted as musical consultants – Lewis was also consultant to the Monterey Jazz Festival, one of the world's foremost jazz events, which Harold and Chris had attended two years previously and loved. Not that the Richmond festival required much consultation because it was basically a roster of Marquee regulars enticed out of their Oxford Street basement for a couple of days in the sun. The bill of festival performers included Chris Barber and Ottilie Patterson, Johnny Dankworth, Joe Harriott, Ken Colyer, Tubby Hayes and Ronnie Ross. The event offered almost thirteen hours of non-stop jazz on each of the two days.

Heralded as a great success, the festival returned to Richmond the following summer with a similar line-up, but with the addition of another couple of big names in Humphrey Lyttelton and Kenny Ball. Both festivals passed off without incident but the stigma of Beaulieu remained; local newspapers were quick to blame every local break-in or bit of vandalism that happened over the weekends at the door of jazz fans.

By the third edition of the festival, in 1963, the line-up began to reflect the musical changes taking place at the Marquee. Joining the jazzers at Richmond were a handful of R&B artists in the form of Long John Baldry, the Cyril Davies All-Stars and, most notably, at the bottom of the bill, the Rolling Stones. Following their ignominious exit from the Marquee, the Stones had come into the orbit of self-mythologising jazz fan Giorgio Gomelsky, a Georgian émigré with a Swiss passport and a heavy accent who came to London in 1955 looking to break into movies. Harold first met him when he showed up one afternoon at his office pitching to shoot a film about Chris Barber. 'At that time Gomelsky was dreaming of becoming a famous film director. It never happened. In fact, he became quite a nuisance,' recalls Harold, who used to refer to the Georgian as Rasputin. Setting film aside for the moment, Gomelsky decided he would become a music promoter instead and hung out at the Marquee, checking out the bands. It's probably where he first saw the Rolling Stones.

He set up a few R&B gigs of his own at the Piccadilly Club, in Ham Yard, in Soho. Which was fine, except Gomelsky leafleted his shows at the Marquee, which brought down the wrath of Harold. Gomelsky beat a retreat and decided to relocate his efforts as far from Soho as possible; he settled on the Station Hotel in Richmond, five minutes from the rugby grounds where Harold held his summer festivals. He was given a Sunday night spot in the pub's back room and the band he hired to fill it was the Rolling Stones. There were possibly as few as three people at the first gig, certainly no more than thirty, but word of mouth spread quickly and within a few weeks large numbers of young people were being turned away from what was now known as the Crawdaddy club. When the owners of the Station Hotel learned of the youth revolution taking place on their premises they had a fit and told Gomelsky to pack it in. 'Giorgio came crying to me,' recalls Harold, 'asking if I could help him find new premises.' Harold introduced him to Commander Wheeler, who headed the Athletic Association and suggested the Crawdaddy could relocate to the club house used by Richmond and London Scottish rugby clubs.

When the festival came around in August 1963, the Stones would have been playing the club house on the Sunday night as part of their Crawdaddy residency. Harold agreed to add the band to the official festival line-up and pay their fee (many years later the cheque for £30, signed by Barbara, was sold at Sotheby's). To everyone's surprise when the gates opened that Sunday morning, instead of the usual jazz crowd, in poured a mass of screaming young girls – Stones fans. 'They all jammed into the club house till it was packed out,' recalls Harold. 'I thought, this is downright dangerous – it was like the black hole of Calcutta. So, we moved the Stones into a large outdoor tent and because of that an audience other than their usual crowd saw them and it ended up a really good move for them.' That evening, Acker Bilk's band took to the main stage as the closing act of the festival. They'd barely begun when a voice came over the public address system to announce the start of the Rolling Stones set. Bilk's audience instantly drained away to the far side of the field to the tent from which heavy rumblings could be heard. Journalist Chris Welch was present; he remembers the Stones at Richmond in 1963 as a seminal moment, when young people visibly abandoned jazz en masse in favour of an electrifying new sound in popular music.

THE YARDBIRDS

John Mayall and the Bluesbreakers I The Cyril Davies All-Stars
I Long John Baldry and the Hoochie Coochie Men I Rod Stewart
I The Yardbirds I The Cheynes

R&B was an explosion with an aftermath that sucked in musicians the length and breadth of Britain. It was estimated that between mid-1963 and mid-1964 more than 280 trad jazz clubs around the country switched over partly or wholly to R&B. While it wasn't confined to London, the capital was definitely the epicentre of the blast. 'It was thrilling to be a part of it,' says Paul Jones, 'because R&B had been niche music for so many years in Britain and suddenly to find it was in the charts and in every possible club was great.'

After Blues Incorporated, the other most influential early act – at least in terms of the musicians who passed through its ranks – were John Mayall and the Bluesbreakers. In November 1963, they made the first of what would be close to fifty appearances at the Marquee, initially as the interval band for Manfred Mann. They landed the gig in part due to the patronage of Alexis Korner, who persuaded Mayall to leave his job in Manchester as a graphic designer and take the plunge to become a full-time musician in London. Korner introduced Mayall to the clutch of musicians from which the first version of the Bluesbreakers was assembled. Over the years, there'd be a rotating door of personnel, among them Eric Clapton, Peter Green and Mick Fleetwood, both later of Fleetwood Mac, Mick Taylor, of the Rolling Stones, and Andy Fraser, of Free. In the original line-up were guitarist Bernie Watson, fomerly of the Cyril Davies All-Stars, and seventeen-year-old bassist and future Fleetwood Mac member John McVie. Mayall had to reassure McVie's parents that their son would come to no harm joining a blues band. As it happened, McVie needed little encouragement to misbehave and he was fired and re-hired several times by Mayall. The Bluesbreakers pioneered an audaciously modern and exciting interpretation of American blues music. 'Trad jazz ruled the roost for a good ten years and it had just run its course,' says Mayall. 'You had younger people in the audience looking for something new that was fun and invigorating. And it wasn't just in music, it was in fashion and film. There was a big change in social and cultural habits going on. It was a fantastic time in British musical history and it did feel special to be part of it.'

The Cyril Davies All-Stars continued with their Thursday night residency right through 1963 but this came to an abrupt halt in the first week of '64. Audiences would have noticed how frail Davies was looking – he had taken to walking with a cane. Some of those around him put it down to the amount he drank. In fact, Davies was suffering from pleurisy. Against the advice of doctors, he continued with a remorseless schedule of gigging, drinking to ease the pain. Nicky Hopkins, who had replaced Keith Scott on piano, recalled in a 1974 *NME* interview hearing a loud crash from the dressing room at the Marquee one night. Running in he saw that Davies had smashed his fist through a mirror. 'His eyes were really tight shut and everything tensed in his face. You couldn't have moved him. He looked like a statue. You could see the pain in his face – not physical, but mental pain.' Davies collapsed on stage and died in January 1964. He was only thirty-one. 'I do not think that Britain will produce another bluesman of his stature,' wrote Alexis Korner in an obituary for his former partner.

Davies's regular singer, Long John Baldry, took over the All-Stars, renaming the band the Hoochie Coochie Men. Serendipitously, on the same night that Baldry led a musical tribute to Davies he discovered a new talent to add to the band in the unlikely setting of Twickenham station. The gig had been at Eel Pie Island, in Twickenham, and afterwards Baldry was waiting for the Waterloo train when he heard a harmonica riffing on Howlin' Wolf's 'Smokestack Lightning'. It was being played by a dishevelled teenager huddled against the cold on a bench further down the platform. Baldry went over and introduced himself and discovered the youth's name was Rod Stewart and he'd been at the gig. They both got on the train and by the time it pulled into Waterloo Baldry had talked the nineteen-year-old into joining the Hoochie Coochie Men.

Harold was happy for Baldry and his Hoochie Coochie Men to take over the Thursday night residency. Not everyone was as appreciative: Stewart describes in his memoirs how one night a member of the audience made a point of reading a newspaper in front of the stage while the band was on. Baldry took out a cigarette lighter and set fire to the paper. Stewart called his time with the Hoochie Coochie Men a great apprenticeship. And Baldry knew he had something special on his hands in Stewart – in addition to the harmonica, he let his protégé share vocals on a few songs. With a sharp dress sense, bouffant hairdo and bags of natural showmanship, it was obvious Stewart was on his way to the top, and it was at the Marquee that he was talent spotted and acquired his first manager.

Support at the earliest Hoochie Coochie Men gigs came from a new R&B group, who were graduates of Giorgio Gomelsky's Crawdaddy club. Gomelsky had had the Rolling Stones poached from under his nose by a young, ambitious, would-be impresario by the name of Andrew Loog Oldham. Gomelsky had gone off to Switzerland to attend his father's funeral and by the time he got back Oldham had the Stones' signatures on a contract – something Gomelsky had neglected to do. Scouting around for a replacement, Gomelsky's assistant, Hamish Grimes, saw a promising band at Ken Colyer's Studio 51. They were the Yardbirds, who'd formed only a few weeks earlier and had played no more than a handful of gigs. They had all grown up around the Kingston/Richmond area of southwest London: blonde-haired Keith Relf played harmonica and sang, Jim McCarty was on drums, Chris Dreja played rhythm guitar, Anthony 'Top' Topham was on lead guitar and Paul Samwell-Smith played bass. Gomelsky went along to watch them rehearse in a Richmond pub and immediately offered them the gig as the replacements for the Rolling Stones at the Crawdaddy. This was late September 1963.

A few months later, Gomelsky persuaded Harold to give his new band a try-out at the Marquee. They debuted on 23 January 1964, playing the interval slot between Long John Baldry's sets. By this time, original guitarist Top Topham had quit the band to return to his studies; his replacement was someone who'd previously played the Marquee with the Roosters – Eric Clapton. 'We got Eric because he'd been at the same art college [Kingston] as Keith and Chris,' says McCarty. 'They knew all about him because even then he had a bit of a reputation.' It didn't take Clapton long to establish himself as the band's main attraction. 'He made a pretty immediate impression,' McCarty confirms. 'Even before he could play great guitar Eric always looked good on stage and always seemed to captivate people.'

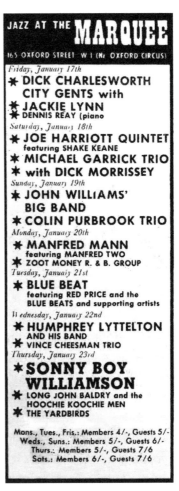

JAZZ AT THE **MARQUEE**
165 OXFORD STREET W 1 (N: OXFORD CIRCUS)

Friday, January 17th
✱ **DICK CHARLESWORTH CITY GENTS** with
✱ **JACKIE LYNN**
✱ DENNIS REAY (piano

Saturday, January 18th
✱ **JOE HARRIOTT QUINTET** featuring SHAKE KEANE
✱ **MICHAEL GARRICK TRIO**
✱ with **DICK MORRISSEY**

Sunday, January 19th
✱ **JOHN WILLIAMS' BIG BAND**
✱ **COLIN PURBROOK TRIO**

Monday, January 20th
✱ **MANFRED MANN** featuring MANFRED TWO
✱ **ZOOT MONEY R. & B. GROUP**

Tuesday, January 21st
✱ **BLUE BEAT** featuring RED PRICE and the BLUE BEATS and supporting artists

Wednesday, January 22nd
✱ **HUMPHREY LYTTELTON AND HIS BAND**
✱ **VINCE CHEESMAN TRIO**

Thursday, January 23rd
✱ **SONNY BOY WILLIAMSON**
✱ **LONG JOHN BALDRY** and the **HOOCHIE KOOCHIE MEN**
✱ **THE YARDBIRDS**

Mons., Tues., Fris.: Members 4/-, Guests 5/-
Weds., Suns.: Members 5/-, Guests 6/-
Thurs.: Members 5/-, Guests 7/6
Sats.: Members 6/-, Guests 7/6

The Yardbirds' Marquee debut.

Following the Yardbirds into the club, less than two weeks later, were the Cheynes. They formed in west London and were named after Cheyne Walk, a fashionable street in Chelsea. The line-up was Peter Bardens, Eddy St John, Pete Hollis and Mick Fleetwood. Their repertoire consisted of Bo Diddley, Buddy Holly and Little Richard covers, plus a handful of originals. They made their Marquee debut on a Monday night, sharing the billing with John Mayall's Bluesbreakers. The following week, they were on with Manfred Mann and Sonny Boy Williamson. 'I have a first, stomach-turning memory of playing the Marquee with my band the Cheynes,' Mick Fleetwood recalls. 'We had no following and it was a miracle to have been asked to back the legendary blues star Sonny

Boy Williamson. We had studied his albums and learned his every note by heart to prepare for this honour.' On the night Sonny Boy went totally off book while the Cheynes did their best to play each song exactly as they'd learnt it. This didn't go down well with the blues legend. 'He stopped playing in mid-song,' recalls Fleetwood, 'and bawled us out in front of the audience for not following his lead.'

Barely had the Yardbirds' Thursday night interval slots and the Cheynes' Monday night residency begun than both were abruptly interrupted.

90 WARDOUR STREET

Long John Baldry and the Hoochie Coochie Men | The Yardbirds | Sonny Boy Williamson | The Grebbels

Sitting in his Carlisle Street office Harold was able to ponder the first five years of the Marquee with great satisfaction. The club was now operating seven nights a week. 'It was perfect. Every night was full blast. I felt I'd achieved everything I wanted.' Regular full houses showed that the club was a hit with audiences and there was a strong loyalty to the place from the close-knit community of musicians who played there. 'You got the sense that it was a real professional venue, just the way it was managed,' says Keith Scott. 'And the way the sessions were presented was pretty up-market compared with some of the other clubs in London. Most other places were dives, a collection of damp basements, or coffee bars and back rooms of pubs. The Marquee was a class act. It even had a grand piano that was in tune and that was a remarkable rarity.'

Harold's contentment came to an end one afternoon in late 1963 when George Hoellering, the owner of the Academy, called on him. 'Harold,' he said. 'I've got some good news for me and bad news for you. That cigarette kiosk next to your club entrance, I've bought it.'

'So?' said Harold.

'It means I can widen the entrance.'

'And?'

'It means I'll have a much wider public access and I can turn the ballroom into a second cinema. I am in the cinema business, after all.'

Hoellering gave Harold a not ungenerous six months to find new premises for his club. 'I went into so many miserable, damp basements you wouldn't believe,' recalls Harold. One afternoon, he was with an estate agent, walking down Wardour Street, when they ran into another property agent and stopped to talk shop. Harold wasn't paying attention until he heard the words, 'Too large.' What was too large, Harold asked. 'This place, here,' said the other agent, indicating a boarded-up building. 'Can I have a look?' said Harold.

He was let inside, into a large space divided by glass and metal partitions. It had been offices and cutting rooms for Burberry, the luxury fashion house, but since they moved out twelve months previously the premises had been empty. As it happened, the owners were Great Universal Stores, who shared a solicitor with Harold. He set up a meeting with GUS at their head office on Tottenham Court Road. 'I gather you've had this place empty for a year,' said Harold.

'Yes.'

'Well, I'll take it.'

'Oh! Really?'

'If you lend me the money.'

There was a slight pause. 'Pardon me?'

'I don't have the money to give you up front,' explained Harold, 'but I'll take the place off your hands and pay you in instalments.'

An agreement was reached and Harold was given the property until the end of the company's lease in twenty-two years time, with no rent review. 'That was miraculous, twenty-two years with the same rent. That was the foundation of the club at Wardour Street. It became the rock on which I built everything.'

Given that Hoellering was converting the Academy ballroom into a cinema, Harold reasoned he wouldn't need the seating or decor or, for that matter, the name. Nor would he have any need of the Steinway piano. Harold negotiated a modest fee for the lot.

On Sunday 8 March 1964, a stellar line-up headed by saxophonist Stan Getz, with support from the Tubby Hayes Quintet, Ronnie Scott Quartet

SOHO

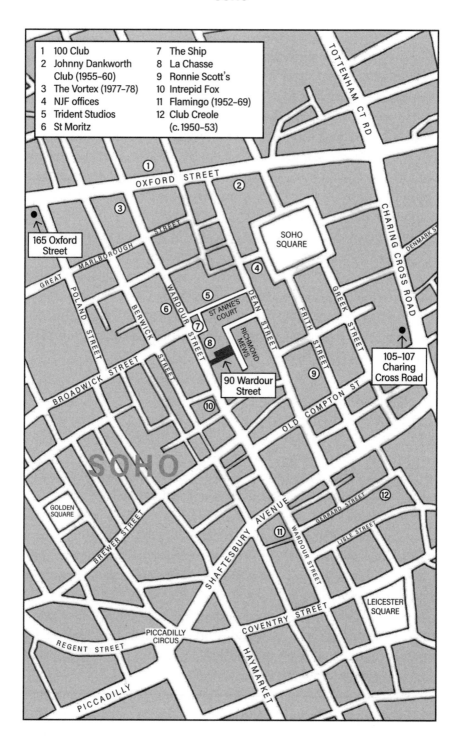

1 100 Club
2 Johnny Dankworth
   Club (1955–60)
3 The Vortex (1977–78)
4 NJF offices
5 Trident Studios
6 St Moritz
7 The Ship
8 La Chasse
9 Ronnie Scott's
10 Intrepid Fox
11 Flamingo (1952–69)
12 Club Creole
    (c.1950–53)

165 Oxford
Street

SOHO
SQUARE

105–107
Charing
Cross Road

90 Wardour
Street

SOHO

GOLDEN
SQUARE

LEICESTER
SQUARE

PICCADILLY
CIRCUS

and American singer Betty Bennett, played a last gig at 165 Oxford Street. 'Afterwards we cleaned the place out,' recalls Harold. 'Furniture, the whole lot, shipped it all to 90 Wardour Street, put up an illuminated sign outside and opened on the following Friday.'

It wasn't done out of choice, but relocating to Wardour Street was the best thing that could have happened to the Marquee. It was only five minutes' walk from the Academy, but the difference in environment was considerable. The club moved from an address on central London's busiest shopping street, dominated by department stores and high street drabbery, clogged by double-deckers and delivery vans, to a characterful patch of central Soho. Wardour Street was at this time still the home of the UK film industry. Film offices lined both sides of the street, from big international outfits, like Warner Brothers and the Rank Organisation, to small one-man operations. Hammer House, home of Hammer Films, was just across the road. The Wardour Street windows were filled with film posters, and runners dashed in and out of doors delivering film cans. Down in the basements were the screening rooms, busy from morning until night with publicists and critics viewing the new releases. Underneath the street was a network of tunnels linking the screening rooms. Squeezed into the premises not occupied by the film business were pubs, small cafes and restaurants, typically run by Greeks or Italians, along with a scattering of strip clubs, massage parlours, sex cinemas and other assorted businesses that periodically attracted the attention of the vice squad. The street was a haunt of low-lifers, drunks, chancers and dreamers, wannabe starlets and wide boys, to which the Marquee now added jazz fiends, beatniks and blues fans.

There was already a music club on the street, south of Shaftesbury Avenue, in the Flamingo. A former jazz haunt, it had a growing reputation as a hub for R&B and was famed for its weekend all-nighters, when the doors stayed open until six in the morning. 'Everybody who went to the Flamingo thought they were much hipper than everybody who went to the Marquee,' says Paul Jones of Manfred Mann. 'American GIs went there and West Indians.' It was also a hangout for gangsters, pimps and prostitutes, and there were brawls and violence, but the music was excellent. 'There was some top-quality shit in there,' says Geno Washington, who fronted the R&B/soul outfit the Ram Jam Band and who played the Flamingo regularly. 'The Rolling Stones used to come down there to drink and hang out because they liked the bands.'

Harold would not be bothered by gangsters or any of Soho's criminal fraternity because the Marquee closed at eleven and didn't have a drinks licence. 'Harold's view was that they should all go home to bed early because they had to go to college or work the next day,' says Barbara. 'And we wanted to go home to bed early, too.'

The new premises occupied the ground floor of two blocks but the club had barely any street frontage beyond a plate-glass-filled brick arch, which accommodated the main entrance, with just a little bit of display space for schedules and posters. Immediately through the door on the left was a hatch to the box office and cloakroom, and then a long corridor leading to a set of double doors, with glass portholes, that opened into the main room. This was a low-ceilinged space, where Harold built a low stage off to the left. Laying a new floor, workers made the discovery that the room sat over wine storage cellars belonging to Fortnum & Mason. At the rear, the main room bled into another low, squareish room, off which was a corridor connecting to the exit doors, which in turn opened onto Richmond Mews. Journalist Chris Welch, who by now was writing for *Melody Maker*, remembers that whereas the old Marquee felt like a nightclub, the new place almost felt like going to the cinema: a box office just inside the door then a long dark corridor and heavy doors through into a large dark room.

Harold went to great lengths to make sure that the interior of the new Marquee looked much like the old one. 'When the punters came in, they took one look and said, my God, how did you move it?' The walls were painted the same shade of green, while the stage lay beneath the same red-and-white striped canopy. There was banquette seating on both sides of the room and at the back, although as the club's regular crowd shifted from adult aficionados of jazz to student R&B fans, punters took to standing on the furniture for a better view, and the decision was quickly made to remove it all. Instead, a couple of rows of folding chairs were set out at the front for each show, a policy that remained until the mid 1970s. 'Not many clubs had a seated audience,' remembers Ian Anderson of Jethro Tull. 'The

The entrance to 90 Wardour Street.

bulk of the audience were standing but there was this area in front which was seated and you could actually develop a little bit of camaraderie, a bit of patter between the audience and the performer.'

On stage there were no technical frills. Stage lights were just a few white lamps that were either on or off – no colour filters, follow spots or strobes. There were no stage monitors and no mixing desk. Sound balance was achieved by the band turning their amps up or down. In this respect, the Marquee was no different to any other club at the time, no better, certainly no worse. The one thing Harold got wrong was the flooring: 'I installed

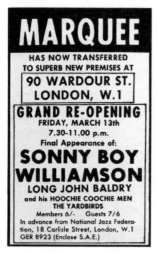

MARQUEE

HAS NOW TRANSFERRED TO SUPERB NEW PREMISES AT

90 WARDOUR ST. LONDON, W.1

GRAND RE-OPENING

FRIDAY, MARCH 13th
7.30-11.00 p.m.

Final Appearance of:

SONNY BOY WILLIAMSON

LONG JOHN BALDRY

and his HOOCHIE COOCHIE MEN
THE YARDBIRDS

Members 6/-   Guests 7/6

In advance from National Jazz Federation, 18 Carlisle Street, London, W.1
GER 8923 (Enclose S.A.E.)

The grand reopening night on Wardour Street.

a beautiful green carpet and the morning after our grand opening I saw it and nearly wept – there were patches of chewing gum everywhere. We tried everything to remove them, we even put ice cubes on the gum. In the end I gave up. A year or two later we took up the carpet and put in a rubberised floor covering.'

The grand opening took place on Friday 13 March 1964. The acts that night were Long John Baldry and the Hoochie Coochie Men, along with the Yardbirds and Sonny Boy Williamson. At the end of his set, Williamson took his stage bow in a magnificent fireman's helmet presented to him by Lawrence Coombs, the recently retired chief fire officer of Richmond. Six hundred fans were turned away after the 'House Full' notice went up.

What constituted full was a matter of debate. The official capacity was 400, as set by Westminster City Council and based upon Harold's original application for a Singing, Performing and Dancing Licence, which was the only suitable licence available to apply for in those days. The 400 was arrived at because the council set a minimum requirement of six square feet per dancer, and they reasoned fifty percent of the approximately 4,500 feet of club space should be considered for 'dancing'. Harold, with the help of his father-in-law, the former chief fire officer, showed that because the club was on the ground floor only, with no steps or stairs, and with two exits, more than twice that number could be vacated in under the prescribed two minutes. So, in practice the auditorium could comfortably fit 500 to 700 people and never put anybody's life in danger. Later, there would be occasions on which that number was massively over exceeded, when the Marquee squeezed in something like a thousand or more compressed and sweaty souls.

'The only thing I lost in the move was jazz,' says Harold. 'Jazz never really transferred to the new Marquee. Blues had already taken over. I remember Humphrey Lyttelton complaining to me that I wasn't advertising his appearances. I said, "Sorry Humph, I have advertised, they know you're on, they just don't want to come."'

1964 was peak R&B. The Rolling Stones' first LP, released that April and composed mostly of R&B covers, became one of the year's biggest sellers, staying at No.1 for twelve weeks. The Yardbirds also put out an album. After playing at the club's Wardour Street opening night, they were bumped up to regular Friday headliners. It was Giorgio Gomelsky's suggestion that the group cut a live recording in order to capture the raw excitement the band generated at gigs. 'It was always so cold trying to record our songs in a regular studio,' says Jim McCarty. 'We all agreed a live album was the best approach.' The venue chosen was the Marquee and the recording was set for 20 March, the first night of the band's headline residency at the club. No special planning went into the recording session, it was just a regular gig with regular punters – or, as Gomelsky called them in his sleevenotes, 'mody-bodies'. 'We always used to get a great crowd,' recalls McCarty. 'They always used to go mad, so we were pretty much guaranteed the right kind of atmosphere.' Engineer Philip Wood took charge of the recording equipment, housed in the dressing room at the back of the stage, and there was Keith Relf's dad, Bill, stood at the edge of the stage holding out what looked like a fishing rod with a mic on the end to capture the audience noise. 'It was all pretty low tech,' says McCarty. 'But it worked.' The only fuck-up came courtesy of human error: bassist Paul Samwell-Smith noticed a button on the equipment and, saying, 'What does this do?' pressed it and erased one of the tracks. Released later that year, *Five Live Yardbirds* failed to chart but received respectable critical praise. Its reputation has grown over time: *Ultimate Classic Rock* magazine included it in its list of 'Top 100 Live Albums', and it was ranked No.6 in *Classic Rock*'s 'Top 30 British Blues Records'.

What the recording does do is brilliantly capture the energy and barely restrained chaos of a Friday night session at the Marquee, beginning with the stumbled introductions by compere Hamish Grimes and climaxing in the bass-driven 'rave up' that was the band's version of Howlin' Wolf's 'Smokestack Lightning'. The album contains some of the earliest recordings of a young Eric Clapton ripping loose. Aerosmith's Joe Perry describes himself as 'a huge fan' of Clapton's work on *Five Live Yardbirds* and the album's version of Chuck Berry's 'Too Much Monkey Business' was a blueprint for a lot of what Aerosmith would later do. 'It was like the band was a slingshot and, as soon as it hit that pocket, [Eric] went sailing,' says Perry. 'Those parts of the songs still give me goosebumps.'

That Marquee residency was key to building the Yardbirds' reputation. 'Mick Jagger was in the audience for one of our sets and came on stage to do a number with us,' recalls McCarty. The first band Phil Collins ever saw, aged fourteen, was the Yardbirds at the Marquee. They were usually supported at the club by other Gomelsky-managed acts, including the Grebbels, who featured guitarist Roger Pearce, a friend of the Yardbirds who'd stood in for Clapton when he was absent for a few gigs, and the Authentics, from Bedford, another forgotten band, who once recorded two tracks, both unreleased, with guest guitarist Jimmy Page.

In early 1965, the Yardbirds lost their lead guitarist. 'Eric was his own man,' says Harold. 'He knew what he wanted, and when he was in the Yardbirds he argued with Giorgio. Now, you don't do that with Giorgio. Giorgio was the only manager I know who was more temperamental than any artist. He fired Eric for arguing with him.' Except, unwilling to do it himself, Giorgio sent Eric over to the Marquee office for Harold to act as executioner. 'I thought the saddest thing,' says Barbara, 'was after Harold said to Eric, sorry you've got to go, we then had to say to him, and you've got to give back your guitar, because the band owned it.' Clapton's replacement was Jeff Beck, who was privately auditioned at the Marquee on 17 February 1965. Clapton played his last gig with the band on 3 March, in Bristol, and Beck made his Marquee debut five days later on 8

March. If anything, the band became even more popular with audiences, wowed by Beck's pyrotechnical playing and the new directions their music was taking, prime evidence being their recent hit, 'For Your Love' (written by a young Mancunian sales assistant called Graham Gouldman, later to constitute one quarter of 10cc). National success meant more time on the road and less time on stage at the Marquee but when they did appear they could be incendiary: on their final appearance at the club (not counting a 1983 reunion), in June 1966, both Jeff Beck and his soon-to-be replacement in the band Jimmy Page featured in the line-up.

JOHN GEE

Following the move to Wardour Street, Harold decided it was time to bring in a full-time manager to run the club. The person he appointed was John Gee, and he would come to play a major role in the development of the Marquee. Born in 1927 in east London, Gee spent most of his formative years in Berkhamsted in Hertfordshire, twenty-five miles northwest of London, near the RAF base where his father was stationed. An only child, Gee won a place at the local grammar school, where he discovered a love for literature and jazz. His first job in the music business was as tour manager and publicist for two of the great dance-band leaders of the day, Ted Heath and Bert Ambrose. He moved into journalism (he was the first British journalist to interview Duke Ellington), writing for various publications including the NJF's *Jazz News*, which brought him to the attention of Harold, who hired him to write the Marquee newsletter, as well as the programmes for the National Jazz Festivals.

Harold obviously thought Gee had the qualities to make a good club manager, but he cut an unlikely figure at the Marquee. He was always immaculately dressed in a pressed suit, white shirt and tie. 'In a way he fantasised about himself as a cool New York jazz kind of guy,' says Ian Anderson of Jethro Tull. 'He modelled himself on Frank Sinatra and would often be seen carrying an overcoat over one arm and wearing a hat cocked at a jaunty angle.' As Alan Whitehead of the band Marmalade recalls, 'John wasn't a typical club manager. He spoke in a very upper-class accent. He wasn't at all hip.' For singer Dana Gillespie that wasn't such a bad thing: 'John was the right man to run that club. You need one person with their feet on the ground. As a musician I never would've wanted a manager to be more off his rocker than the artist.'

Gee required all musicians to be in the dressing room fifteen minutes before the show started. They had to be off stage just as promptly – if they weren't finished playing by eleven, Gee was likely to switch the power off. 'The club was run like a very well-oiled machine and a lot of that was due to John Gee,' says Colin Richardson, who was brought in as a night manager. 'He ran a tight ship.'

Gee was also the club's main booker, the man a band had to schmooze to get a gig. Apparently, the best way into the Marquee was for a band to profess admiration for Frank Sinatra – Gee was president of the singer's British appreciation society.

Despite coming across like some funny old uncle, Gee revelled in his front-of-house role, which he decided would extend to introducing the bands on stage. Being of an age where he'd done national service – spent in the RAF, like his dad – he brought a military bearing to the role. Sometimes, when faced with a particularly keyed up crowd – this was a live music venue, after all – Gee would warn the room that he wasn't going to continue until everyone quietened down. At one point he confessed to Harold that he was worried about his receding hairline, so the club bought him a wig and Gee paid back the money via deductions from his salary. Manfred Mann remembers an occasion when Gee was doing his introductions and the lead singer of whichever band was on that night came up behind him and whipped off his hairpiece: 'Poor John was left exposed in front of the audience, bald.'

Carl Leighton-Pope's first encounter with John Gee was on the night the Marquee opened on Wardour Street. Leighton-Pope was an eighteen-year-old coal miner's son and had been asked by a friend if he could help out at the club. When he turned up he found Long John Baldry up a ladder fixing some lights. Leighton-Pope gave him a hand, until Gee appeared and put Leighton-Pope to work in the cloakroom. Once the music started, Leighton-Pope asked Gee if he could find someone to cover for a bit so he could watch some of Baldry's set. He ended up working at the Marquee five days a week. 'I worked the door and I worked on stage humping gear. I just did whatever was needed.' One of his tasks was chucking people out. Anyone could find their way to Richmond Mews, round the back of the Marquee, where the bands and crew unloaded their gear and brought it in. It wasn't unknown for a fan to grab a mic stand and saunter in, hoping to pass themselves off as a roadie. Then they'd find a place to hide inside. 'They always hid in the same places,' says Leighton-Pope, 'usually the toilets. You'd give a push to the cubicle doors and one of them wouldn't open so you'd climb on the seat in the next cubicle and look over the top and there'd be four or five guys crammed in.' One time there was a guy Carl hauled out of a cubicle who insisted he was in the band but Carl had heard that one before and he marched him off the premises. Muff Winwood had to walk around to the front of the club, explaining, 'The big guy has just thrown me out,' and heading back inside to continue his soundcheck with the Spencer Davis Group.

Like the old premises, the new Marquee didn't have an alcohol licence. This wasn't a problem for punters, who got tanked up beforehand at one of several nearby pubs, typically the Ship, which was the closest boozer to the club. It was just around the corner from the back entrance to the Marquee, so it was a hangout for musicians and crew, too (it was also the main watering hole for Wardour Street's film industry). 'You would often meet a Yardbird in there or a Kink,' says Tom McGuinness. Johnny Warman, of rock band Bearded Lady, was in there one night in the early 1970s, 'and standing next to us was Freddie Mercury in his black outfit with bat-like wings on the shoulders.' Obviously, Harold preferred that the punters spent their money at the club. He enquired into a licence but it wasn't straightforward, not least because his application would be challenged by local publicans who wanted to avoid the loss of any trade. Harold was told that the Marquee could apply for a private licence, the kind reserved for members-only drinking clubs, but that would mean everyone in the audience would have to apply in advance for membership before they could attend a gig. That wasn't going to work.

To offer something in the way of refreshments at the Marquee, Harold installed a coffee bar at the back of the club, complete with a state-of-the art Gaggia machine. Barbara's dad was given the responsibility of looking after it. Hauled out of retirement, Lawrence Coombs was roped in to serve as a general maintenance man for the club. The Marquee was quite a family affair: Barbara's mum, and sister, Laurie, and her boyfriend all worked the coffee bar. Her dad had an assistant for odd jobs named John Palmer, and John's wife, Rose, and daughter, June, both worked in the cloakroom and ticket office, while son-in-law Bob Brooks was a duty manager.

More popular than the coffee was Coca-Cola, so much so that the club became one of the biggest sellers of the fizzy drink in the West End. 'They were delivering to us nearly every day,' remembers Harold. The problem was keeping so many bottles chilled. Barbara's father came up with the solution of a butcher's safe – basically, a walk-in chiller – and Harold had one installed. Another food and drink innovation came about because of a neighbour. An entrepreneur by the name of Peter Boizot had an office next door to that of the NJF on Carlisle Street, which is how he became friendly with Harold and Barbara. When Boizot set about promoting proper Italian pizza to the British public, Harold agreed to trial it at the Marquee. It didn't work at the club, but later Boizot opened a restaurant on Wardour Street in 1965 calling it Pizza Express. That did okay.

John Gee, always the consummate professional, used to plug the club's refreshment offerings as he introduced the night's headliner. He would draw attention to the coffee bar at the rear, where one could purchase 'splendid coffee', a 'cooling Coca-Cola' and, with theatrically rolled rrrrs, a 'Marrrrs barrrr'. It always got him a laugh.

THE STUDIO

The Moody Blues | Paul McCartney | The Beatles | The Troggs

Along with the main performance space, 90 Wardour Street came with a basement space and upstairs offices. Harold sublet some of the offices, although over time they would fill with Marquee-related businesses, like artist management (which we'll come to). There was also another large space at the back of the building that used to be an unloading bay for the Burberry cutting rooms. It was separated from the main club area by a thick wall, which was structural and couldn't be knocked out. For the moment it was a redundant space. A mutually beneficial arrangement with an engineer by the name of Philip Wood put it to good use.

Wood was an interesting character. He'd once been a racing driver and participated in the Mille Miglia ('Thousand Mile'), the Italian open-road motor race that was so lethal to both drivers and spectators that it was banned in 1957. He suffered a major accident himself, resulting in head injuries that affected him for the rest of his life. His family owned a large printing company near Newcastle, but Wood was too full of other ideas and schemes to simply step into the family business. He had a knack for acquiring new skills. Besides motor racing he learned to fly helicopters and was one of the first people to start a commercial helicopter service, flying paying customers from Lydd in Kent over the Channel to France. He took up opera singing. His interest in music led to a fascination with recording, and he accumulated mixers, mics and tape machines. He used his equipment to make some demos with local outfit the Alan Price R&B Combo (soon to become the Animals). This brought him into the orbit of Yardbirds manager Giorgio Gomelsky, up in the Northeast to check out the local talent. Gomelsky had Wood bring along a portable tape machine to a club one night to capture the Alan Price outfit live. This led to Wood being called down to the Marquee to record the Yardbirds for their *Five Live* LP, which is how Wood met Harold. The two agreed that the Geordie should ship all his equipment down to London and transform the unused room at the Marquee into a recording studio. With little more than a twelve-channel mixer, some surplus BBC microphones and two second-hand tape machines, Wood created a modest monophonic recording space.

As luck would have it the very first recording made at the new studio turned out to be a bona fide classic and a No.1 UK hit. The Moody Blues were part of a flourishing Birmingham music scene. Comprising of Denny Laine (guitar/vocals), Clint Warwick (bass), Graeme Edge (drums), Mike Pinder (keyboard) and Ray Thomas (flute and percussion), they came together in early 1964 as an R&B covers band. They were talent spotted by former singer Alex Wharton, who together with his management partner,

Tony Secunda, brought the band down to London that summer. It was a lucky break that got them their first gig at the Marquee, in early September. 'Manfred Mann's Paul Jones came down with laryngitis and wasn't able to sing one night,' recalls Ray Thomas. 'We were asked if we could fill in. We hadn't got a gig so we were in there like a shot.' The audience seemed to like them so they were booked to support the Yardbirds the following week. That again went down well and from then on they were given their own headline slots two or three nights a month. (A regular support act were the Muleskinners, with a pre-Small Faces Ian McLagan on keyboards.) 'It was extremely hot and sweaty,' says Thomas, 'a bit like the Cavern in Liverpool. And packed to the rafters every night.'

Already signed to Decca, the band had put out a single, 'Steal Your Heart Away', but it had done nothing. One afternoon at rehearsal, Alex Wharton brought in a box of 45s he'd been sent by an American DJ. One of the tracks, a demo by Bessie Banks called 'Go Now', sounded like something that would suit the Moodys. When the band performed the number for the first time, at a Marquee gig, Wharton remembers it blew the crowd away: 'My spine was electrified. I knew this was the big one.'

The band first attempted to record the song at Chappell Studios in Bond Street but it wouldn't come together in the limited time they had booked. Chappell was expensive, so to save money Wharton decided to take a chance on the new studio still under construction at the Marquee. 'The builders were in the studio during the day so we recorded at night,' recalls Ray Thomas. 'The control room was about ninety percent complete but we recorded among ladders, tools, bags of plaster, you name it.'

'The final result sounded like it had been recorded in a public lavatory, dirty but full of ambience, which was what I was after,' says Wharton. Not long afterwards the band returned to the Marquee to shoot a promotional film for the song. 'Alex filmed that promo with a borrowed eight-millimetre camera,' says Thomas. 'We dressed all in black with a black background so just our heads and faces showed. It turned out so well a band called Queen "borrowed" the idea a few years down the line!' It's now regarded as the first ever pop video, predating the promos the Beatles did for their 1966 singles 'Rain' and 'Paperback Writer' – promos that prompted George Harrison to famously claim the Beatles invented MTV.

'Go Now!' (the Moodys added an exclamation mark) hit No.1 in the UK charts in January 1965. The band continued playing the Marquee once a month until September. 'The Marquee was important to us,' says Ray Thomas. 'It built up our popularity and exposure in London. When we saw the queues stretching down Wardour Street it was very exciting.' After that, the Moodys would return for just one more Marquee date, in October 1968, by which time the former raw R&B band had embraced orchestral rock and the biggest cheer of the night would probably have been for recent chart hit 'Nights in White Satin'.

Sadly, for Philip Wood, his life spiralled out of control. He suffered from periodic depressions and it was only when he was discovered sleeping under the Steinway in the studio, hidden by its dust cover, that anyone realised that he'd somehow become homeless. A little while later he disappeared completely. He was subsequently found to be living in France, where he had reinvented himself as a food critic for French newspaper *Le Parisien* and as a DJ named 'Big Ben' working on the French equivalent of Radio 1 – he lost his radio job when he was arrested for lobbing cobblestones at the police during the student riots in 1968. He died young, partly as a result of the head injuries he received years before in the Mille Miglia.

Wood's position as the Marquee's studio manager was taken by Simon White, who until then had been working towards his finals at law school in London. He was no longer enthused by a career as a solicitor and was actively looking around for other things to do. Living in Sussex Gardens in Paddington he met a bunch of teens who were staying at the seedy hotel next door and they turned out to be a band called Gary Farr and the T Bones. They were playing the Marquee that night and they invited White along and introduced him to Harold. Harold was impressed by White, who was equally taken with the Marquee and the idea of having a go in the music business. He wasn't short of money and offered to become a shareholder, by investing £2,500 in the studio.

White knew nothing about recording music before he bought in, and it was only afterwards he learned that the only person who knew how all the equipment worked was the now-departed Philip Wood. The Marquee brought in other engineers to help but some of the gear had been handmade by Wood, including the twenty-four-channel mixing console,of which only about eight of the channels worked at any given time. The desk was powered by turning a key, a bit like starting a car. 'It was unique,' says White, 'but useless.'

It was obvious the equipment had to be replaced and competent people brought in to staff the studio; the new recruits included Gerry Collins who had been at CBS Studios in London. He took on the job of getting everything upgraded and making the decor more presentable – as it stood, the walls were covered with rockwool secured with chicken wire and the floor laid with linoleum. 'Before the various technical problems were sorted out, Chris Barber tried to support the studio by using it whenever he could, although I don't think he recorded much that was released,' says White. 'On one occasion, Paul McCartney, producing for possibly the first time, came into the studios to produce Chris and his wife Ottilie Patterson.' McCartney, along with John Lennon and Ringo Starr (George Harrison was not present), also used the studios in October 1965 to record the band's annual Christmas fan club message. The trio worked from a prepared script, with ad-libbed exchanges thrown in, before gathering around a piano to sing various improvised lines. The session was not a success, and while around twenty-six minutes of material was recorded, none of it was judged suitable for release.

The Troggs also used the Marquee's studio around this time to record a song provisionally titled, 'The Lion'. Someone came up with the idea of using a real lion's roar for the recording and so the band contacted Mary Chipperfield, of the Chipperfield circus family. She had a lioness called Marquess who she said could do the job. 'We met up at the Marquee,' recalls Pete Staples, the band's bass guitarist, 'and were pleased to see so many press and photographers there.' The lion was there, as promised, securely tethered, with a microphone in front of her. 'They say never work with animals,' says Staples. 'Well Marquess decided to lick the mic and got a shock. She let out an enormous roar and everyone scattered. I've never seen the press run so fast, pushing and shoving to get out the door.' Mary Chipperfield was on hand to calm the animal down, and slowly the press and photographers crept back in and the band got the centre spread in the *Daily Mirror* the following day.

THE WHO

It was in the Marquee's studio that Harold first encountered the High Numbers. They were making some demos, covers of Tamla Motown and blues numbers. He didn't pay the group much attention because he was far more intrigued by their two managers. Chris Stamp was the brother of Cockney actor Terence and Kit Lambert was the Oxford-educated son of composer Constant Lambert. Harold was impressed by their smarts and ambition, and sensed very quickly that he could do business with them. He asked if their band wanted a night at the Marquee. 'Absolutely,' they said. 'But we're changing their name, by the way, to the Who.'

The night set aside for the Who's Marquee debut was a Tuesday, 'Which was a rubbish night,' admits Harold. 'Tuesday was the night all the pub managers took off.' It was a night when there was little to be lost in taking a gamble on a new band.

'The Marquee meant nothing to me when we started,' the Who's guitarist and chief songwriter Pete Townshend told *Uncut* magazine in 2013. 'I thought it was a jazz club. It was a dump, but it was a good venue for sound and it made us appear to be cool.'

It wasn't Marquee policy to promote gigs. Since launching, the club had always run ads in *Jazz News* and *Melody Maker* listing the coming week's attractions but, beyond that, it was up to the individual bands to do their own promotion. Motivation came from the Marquee's payment policy. The club never paid headliners a set fee, only a percentage of the door takings. That percentage varied from band to band, depending on their ability to pull in the punters. Ironically, often the support act could go home with more money than the headliner because the Marquee was obliged under rules set by the Musicians' Union, to pay the musicians in the support band a set fee per head. If the headliner couldn't draw a crowd, they made nothing.

'Kit and Chris created a real buzz for that first show,' remembers Harold. 'It was a case study of clever marketing, how they mobilised and created that buzz to get people to turn up.' Lambert and Stamp commissioned a striking monochrome poster for the shows featuring the Who logo above the words 'Maximum R&B' with an image of Townshend with his arm

Poster for the Who's Marquee residency, beginning November 1964.

raised, posied to strike his guitar. They drove around London every night in a van sticking them up anywhere and everywhere. As they were torn down, a crew would be out the next night replacing them. To help spread the word further, Lambert and Stamp devised an exclusive fan club known as the 'Hundred Faces' – echoes of the Homeless Network of street people used by Sherlock Holmes as his eyes and ears across London – who would be given reduced admission to gigs in exchange for handing out flyers. Despite all this, no more than thirty to forty people were persuaded to show up for the first Marquee gig on a wet Tuesday 24 November 1964.

One of those who was there that night was club employee Carl Leighton-Pope. He'd followed the group since he was sixteen. 'I used to go out to the Old Field Tavern in Greenford on a Thursday night to watch them when they were the High Numbers.' He remembers that at the first Marquee gig, 'we all sat on the floor, along with Kit Lambert and Chris Stamp'. Because the Marquee had no drinks licence, Lambert handed out tots of whiskey. Despite the poor turnout, John Gee deemed the show enough of a success to give the band the Tuesday night slot on a regular basis. Over the following weeks the advertising began to pay off.

'It was the posters that did it,' says Pearce Marchbank, a young art student at the time. 'I was walking down Wardour Street and I saw loads of them outside this club, so I went one Tuesday. I went back almost every week and the queues got longer and longer each time.'

The Who made the absolute most of their central London residency, delivering a weekly programmed explosion of high-volume attitude and controlled aggression. They played 'Smokestack Lightning', 'I'm A Man' and Martha and the Vandellas' 'Heat Wave'. 'I'd never heard such a loud band in such a small room,' says Pearce Marchbank. Rock writer Mick Farren described the scene: 'Tuesday nights at the Marquee were an unreal spectacle of nearly a thousand mods watching transfixed, packed shoulder to shoulder, bopping and gum chewing as at deafening volumes the Who go through their act, culminating in an orgasmic ritual of fantastic destruction as Keith Moon climbs onto his drums and swings at them with an axe and Pete Townsend drives his guitar into his speakers until it splinters.' Dedicated mod Dave Goodman, who later produced the Sex Pistols, recalled, 'I'd never seen anything like it. The set was so fucking violent and the music so heady it hit you in the head as well as the guts. It did things to you. I went straight out and broke a window.'

The residency ran for five months, twenty-three consecutive Tuesdays in all. During that time, Shel Talmy, producer of the Kinks, caught a show and on the strength of what he saw offered the band a contract to cut their first single, the Townshend-penned, 'I Can't Explain'. Additional guitar on the session came from Jimmy Page, who had also dropped by the Marquee to see the show: 'To be a kid, in the room, right there in the middle of the sound Pete, John and Keith created, was phenomenal.' A producer from *Ready Steady Go!* came by one Tuesday resulting in the Who's first appearance on the pop show, followed by two appearances on the BBC's *Top of the Pops*. They received their first write-up in *Melody Maker*, which noted the 'weird and effective techniques of guitarist Paul [sic] Townshend, who expertly uses speaker feedback to accompany many of his solos' and declared the Who to 'surely be one of the trendsetting groups of 1965'. Lambert and Stamp filmed the band miming to 'I Can't Explain' at the Marquee and on 16 February the band's performance at the club was filmed for French television. In April, the Who also managed to record a new single, 'Anyway Anyhow Anywhere', and practically an album's worth of material at IBC Studios in Portland Place. The final show of the residency, on 27 April 1965, was recorded for later broadcast on Radio Luxembourg's *Ready Steady Radio!*

While the Who played gigs at other venues during this time, beginning a UK-wide tour in mid April, the Marquee remained special, as Keith Moon confirmed in a 1973 interview: 'Playing the Marquee was the biggest thing ever for the Who, when we started. The only place that had any influence, where the managers and promoters and press could see us, was at the Marquee. They had a very discerning audience there, and it helped us develop our musical ideas. We were finding our feet – and the Marquee put us on our feet.' Roger Daltrey has said much the same: 'We were just a pub band but the great thing about the Marquee was it was in the West End of London. It expanded our audience by literally a million.' It was at the Marquee that the Who staked their claim to be the greatest live rock band in the world.

While the music the Who played – and the volume they played it at – wasn't to Harold's personal taste, he did appreciate the band's talents and even more so their work ethic. 'They worked like hell to build up that Tuesday residency,' recalls Harold. 'So much so that when the Who moved on, Tuesday was the night everybody wanted.' Considering their poles-apart personalities, Harold got on notably well with the Who's legendarily lunatic drummer Keith Moon. The two sometimes shared a drink over at neighbouring drinking club La Chasse, where Moon once reputedly arrived via the window after climbing over the rooftops from the Who's management offices in nearby Old Compton Street.

The Who on stage at the Marquee in 1965.

The end of the residency did not mean the end of the Who's Marquee appearances; they played five more shows at the club later that year. At a gig on 2 November they played 'My Generation' live for the first time. On 23 April 1968, they returned to honour the Marquee's tenth birthday.

By the last weeks of the Who's residency, the Marquee was easily the best music venue in London, if not the whole of the UK. Over eight days in May 1965 punters at the club could catch the Who, the Yardbirds, Long John Baldry, Manfred Mann, Jimmy James and the Vagabonds, and the Alex Harvey Soul Band. Jazz wasn't entirely gone from the programme, but it was now confined to weekends. Regular appearances by long-standing favourites, including Johnny Dankworth, Joe Harriott, Ronnie Ross and, of course, Chris Barber, were boosted by occasional heavyweight international guests, such as in May 1965 when leading American pianist and composer Bill Evans and his trio made two appearances at the club. The Marquee was one of the venues used for filming of the BBC Two TV programme *Jazz 625*, which was broadcast between April 1964 and August 1966. This marked the end of the long-standing deadlock between the Musicians' Union and the American Federation of Musicians, which meant that big names from the US were coming over to Britain for the first time since the 1930s. Harold must have been overjoyed that the club could host the filming of a set by the Thelonious Monk Quartet – Monk was one of the artists featured in the documentary film *Jazz on a Summer's Day* about the 1958 Newport Jazz Festival, a film Harold liked so much that it was occasionally screened on a Sunday night at the club instead of a live band.

THE SPENCER DAVIS GROUP

Rod Stewart and the Soul Agents I Buddy Guy I The Spencer Davis Group

Rod Stewart was a member of the Hoochie Coochie Men for less than a year before he decided that Long John Baldry cast too tall a shadow. Stewart already had his own management and they decided he needed to be fronting his own band. They settled on a Southampton outfit called the Soul Agents, who'd played support to the Hoochie Coochie Men on a few occasions and who were looking for an upgrade on their current singer. 'Our vocalist, Johnny Keeping, had a good voice but was never really into the blues,' recalls the bassist Jim Sach.

Stewart joined the Soul Agents on 3 December 1964 and they performed that very same night at the Marquee. They were playing support to Rod's ex, Long John Baldry, which you imagine might have been awkward. As well as fronting the band, Stewart also performed a solo set of acoustic blues. Within a few weeks, they had their own Thursday-night headline slot. 'Wherever we performed,' remembers Sach, 'as soon as Rod appeared on stage the dancing and talking in the audience would stop and all eyes and ears would be on this charismatic figure.' A short time later, the Soul Agents were hired to back American blues guitarist and singer Buddy Guy on a UK tour. Rehearsals took place at the Marquee. On the tour, Stewart and the band played an opening set and then, after the interval, the band returned, minus Stewart, to back Guy. On 25 February 1965, at the Marquee, Buddy Guy fans Eric Clapton and Jeff Beck were both in the audience.

Four nights later, the Marquee gave a club debut to the Spencer Davis Group. Bass-playing Mervyn 'Muff' Winwood and his younger brother, vocalist and organist Steve, had played in their father's dance band before forming their own amateur jazz, blues and skiffle group in their hometown of Birmingham. They were seen at a local pub by Welsh guitarist Spencer Davis who recruited the brothers, along with Pete York on drums, to form an R&B band. 'After two or three gigs everybody who was anybody in Birmingham knew who we were,' says Muff Winwood. In the audience at one gig was Chris Blackwell, founder of Island Records, and he immediately snapped up the band. Blackwell set them up with a booking agency to find them more gigs. Getting into the Marquee was no breeze. 'We had to prove ourselves before they accepted that we were good enough to play there,' recalls Winwood. After that first gig, in March 1965, it was another couple of months before they could get another Marquee booking, but from May onwards they played regularly once or twice a month through into the following year.

For journalist Chris Welch, the Spencer Davis Group were one of his favourite Marquee acts. 'Some of the most exciting nights were the spontaneous jam sessions. I remember one night [16 November 1965] when Stevie Winwood and Eric Clapton both played lead guitar together on stage. They were both as good as each other. Everyone thought that was amazing because normally Stevie Winwood would be playing piano.' Blackwell used to send his Jamaican artists to sit in with the Spencer Davis Group, leading to some of them, including Millie Small and Jimmy Cliff, landing gigs of their own at the club.

What marked the Marquee out from other popular clubs around the country, like the Twisted Wheel in Manchester or Newcastle's Club a'Gogo, which both had reputations for great music, was that it was in central

London, and London was the centre of the music industry. 'Business could be done there,' says Winwood. 'People could come and see you and offer you gigs, or your manager could send down a TV producer or a photographer. And the audience were very cool. They knew their stuff.' What he remembers most of all, though, was the heat and humidity. 'The only way you could get dry was to walk outside into the cold and hope you didn't get the flu.' The hot stuffy air was a perpetual problem on busy nights. 'People always used to ask me why we hadn't got air-conditioning,' says Harold, 'but you have to get the room cold to start with, so you have to run it for hours before you open. Then when the punters come in, they start shivering because it's like the bloody Arctic. It would have been a waste of money trying to put air-conditioning in. The only thing I could do was to put two great big vents in the ceiling to take the hot air out.'

At the end of 1965, the Spencer Davis Group released the single 'Keep on Running', penned by Jamaican ska singer Jackie Edwards, which went to No.1 in January 1966. For the follow-up Chris Blackwell encouraged the band to come up with their own material and booked them into the Marquee's studio. 'We had to be there at nine o'clock in the morning,' says Muff Winwood. 'When we arrived, there was nobody there so we started fiddling around and within ten minutes we'd come up with "Gimme Some Lovin". We looked at one another and went, bloody hell, that don't half sound good. It was that thing where people say they wrote a hit on the back of a cigarette packet. Those things do happen.' When Pete York said he hadn't had any breakfast the band took off for a cafe on Wardour Street, which is where Chris Blackwell found them and threw a fit over the wasted studio time he was shelling out for. 'We walked back to the Marquee,' recalls Winwood, 'picked up our instruments and played him the track. His jaw just dropped.'

Driven by Muff Winwood's hammering bass riff and brother Steve's Hammond organ, 'Gimme Some Lovin" reached No.2 in the British charts and made the American Top 10, becoming the band's most instantly recognisable song. It has been covered by everyone from the Grateful Dead to Olivia Newton-John, and has featured on the soundtracks to over fifteen films, including prominently in the 1980 John Landis film *The Blues Brothers*. Whenever Muff Winwood heard that a movie producer was going to use the song, he always made a point of taking his wife for an evening at the Marquee to celebrate. 'It's how I marked the fact that this key thing in my life happened at the Marquee.'

STEAMPACKET

The Animals | The Mark Leeman Five | Gary Farr and the T-Bones | Stevie Wonder | Steampacket | 5th National Jazz and Blues Festival, Richmond 1965

Glancing through the monthly calendar of gigs during 1965, so many names jump out – the Who, the Moody Blues, Manfred Mann, the Yardbirds, the Spencer Davis Group, and the Animals, who made their first appearance of six at the club in July 1965. But packing the dates between them are countless other acts now wholly forgotten. Some of these bands played the club every week, usually as support but in some cases enjoying headlining residencies. Many must have had a decent following and set the box office cash till ringing otherwise John Gee wouldn't have had them back. The Mark Leeman Five, for example, who came from Woolwich and from 1964–1966 smashed out their signature brand of jazzy R&B on eighty-seven occasions on the Marquee stage. They were the regular support band for Manfred Mann, with who they shared the same manager in Kenneth Pitt; they also occasionally backed the Moody Blues and the Who, and played a few headliners of their own. They were tipped by their peers as the band most likely to succeed but the band's promise fizzled out when frontman, Mark Leeman, was killed in a car crash on the way home from a gig in Blackpool. The band's drummer, Brian 'Blinky' Davison, went on to play with the Nice.

Gary Farr and the T-Bones were a top-class draw who held a prestigious Friday-night residency through much of 1965 and 1966, regularly playing to packed houses. They were an energetic live act but a lack of songwriting ability meant their record releases were unimaginative covers of R&B standards that never troubled the charts. Radio Luxembourg used to have a short show that was recorded just before the T-Bones' set and which often featured guests over from the US, including Sonny Boy Williamson and a very young Stevie Wonder. On the latter occasion, when the T-Bones did their set, Wonder joined them, asking if he could sit in on drums for a couple of numbers. 'It was incredible,' recalls T-Bones drummer Brian Walkley, 'because all drummers set up their kit in a different way, but he just knew where everything was. Later I was told that he'd been listening to me playing and worked it all out.'

The year after drumming with the T-Bones, Little Stevie Wonder, then aged fifteen, played his own date at the Marquee, on Monday 7 February 1966. It was part of a UK tour of small club dates promoting his new single 'Uptight (Everything is Alright)'. John Lennon was in the audience that night (fellow Beatle Paul McCartney caught the show at the Scotch of St James club five nights earlier).

The T-Bones were represented by Giorgio Gomelsky, and Brian Walkley remembers Gomelsky had an attractive young assistant who would hand over the band's wages every Friday in little brown envelopes. Her name was Julie Driscoll. In July 1965, Driscoll made her own Marquee debut. She was the surprise element in a 'supergroup' assembled by Gomelsky. Long John Baldry's Hoochie Coochie Men had disbanded and Rod Stewart had recently parted company with the Soul Agents, and Gomelsky brought them together again. They were teamed up with another of his artists, organist Brian Auger, a regular at the Marquee since 1963 with first his Trio, then his Trinity. Rounding out the group were guitarist Vic Briggs, who'd played with Dusty Springfield, and drummer Micky Waller and bassist Ricky Fenson, both former Cyril Davies All-Stars. Gomelsky had heard Driscoll singing along to the radio and thought she had a fine voice, so she was in, too. Steampacket were more musical revue than group, with the three vocalists doing solo spots and backing each other on a mix of blues, soul and Tamla Motown numbers.

It was usually packed whenever Steampacket played the Marquee, but night manager Colin Richardson never looked forward to their gigs. Unlike some other venues, the Marquee was known for its scrupulously fair accounting and this was good enough for most bands, but not Steampacket, as Richardson recalls: 'There was always this inquest with

Fifteen-year-old Stevie Wonder backstage at the Marquee on 7 February 1966.

them after the gig. The club closed at eleven and there was half an hour to sort the money out and pay the band, and they just used to argue all the time, mainly Baldry and Rod Stewart, who was quite a volatile young man. Quite often I had to practically throw them out so I could catch my last train home.'

Steampacket had barely been in existence a month when they made their way out to Richmond to appear in what was formerly the National Jazz Festival but was now the National Jazz and Blues Festival. For his annual festival, now in its fifth year, Harold had accepted the inevitable and relegated his beloved jazz to the afternoons, leaving the evenings exclusively for R&B. The festival started on Friday evening, kicking off with the Moody Blues followed by the Who. During the latter's set, Roger Daltrey performed a wild dance across the width of the stage and kicked out the front stage lights. Barbara was not pleased and had the cost of the lamps deducted from the band's fee. The headliners were local boys the Yardbirds. Saturday featured Georgie Fame, the Graham Bond Organisation (who'd recently settled in to a Thursday night residency at the Marquee) and headliners Manfred Mann; Sunday was the Spencer

Davis Group, Steampacket and, top of the bill, the Animals. The event was captured by a film crew from *Shindig!*, an American musical variety TV series that aired on ABC. Newspaper reports put the crowd for the weekend at an estimated 33,000, making it the most successful festival yet.

Laurie Coombs was Barbara's younger sister and for her the festival was an eagerly awaited annual event. 'All the staff and security would look forward to meeting each other again every year,' she recalls. She used to help out with folding leaflets and sticking stamps on envelopes. 'One of the things I remember most was when John Lennon and George Harrison arrived. I was very excited and ran to tell Barbara they were on site, and promptly fell over a metal tent peg and had to be carried to the first aid tent. I've still got the scar.' The Beatles were not, unfortunately, on the bill but had come along at the invitation of Eric Burdon to see the Animals.

1965 was to be the last hurrah for the festival at Richmond. There had always been friction with the local council caused by fans sleeping rough around the town. It wasn't helped by local press describing the festival-goers as, 'People… with a penchant for vagrancy and little use for all the conventional paraphernalia of beds, changes of clothes, soap, razors and so on.' As the fame of the festival had spread and ever more people started coming from ever further afield, the problem became more acute. The festival provided a large crash tent but there were far more people turning up with sleeping bags than it could accommodate. Complaints from the good folk at the Royal Mid-Surrey Golf Club, which backed onto the festival site, and whose members objected to beatniks bedded down in the bunkers, finally tipped the balance. Harold was told to go and be a nuisance somewhere else.

JACK BARRIE

In 1965, it was decided to give John Gee a full-time assistant. The man Harold chose was Jack Barrie. Harold met Barrie for the first time in the Ship that summer. John Gee brokered the introduction. Barrie's acquaintance with Gee began with Barrie's repeated requests for Gee to give his band a break with a gig at the Marquee. They were an R&B outfit called Boz and the Boz People, featuring future King Crimson member Boz Burrell on vocals/guitar and ex-Muleskinner Ian McLagan on organ; Barrie was their manager. His perseverance paid off with a string of support slots at the club but then the band had the Ford Transit with all of their equipment in it stolen overnight from outside a B&B in Paddington. The insurance refused to pay out because they considered that leaving equipment in a van overnight on a London street wasn't taking the necessary due care. Everything had been bought on hire purchase, with Barrie as guarantor. John Gee took pity on him and set up a meeting with Harold and Barbara. The result was that Barrie was offered the job of tour manager for a Marquee-promoted package of Manfred Mann, the Yardbirds, Gary Farr and the T-Bones, American all-girl group Goldie and the Gingerbreads, teenage identical twins Paul & Barry Ryan, and the Scaffold, a comedy-poetry-music trio from Liverpool featuring poet Roger McGough, comic entertainer John Gorman and musician Mike McGear. 'Mike spent most of the time trying to keep quiet about being Paul McCartney's brother,' recalls Barrie. 'But Paul kept coming back stage to say hello at their London shows.'

The tour went off without incident, and having proved himself to be dependable and hard-working, Barbara offered Barrie a more permanent position as assistant to John Gee, starting 2 January 1966. Another factor in Barrie's favour was that his musical taste was more flexible than Gee's. The premier Sinatra fan was displaying irritation with a lot of the music that was drawing the crowds at the Marquee. 'We realised that perhaps John's days were numbered,' recalls Harold. 'And we had to have a replacement waiting.'

Barrie's duties involved arriving at 10am to do the paperwork and banking from the previous night's operation, book any rehearsal slots and arrange auditions for John Gee to view when he arrived at 4pm. Barrie would finish at 6pm, which allowed him to take on some extra work – a financial necessity at the time – as coffee bar assistant, cloakroom attendant or, the best job of all, cashier. The cashier was paid five shillings more because of the responsibility. His weekly salary was £15, which after tax and insurance, left £11.70. Years later, at one of Harold's boardroom

Jack Barrie running the bar at the Windsor festival in 1966.

lunches, with John Peel and George Melly as guests, Barrie produced one of his old pay packets with the financial breakdown written on the front of the envelope: Harold's comment was, 'It appears I even overpaid you back in those days as well.'

While working as John Gee's assistant, Barrie was introduced to the owners of a small, members-only drinking club called La Chasse, which was on the first floor above a Ken Munden betting shop at 100 Wardour Street, half-way between the Marquee and the Ship. The club owners told him that they were selling up and moving to Spain. Barrie decided running a place like that would be more rewarding than overtime at the club. Being broke, he managed to sell the idea to two friends, Kenny Bell, who owned his own booking agency, and Simon White, part owner and managing director of the Marquee's recording studio. Between them they put up the finance for the purchase. Starting in May 1967, under Barrie's management La Chasse became the unofficial green room to the Marquee.

It was accessed from the street by the narrowest of staircases. Up one flight, it was a single room about the size of a large living room. There was a payphone on the landing and a toilet up half a flight up again, shared with the top two floors, which were taken by more bookmakers' offices. Beside the bar, La Chasse had a jukebox of choice cuts and a couple of couches, with room for about thirty drinkers, tops, and, after the first ten, the rest would be standing. Writer Dan Hedges described what it was like: 'Dark. Cramped. Thick with cigarette smoke and the low rumble of the clientele. It's people making promises, people making deals, people bullshitting each other stiff about albums that never quite seem to get recorded, and coast-to-coast American tours that never quite seem to get off the ground. A drink at the tiny bar will set you back the equivalent of a small bank loan.' Musician Stan Webb recalls, 'There were people there drinking for England. That's what it was like.'

'About ninety per cent of the people in La Chasse were Marquee bands,' says Lee Jackson of the Nice. 'It was a great bar.' Those who weren't musicians were road crew, producers, studio personnel (particularly from Trident Studios on nearby St Anne's Court), journalists and groupies. Some of the musicians would take it in turns to work behind the bar. 'I used to have to put in one night a week serving drinks,' recalled Long John Baldry. 'They got rid of me pretty quickly because I was giving people far too hefty a shot in their glass.' A young Phil Collins remembers dropping in one evening and being served by Keith Moon. 'I buy a round from him and he gives me back more money than I'd handed over.' In an article for the *Mail Online*, David Bowie said of his song 'The Bewlay Brothers', 'I do believe that we finished the whole thing on that one night. It's likely that I ended up drinking at the Sombrero in Kensington High Street or possibly Wardour Street's crumbling La Chasse. Cool.'

In early 1970, Jack Barrie handed the running of the bar to one of the regulars, Roger Nickson, whose family had the Morning Star pub in Peckham. 'We opened regular pub hours – eleven until three, then five-thirty until eleven. I only opened on Saturdays when it suited me.' Keith Moon was a mainstay of La Chasse and so the club was always accommodating to the Who. One time they were due to play the Roundhouse on a Sunday and Nickson opened up specially so the band and crew could get in the mood before heading up to Camden. When the Who were recording nearby, Nickson stuck around the club to ferry boxes of booze over to the studio. 'There was a summer Saturday night,' recalls Nickson, 'when I got a call from Terry Doran, George Harrison's chauffer and personal assistant, to say George was coming up to town and wanted a quiet drink with friends. I opened for him.'

Nickson says the club never served out of pub hours because Harold and Barbara were co-licensees, and the Marquee didn't want trouble with the police. Instead, come eleven, folk would move on to the Speakeasy, north of Oxford Street at 48 St Margaret Street, or to Blaises or the Cromwellian in South Kensington, all of which were music scene hangouts and were open into the early hours.

Avoiding trouble was always going to be difficult for any club that counted Keith Moon as a regular. He and partner-in-crime Vivian Stanshall, of the Bonzo Dog Doo-Dahs, liked to swing by the theatrical costumier on their way to the club and hire Nazi uniforms in which they'd goosestep through Soho and up the staircase to La Chasse, announcing their arrival by rapping their leather gloves on the door. They liked to stand at the open windows looking down on Wardour Street and across at the offices of the Rank Organisation, and give Nazi salutes to passers-by. 'People on the street would be flicking V-signs at them and shaking their fists,' says Nickson.

At one time, La Chasse had its own football team, made up of roadies, plus Phil Collins and Jon Anderson, and one or two professional ringers the well-connected Nickson would draft in. A team picture made the pages of the *NME*. The roadies who used the club – La Chasse was a prime place to pick up work – organised an annual van race from Soho to the Blue Boar services at Watford Gap on the M1, a fixture for gigging bands hacking it up and down the motorway between London and the North. The club put up fifty quid for the winner.

BOWIE

David Bowie and the Lower Third | David Bowie and
the Buzz | The Action | The Move | The Summer Set
| Bluesology | The Herd

By 1965, eighteen-year-old Bromley boy Davy Jones had already released a couple of singles, recorded with two short-lived bands, the King Bees and the Manish Boys. Neither act had made any sort of splash and the ambitious Jones had moved on. Now he had been invited to join a mod band called the Lower Third, narrowly beating out his pal Steve Marriott at the audition. Put together by schoolmates from Margate in Kent, the Lower Third went from gig to gig in a battered old diesel ambulance. 'We used the bell a few times when we were late getting to a venue and had to cut through traffic,' confesses drummer Phil Lancaster.

Lancaster thinks it was Davy Jones's connections with the Marquee that led to the Lower Third's first booking at the club. 'He'd played there with the Manish Boys as early as 1964 and befriended the management, and they'd let him see gigs for free whenever he rolled up at the door.' The first Marquee dates with the Lower Third came in September 1965. These were part of a series of Saturday afternoon concerts put on in partnership with the pirate station Radio London and billed as the Inecto Show, so called because they were sponsored by the Inecto shampoo brand. The Lower Third were the warm-up act for the week's star guest, who would perform their new single before being interviewed by Radio London DJ Kenny Everett. 'Lulu was a guest one week,' remembers Barbara Pendleton. 'But the one that really stood out was Tom Jones. He only had to open his mouth and it was, my God, what a voice!' A lot of the guest stars came straight from the *Ready Steady Go!* TV studio a mile away on Kingsway in Holborn. 'We used to poach some of the artists and collect them after they'd recorded their segment and whistle them round to the Marquee,' recalls Harold.

Eventually, on Friday 8 October, the Lower Third graduated to an evening slot, supporting Gary Farr and the T-Bones. By this time their frontman was no longer calling himself Davy Jones, he was David Bowie.

A typical Lower Third gig mixed original songs by Bowie with covers, such as the Kinks' 'You Really Got Me'. 'We also did some very wacky numbers,' says Lancaster, 'like a mad rocked-up version of Holst's "Mars, the Bringer of War".' That wasn't even the weirdest of their numbers: the band also did a version of 'Chim Chim Cher-ee' from the recently released Walt Disney film *Mary Poppins*. 'Dave was already experimenting in that sense, but audiences away from London were often more bemused by us than excited. The Marquee is where we did best, and where we built up a good little following.'

In the audience one night was a schoolgirl called Dana Gillespie. A blues fan, she was first taken to the Marquee by a friend and instantly fell in love with the place. 'I'd never been to that type of club before. Here was a venue where you could sit right up close and hear the blues played by these young English bands.' Often the doorman let her in for free before the venue opened so she could catch the band setting up and doing their soundcheck. All this despite the fact Dana was under age. 'I was only fifteen or sixteen but I looked much older. I also looked good – nothing wrong

MARQUEE

**90 WARDOUR STREET
LONDON, W.1
Phone: GER 8923**

Thursday, Oct 7th (7.30-11.0)
★**GRAHAM BOND
ORGAN-ISATION**
Friday, Oct. 8th (7.30-11.0)
★**GARY FARR and**
★**THE T-BONES**
★ DAVID BOWIE and the LOWER THIRD
Saturday, Oct. 9th (2.30-5.00)
★**THE MARQUEE
SATURDAY SHOW**
Top of the Pops with guest D.J.s
and Star Guests
Saturday, Oct. 9th (7.30-11.0)
★**TONY KINSEY QUINTET**
★**JOHNNY BURCH TRIO**
with BOBBY WELLINS

David Bowie's first Marquee headliner.

with having a bit of a cleavage and lots of long blonde peroxided hair.' She was a big fan of the Yardbirds. 'I remember Jeff Beck came on stage in his pyjamas one night. The story was that his wife was so pissed off with him she locked him in the house and hid his clothes, so he climbed down the drainpipe in his pyjamas and still made it to the gig.' She was also a fan of the T-Bones and it was possibly at one of their gigs that she was standing at the back of the club brushing her hair when someone snatched the brush out of her hand. She turned to confront a guy with long Veronica

Lake blonde hair and knee-length suede boots. This was David Bowie. There was an immediate mutual attraction and the pair started to hang out together. 'David taught me a lot of my first chords on the guitar, and he taught me a few songs.' In the late 1970s Gillespie would play a couple of headline gigs of her own at the Marquee – 'And what an honour that was, especially having been so in love with the place,' she recalls.

In January 1966, Bowie and the Lower Third parted company; their final gig together was at the Marquee. Phil Lancaster was left wondering what had gone wrong: 'Now it's fairly easy to see that we, like all the other bands he worked with in the Sixties, were just transient experiments. Dave was barely with any of his line-ups more than a year. I think the Spiders from Mars lasted the longest and even they got the chop eventually.' Set on a solo career, Bowie booked three consecutive afternoons at the Marquee during the first week of February and held auditions for a new backing group. A couple of days earlier a young out-of-work musician named John Hutchinson, recently returned from Sweden, pushed through the doors into the Marquee. 'Behind the cash desk was Jack Barrie and I asked him if he knew of anyone who needed a guitarist. He gave me a phone number and said to call immediately as the auditions were that week.'

'I turned up as instructed,' remembers Hutchinson, 'dressed in my best outfit of a suede leather jacket, matching suede jeans and blue clogs. This was more or less standard-issue in my recent hometown of Gothenburg, but I was probably well ahead in the fashion stakes in London.' When it came to his audition a voice from the back of the room shouted that he should play some Bo Diddley. 'My Bo Diddley was pretty good,' says Hutchinson, 'but without bass and drums it sounded a bit weak in the empty club.' It was no surprise, he says, when another voice from the darkness shouted, 'OK. Thank you.' He was packing his guitar in its case and about to leave when Spike Palmer, Bowie's assistant, came over and said, 'David says you're in.'

'I think the clothes probably got me the gig,' says Hutchinson.

The new band was called the Buzz, and the act was billed as David Bowie and the Buzz. Their second-ever gig was at the Marquee on Friday 11 February, the same week that both Little Stevie Wonder and Georgie Fame also made their Marquee debuts (Fame would only play the club twice during the Sixties – his regular London gig was down the street at the Flamingo). Starting 10 April, Bowie and the Buzz began a nine-week run of Sunday afternoon performances. These kicked off at 3pm and promised 'three hours of music and mime' under the banner of the 'Bowie Showboat'. Hutchinson says that the residency gave them the chance to try out new material in relaxed surroundings. As with the Lower Third, sets were a mix of Bowie originals and covers, delivered in an increasingly theatrical fashion. The afternoon's closer was usually a melodramatic version of 'You'll Never Walk Alone', the Rodgers and Hammerstein show tune that Gerry and the Pacemakers had taken to the top of the charts a couple of years before. For the Marquee, the shows generated business at a time of the week when the club would normally be closed. Most of the Sunday concerts were sparsely attended and then chiefly by young female fans of Bowie. 'There were a lot of clubs to go to in the Soho scene of the 1960s,' he told an interviewer in 2001, 'but the Marquee was top of the list because musicians did hang out there, pretending to talk business and pick up gigs – but picking up girls mostly. One of my keenest memories of the Marquee in the Sixties was having a permanent erection because there were so many fantastic looking girls there.'

Among the screaming teens one Sunday was Kenneth Pitt, manager of Manfred Mann. He thought Bowie 'oozed confidence and was in total command of himself, his band and his audience.' That same evening Pitt became Bowie's manager, a role he'd fill for the next five years. He'd find himself working in tandem with the Marquee because not only was the club a regular gig for Bowie, it had an agreement to also secure bookings for the singer at other venues.

In addition to the club and studio, by this time the Marquee empire also extended to a publishing arm, Marquee Music, a press and public relations operation, called Marquee Publicity, and the Marquee Artists Agency, which handled bookings and looked after artists. The original Agency clients were Kenny Ball and His Jazzmen, Chris Barber's Jazz Band and the Yardbirds, and the list steadily grew through the 1960s. 'There were five of us working in Carlisle Street for Marquee Artists,' recalls Barbara Pendleton, 'myself and my old school friend Eve Holroyd, and Jo Chester, Trevor Whitchello and Julie Driscoll, before she became famous.' It was a busy office, says Barbara, filled with people hustling: Giorgio Gomelsky on behalf of the Yardbirds, Ricky Farr for brother Garry Farr, Alex Murray for the Moody Blues, Reg Tracey for Kenny Ball.

Other Agency artists included Marquee regulars Jimmy James and the Vagabonds, and the Action. After the Who outgrew the Marquee, the club was on the lookout for a replacement band with the same energy and excitement. For a while, in 1966, that was the Action. As the Boys, they'd supported the Who during their Marquee residency, so they already had a following at the club. They had an excellent vocalist in Reg King, regarded by some as one of the best UK soul singers of his era. They'd already caught the attention of no less a person than George Martin, producer of the Beatles, who'd signed on to produce the Action and would collaborate with the band on five singles. Despite Martin's involvement, none of the songs were hits and the band split up in mid-1967. They have since acquired cult status and are seen today as one of the most important bands of the 1960s mod subculture.

Following their relocation from Birmingham to London, Marquee Artists also took on the Move. They'd been spotted by former Moody Blues manager Tony Secunda, who had a tight working relationship with the Agency. The Move made their Marquee debut in April 1966. Led by big-voiced Carl Wayne and lead guitarist and orchestrator-in-chief Roy Wood, they played with volume and speed, employing handbrake turn tempo changes and rich harmonies delivered by four voices. Sets ended with screaming feedback, a drum solo and an enormous firecracker that left the audience dumbfounded, ears ringing and choking on smoke. In June, they began a Thursday-night headline residency. Eric Clapton, Spencer Davis and Muff Winwood dropped in to see them in July. Ever wilder stage antics, encouraged by Secunda, included flash bombs and smashing up TV sets with an axe. The resulting publicity grabbed the attention of the record companies and secured a contract with Deram.

London-based American producer Joe Boyd had a Thursday evening ritual for any visiting music business dignitaries: Chinatown for dinner followed by a walk up Wardour Street to the Marquee to catch the Move, 'for the Move in their prime were a phenomenon few Americans had the privilege of seeing,' he recalls. It all came to an abrupt end when the fireworks at one gig in November 1966 resulted in firemen turning up to clear the club. John Gee condemned the 'cheap, vulgar publicity stunt'. It was the last time the Move would play the Marquee.

The Summer Set were another outfit with mod sensibilities, who were also very obviously influenced by the Beach Boys. They sang in close harmony and were pioneers of the little-known UK 'surf sound' (appropriately, they came from the south coast). Keith Moon was a fan, apparently. The Marquee saw enough promise that they were added to the Management books. Like Davy Jones and the Lower Third, the Summer Set were put to work as a warm-up for Radio London's Saturday afternoon 'Live from the Marquee' sessions, as well as backing other artists' demos in the Marquee studio. Harold thought they might do for the surf sound what the Rolling Stones had done for R&B and introduced a weekly 'Surfin' Night' to the Marquee MC'd by toupée-wearing John Gee in a Hawaiian shirt. It never caught on.

Another Marquee Agency client was described as 'An eight-piece group steadily building a big reputation for themselves… personally requested by such artists as Solomon Burke and Patti LaBelle to accompany them on their British visits'. This was Bluesology. They'd been around for a few years but only turned professional in 1965, making their Marquee debut that December. Their two singles up to this point, issued by Fontana Records, had done nothing but they showcased the talents of songwriter, pianist, vocalist and Bluesology co-founder Reg Dwight.

Len Crawley, a fellow professional pianist, knew Dwight, a mild-mannered boy from Middlesex, and remembers going to see him play the Marquee. 'After the gig Reg introduced me to his mum. She was thrilled to bits that he had started making a name for himself. It was one of the few times she had seen him perform.' The young Dwight hung out at La Chasse, where he was often seen in the company of John Gee, who referred to the drinking club as the 'Pooverama' because the place had a contingent of gay regulars (the club's three owners were all gay). Bluesology played the Marquee at least once a month through 1966, usually as the support act, before becoming the regular backing band for Long John Baldry. Dwight left Bluesology in 1968, feeling that they didn't share his own broadening ambitions, and branched out as a solo artist under the name Elton John.

'The Marquee was a great magnet for talent,' says Steve Rowland, an American singer and actor who arrived in London in December 1965 and found employment producing for the Fontana label. He was often at the Marquee looking for new acts to sign. It was Rowland's partner, Ronnie Oppenheimer, who told him to go check out an act with a young guy, only fifteen years old, but who could really play guitar. 'Back then the Marquee used to hire itself out for afternoon auditions and rehearsals. I went down there with Ronnie and saw this band run through a couple of numbers and I said, man, we've got to sign these guys.' The band was the Herd and the teenage wonderkid was Peter Frampton. Rowland got the band's signatures on a contract and they went on to have three UK Top 20 hits. In the meantime, the Herd played the Marquee more than forty times through 1966 and 1967.

Bowie's final Showboat was in November 1966. His appearances at the Marquee after that were few but highly significant. On 15 June 1969, he appeared on a bill of the 'Strawbs and Friends', one of two support acts for the west London folksters; the other was a new American singer-songwriter recently signed to the Beatles' Apple label and making his UK live debut – James Taylor. On 3 February 1970, Bowie shared the bill with Junior's Eyes, whose members Tim Renwick (guitar) and John Cambridge (drums) formed part of his backing band along with Tony Visconti on bass. In the audience was Mick Ronson, who'd come down from Hull for the gig at the invitation of old friend John Cambridge. After the show, everybody gathered at La Chasse, which is where Bowie was introduced to Ronson, his future guitarist and collaborator on the run of early '70s albums that would make Bowie's name. On Sunday 1 August 1971, Bowie and Ronson performed a low-key Marquee date as a duo, debuting some of the songs that would shortly appear on *Hunky Dory* (released in December). Later that week they would record one of Bowie's career-defining songs, 'Life on Mars?', just up the street at Trident Studios. But that Sunday night, the club was only two-thirds full.

Bowie's final live appearance at the Marquee, on 20 October 1973, ended the era that began in the same room just over three-and-a-half years earlier. It marked the death of Ziggy Stardust and it was the last full gig Ronson would play with Bowie – more of which later.

THE SPONTANEOUS UNDERGROUND

Donovan | Pink Floyd | Phil Ochs | Sandy Denny |
The Spinners | Johnny Silvo | Bert Jansch | John Renbourn
| Al Stewart | Simon and Garfunkel | Cream | Small Faces |
6th National Jazz and Blues Festival, Windsor 1966
| Paul Butterfield Blues Band | Alan Bown Set | Jimmy James
and the Vagabonds | Episode Six | Neat Change | The Syn

You could argue that 1966 was the year music grew up. Several acts emerged this year that would heavily influence future sounds and styles, while a number of established artists produced era-defining albums. But at the Marquee, 1966 started with fun with jelly and a lot of dressing up. These seemingly frivolous goings on would turn out to be dress rehearsals for the coming counter-cultural revolution.

New Yorker Steve Stollman's interests leant toward the avant-garde. He hadn't been in the UK long when he picked up on promising undercurrents on the London scene. His response was to organise a 'happening'. His idea was that if you provided a space for people to get together and perform, then things would just 'happen'. He hired the Marquee for a Sunday afternoon and the inaugural event took place on 30 January under the hopeful billing of the Spontaneous Underground. Stollman distributed flyers promising, 'Costume, masque, ethnic, space, Edwardian, Victorian and hipness generally... face and body make-up, certainly.' A preview in *The Sunday Times* further expanded on the offerings with, 'Poets, painters, pop singers, hoods, Americans, homosexuals (because they make up to 10% of the population), 20 clowns, jazz musicians, one murderer, sculptors, politicians and some girls who defy description.' The audience, proclaimed Stollman, would be its own entertainment.

He was right and the Spontaneous Underground was a surprising success. According to a report in counter-culture newspaper *International Times*, on that Sunday Pete-the-Rat turned up in top hat and tails pushing a pram containing a gramophone on which he played old 78s; a couple performed 'anti-conjuring' acts, pulling broken eggshells from a top hat, setting things on fire and throwing buckets of water about; poetry was read and pick-up bands assembled to play in all manner of styles; people had their hair cut on stage; folk musician Donovan performed wearing Egyptian Eye of Horus make-up and sat cross-legged on the stage accompanied by six sitar players and a conga drummer. *Melody Maker* called it 'highly pretentious nonsense', but the Spontaneous Underground continued as regular Sunday attraction at the Marquee through until the early summer. The second week a classical pianist played her way through a Bach prelude surrounded by Ginger Johnson and his African drummers drumming. Music was also provided by experimental group AMM, led by Cornelius Cardew, professor of composition at the Royal College of Music, who had worked with John Cage and David Tudor, and spent two years as Karlheinz Stockhausen's assistant. For their Marquee appearances they had no prepared music and went on stage in white butchers' coats, and improvised using whistles and sirens, radios, tapes and electric toys that vibrated on steel trays. With no alcohol available, punters made do with pot and acid. A highlight most weeks was the creation of a large mound of jelly that members of the audience were invited to dive into. The magazine *Titbits* covered one event declaring, 'What a rave! A man crawling naked through jelly. Girls stripped to the waist. Off-beat poetry. Weird music. It all adds up to Raving London. For the capital no longer swings. It goes berserk!'

For the third happening, in March, Stollman decided to add a band who had to that point only performed at rag balls, private parties and dances. They called themselves the Pink Floyd Sound. The Floyd's Spontaneous Underground appearance on 12 June was watched by Peter Jenner, a disillusioned lecturer at the London School of Economics, who along with his friend Andrew King had set up a management company in the hope of making their fortunes in the music industry. The Pink Floyd Sound's unique combination of R&B and primitive electronica was sufficiently intriguing that Jenner talked his way into becoming their first manager. He immediately booked them to play some fundraisers at All Saints Church Hall in Notting Hill on behalf of the hippyish London Free School, and he brought them back to the Marquee for a couple of gigs in December and two more in January 1967. However, without the context of the Spontaneous Underground the venue felt wrong. Drummer

Nick Mason wrote in his 2004 memoir, 'We had a fairly uncomfortable relationship with the club and its audiences.' Mason felt that John Gee in particular didn't like them. 'With our weird music and funny lights, as well as our particularly amateur brand of musicianship, we must have been a total anathema to him.' But by then Gee had taken a strong disliking to many of the noisy and unwashed bands that were becoming popular.

One of the Floyd's final Marquee appearances was attended by a journalist from society magazine *Queen*. She noted that the group's apparatus took up more space in the club than the audience. She described a giant screen at the back of the stage projecting fantastical imagery: 'great blobs of red and white and purple and blue that diffused and switched and exploded. The effect was like an endless series of action paintings.' The music itself bored the journalist and she left after half an hour. By now, the Floyd had found a more suitable venue in the UFO club in Tottenham Court Road, launched in December 1966 as a 'sort of psychedelic version of the Marquee' by some of the same crowd involved with the London Free School. The Floyd shared the bill at the first two UFO nights with fellow psych band Soft Machine, who earlier in the year had also played one of their very first gigs at a Marquee Spontaneous Underground event.

There was more experimentation at the Marquee around this time in the form of folk and acoustic sessions on Wednesday nights. Artists included most of the luminaries of the scene: Phil Ochs, Sandy Denny, the Spinners, Johnny Silvo, Bert Jansch, John Renbourn. Al Stewart, still ten years away from his hit single 'Year of the Cat', was a regular all through 1966 and into 1967; he made the most appearances at the club of any folk artist. In July 1966, there was a one-off Sunday-night show by Simon and Garfunkel. It was arranged in association with Rik and John Gunnell of the Flamingo club, who had organised the gig but decided their own club was too small given the duo had already had international hit singles with 'The Sound of Silence' (which had reached No.1 in America) and 'Homeward Bound'. Jack Barrie claims that Paul Simon also made one or more unbilled Wednesday night solo appearances. Other American artists at the club around this time included foundational bluesman John Lee Hooker (he made his first Marquee appearance in May 1966, with a second and last in July 1967), boogie-woogie pianist Champion Jack Dupree (in May

1966 he made the second of what would be five appearances on Wardour Street) and soul man Ben E King, whose only date at the club was in May 1966. There was also 'Godmother of Soul' Patti Labelle, who made a one-off appearance on 17 May. Jack Barrie remembers it started out as a very quiet night: 'There was a very small audience of no more than a hundred. But once she came on the atmosphere was unbelievable. We couldn't get them off the stage. The crowd kept calling them back and they did nine or ten encores before calling it a day at half past midnight.'

By the time the Small Faces made their Marquee debut, in March 1966, they already boasted a hit single ('Sha-La-La-La-Lee') and a screaming teen fanbase. Before then, some of the future members of the band were already regulars at the club. 'Ronnie [Lane] and I saw the Who there, at the start of their long Tuesday night residency towards the end of 1964,' recalls drummer Kenney Jones. 'Afterwards, Ronnie and I headed home, talking very little, both occupied with the same thought. We've got to make that happen for [us].' Jones recalled the Small Faces' Wardour Street debut in his autobiography: 'The audience that night was not screaming girls. They were kids who were into the music, not the image. They were critical, not easy to please. You had to be good musicians to make it at the Marquee.' Part of the concert was filmed for broadcast in Europe. The Small Faces played a second Marquee date three months later. Harold recalls the band attempting a discreet exit via the back door into Richmond Mews where they were met by a mob of fans who had sabotaged their van by taking out the starter motor. They were too big for the club.

That summer three familiar Marquee faces came together in a new group, one that briefly defined the zeitgeist with an explosive attack of improvisational pop, psychedelia and blues played at high volume – and set the musical genre of rock on its way. Jack Bruce and Ginger Baker had previously played the Marquee as part of both Blues Incorporated and the Graham Bond Organisation, while Eric Clapton had appeared at the club with the Roosters, the Yardbirds and most recently with John Mayall's Bluesbreakers. Clapton was also given to turning up at the Marquee looking to jam, joining the Spencer Davies Group on several occasions and, in April 1966, reuniting with old bandmates the Yardbirds and sparring with Jeff Beck – a teenage Brian May was in the audience on

MARQUEE CLUB

FEB. 1966 PROGRAMME

90, WARDOUR STREET, LONDON, W.I. (GER 8923)

Every Saturday afternoon, 2.30-5.30 p.m.

"THE MARQUEE SATURDAY SHOW"

Top of the Pops both Live and on Disc
Introduced by Guest D.Js., featuring Star
Personalities

MEMBERS : 3/6   NON-MEMBERS : 4/6

Tue.	1st	INEZ and CHARLIE FOXX
		The League of Gentlemen
		Herbie Goins and the Night Timers
		(Members: 7/6, Non-members: 8/6.)
		* Members' Tickets in advance from
		January 25th.
Wed.	2nd	THE FRUGAL SOUND
		AL STEWART
		The New Harvesters etc.
Thur.	3rd	GOLDIE and DAVE ANTONY'S
		MOOD etc.
		RAM HOLDER BROS.
Fri.	4th	Gary Farr and the T-BONES
		The Objects
Sat.	5th	Modern Jazz:
		DICK MORRISSEY QUARTET
		RONNIE ROSS QUARTET
Sun.	6th	CLOSED
Mon.	7th	LITTLE STEVIE WONDER
		The Sidewinders
		Victor Brox Blues Train
		(Members: 7/6, Non-members: 8/6.)
Tue.	8th	THE ACTION
		Roscoe Brown Combo
		* Members' Tickets in advance from
		February 1st.
Wed.	9th	RAM HOLDER BROS.
		Mike Rogers
		and Guests
Thur.	10th	THE STEAM PACKET
		Long John Baldry, Rod Stewart,
		Julie Driscoll, Brian Auger Trinity
		JIMMY CLIFF BIG SOUND
Fri.	11th	DAVID BOWIE and the Lower Third
		BOZ and the SIDEWINDERS
Sat.	12th	Modern Jazz:
		DICK MORRISSEY QUARTET
		RAY WARLEIGH QUINTET

Sun.	13th	Sunday Special:
		GEORGIE FAME
		HARRY SOUTH and his ORCHESTRA
		Featuring Tubby Hayes, Ronnie Scott,
		Dick Morrissey, Phil Seamen etc.
		and Peter Bardens Quartet
		(Members: 7/6, Non-members: 8/6.)
Mon.	14th	Jimmy James and the VAGABONDS
		MARK LEEMAN FIVE
Tue.	15th	THE ACTION
		Bo Street Runners
		* Members' Tickets in advance from
		February 8th.
Wed.	16th	THE SPINNERS
		The Frugal Sound
		Tony McCarthy
Thur.	17th	ALAN PRICE SET
		Felder's Orioles
Fri.	18th	Gary Farr and the T-BONES
		and supporting group
Sat.	19th	Modern Jazz:
		RONNIE ROSS QUARTET
		CHRIS BATESON SEXTET
Sun.	20th	JAZZ 625 (B.B.C. T.V.)
		Members only. Tickets available
		free on personal application
		one week prior to this date.
Mon.	21st	Jimmy James and the VAGABONDS
		MARK LEEMAN FIVE
Tue.	22nd	SPENCER DAVIS GROUP
		Bluesology
		(Members: 6/-, Non-members: 8/6.)
		* Members' Tickets in advance from
		February 15th
Wed.	23rd	RAM HOLDER BROS.
		DORRIS HENDERSON
		and guests
Thur.	24th	THE STEAM PACKET
		Long John Baldry, Rod Stewart,
		Julie Driscoll, Brian Auger Trinity
		JIMMY CLIFF BIG SOUND
Fri.	25th	Gary Farr and the T-BONES
		and supporting group
Sat.	26th	Modern Jazz:
		DICK MORRISSEY QUARTET
		TONY KINSEY QUINTET
Sun.	27th	PRIVATE FUNCTION Closed to Public
Mon.	28th	MARK LEEMAN FIVE
		and supporting group.
Tue.	1st	MANFRED MANN
Wed.	2nd	CHRIS BARBER'S JAZZ BAND

(All Programmes are subject to alteration and the
Management cannot be held responsible for non-
appearance of artists)

1966 was arguably the finest year for new music in the history of the Marquee. Artists featuring in February alone include Al Stewart, Stevie Wonder, Steampacket (featuring Long John Baldry, Julie Driscoll, Rod Stewart and Brian Auger), David Bowie, Georgie Fame, the Alan Price Set, the Spencer Davis Group (supported by Bluesology, featuring the future Elton John) and Manfred Mann. The following month adds Davy

marquee club

GERRARD 8923 | **90, WARDOUR STREET, LONDON W.1.**

MAR. 1966 Programme

Tue. 1st	**MANFRED MANN** The D. J. Blues Band (Members: 6/– Non-members: 8/6) *Members' tickets in advance from February 22nd
Wed. 2nd	**CHRIS BARBER'S JAZZ BAND** with Kenneth Washington **RAM HOLDER BROS.** (Members: 5/– Non-members: 7/6)
Thur. 3rd	Jimmy James and the **VAGABONDS** **THE SUMMER SET**
Fri. 4th	**GARY FARR and the T-BONES** The Objects
Sat. 5th	Modern Jazz: **RONNIE ROSS QUARTET** **TONY KINSEY QUINTET**
Sun. 6th	**SUNDAY FOLK SPECIAL** **Davy Graham, Max and John Le mont** **and Marilla Waesche** (Members: 5/6 Non-members: 6/6)
Mon. 7th	**GRAHAM BOND** Organisation Felder's Orioles
Tue. 8th	**SPENCER DAVIS GROUP** The Explosive JIMMY CLIFF (Members: 6/– Non-members: 8/6) *Members' tickets in advance from March 8th
Wed. 9th	3 City 4, Al Stewart Backwater 4
Thur. 10th	**MARK LEEMAN FIVE** **THE SUMMER SET**
Fri. 11th	From the U.S.A.: **IRMA THOMAS and her Group** **Roscoe Brown Combo**
Sat. 12th	Modern Jazz: **DICK MORRISSEY QUARTET** **RAY WARLEIGH QUARTET**
Sun. 13th	**CLOSED**
Mon. 14th	**THE STEAM PACKET** **Long John Baldry, Rod Stewart,** **Julie Driscoll, Brian Auger Trinity** **Target 66**
Tue. 15th	The Return of **THE YARDBIRDS** **The Clayton Squares** (Members: 6/– Non-members: 8/6) *Members' tickets in advance from March 8th
Wed. 16th	**THE SPINNERS** New Harvesters, Mike Rogers
Thur. 17th	**MARK LEEMAN FIVE** The Objects

Fri. 18th	**DAVID BOWIE and the BUZZ** **THE SUMMER SET**
Sat. 19th	Modern Jazz: **DICK MORRISSEY QUARTET** **TONY KINSEY QUINTET**
Sun. 20th	**JAZZ 625 (B.B.C.-T.V.)** Members only. Tickets available free on personal application one week prior to this date.
Mon. 21st	Jimmy James and the **VAGABONDS** **BOZ and the SIDEWINDERS**
Tue. 22nd	First appearance at the Marquee: **THE SMALL FACES** **The Summer Set** (Members: 6/– Non-members: 8/6) *Members' tickets in advance from March 15th
Wed. 23rd	**RAM HOLDER BROS.** Jo Ann Kelly, Shades of Blue
Thur. 24th	**MARK LEEMAN FIVE** Roscoe Brown Combo
Fri. 25th	**GARY FARR and the T-BONES** Alan Walker Group
Sat. 26th	Modern Jazz: **DICK MORRISSEY QUARTET** **JOHNNY SCOTT QUINTET**
Sun. 27th	To be announced Watch the "M.M." for details
Mon. 28th	**MIKE COTTON SOUND** with Lucas The D.J. Blues Band
Tue. 29th	**THE ACTION** The Loose Ends *Members' tickets in advance from March 22nd
Wed. 30th	**THE FRUGAL SOUND** New Harvesters, The Compromise
Thur. 31st	**MARK LEEMAN FIVE** Bo Street Runners

Every Saturday afternoon, 2.30–5.30 p.m.

"THE SATURDAY SHOW"

Top of the Pops both Live and on Disc
Introduced by Guest D.Js.,
featuring Star Personalities

Members: 3/6   Non-members: 4/6

(All Programmes are subject to alteration and the Management
cannot be held responsible for non-appearance of artists.)

Graham, Graham Bond, Jimmy Cliff, the Yardbirds (with Jeff Beck) and the Small Faces.
Not mentioned on the programme are Sunday afternoon's Spontaneous Underground
events featuring the Pink Floyd. Later in the year there would be debuts for The Lovin'
Spoonful, the Move, Cream, the Herd with Peter Frampton, John Lee Hooker, and Eric
Burdon and the Animals. Note the introduction of a new logo heralding a new era.

that particular night. On 16 August, Baker, Bruce and Clapton made their Marquee debut as Cream, in what was one of the group's earliest public performances. According to *Record Mirror*, over 1,000 people were turned away from the door as the gig broke the club's attendance record. Swedish tourist Henry Björklund was one of the lucky ones who managed to get in: 'It was a kind of music I'd never heard before. It was amazing. It was loud, heavy, precise, breathless, it was everything. For some unknown reason, a stuffed gorilla was on stage in the second set.'

Although this was Cream's first appearance at the club, John Gee and the Marquee management were already familiar with the set because they'd given the new group its first major public exposure when they included them in the line-up for that summer's edition of the National Jazz and Blues Festival, held two weeks previously. Since being turfed out of Richmond after the 1965 festival, Harold had been hunting for an alternative site. At one point he approached the owners of the rugby stadium in Twickenham, but they turned him down. Instead, the solution arrived when the owner of Windsor racecourse got in touch and said he was open to the idea of the festival moving there. Harold presented himself to Windsor council with an application for an entertainment licence but he was refused on the grounds of nuisance and noise factor. Harold appealed and won.

The festival went ahead on the last weekend of July on Balloon Meadow, a large expanse of green that was used as an overflow car park for the racecourse. It brought Marquee stalwarts, including the Who, the Move, the Action and the Spencer Davis Group (the Yardbirds were billed but had to pull out because of illness), along with Marquee casuals Georgie Fame, Chris Farlowe and the Small Faces to the royal borough.

The mood that weekend at Windsor must have been jubilant because as Chris Barber and his band were playing jazz on Saturday afternoon, simultaneously Alf Ramsey's eleven men were playing Germany in the final of the football World Cup at Wembley and earning a famous English victory. Later that evening spirits were dampened by the dire weather and it seemed a poor joke when the Summer Set with their Beach Boys inspired songs took to the stage and attempted to gee up a thoroughly soaked crowd who were grimly holding out for the Who. The audience pelted the stage with missiles and the band were forced to run for cover mid-song. When the evening's headliners appeared the audience was treated to a blistering set that included 'I Can't Explain', 'Anyway Anyhow Anywhere', 'Substitute' and 'My Generation'.

The weather was just as filthy the following evening for the festival's closing performance, delivered by Eric Clapton, Jack Bruce and Ginger Baker – which is how they were billed in the festival's advance publicity because they hadn't yet come up with a name for their new band. They had only performed once together in public, a few days earlier at a low-key rehearsal in Manchester. Windsor was their official debut. The rain never let up for the whole of the set, which was just forty-minutes short – and a substantial part of that was taken up with a Ginger Baker drum solo. When they departed the stage John Gee had to rush on and apologise on their behalf explaining that they had played all the material they had. The real loser was Reg Dwight and his band Bluesology, whose single 'Come Back Baby' had just come out but who were on in a tent at 9.15pm, just as the act everybody wanted to see, Clapton and co, were taking to the main stage.

Cream were back at the Marquee in late September and again on 8 November. After the latter gig, the band drove over to Blaises to catch the second set from the American Paul Butterfield Blues Band, who were over on their first visit to the UK and in Chicago-born Mike Bloomfield had one of America's finest blues guitarists. Two nights later, the Butterfield Blues Band played the Marquee; some of its members were back at the club the following night to watch John Mayall's Bluesbreakers, who were showcasing new drummer Aynsley Dunbar, and Paul Butterfield joined the action on stage. (Other artists appearing at the club this week were the Crazy World of Arthur Brown, Peter Frampton with the Herd, Al Stewart, Bluesology and David Bowie – oh, for a time machine!) Cream would go on to appear at the Marquee a further three times, the last being in May 1967 – a scheduled November gig was cancelled when Baker fell ill.

Appearing along with Cream that Sunday at Windsor, and then launching into a Monday residency at the Marquee, were the Alan Bown Set. Led by trumpet player Bown, the brass-heavy jazz and blues outfit was formed from the remnants of the John Barry Seven, after Barry left to concentrate on film composing. They became a big hit on the club circuit, including regular support slots at the Marquee, where they opened for the likes of Manfred Mann, Blues Incorporated and Steampacket. 'We always got a really great reaction from the crowd,' recalls saxophonist John Helliwell. 'Sometimes even better than the main act. There was always a special atmosphere at the Marquee, I think because the audience always expected to hear something good, such was its reputation.' By summer 1966, the Set were flirting with psychedelia and prog, mixing horns with rock music. Helliwell recalls the band being taken to Carnaby Street to be fitted out in brightly coloured shirts and suits. One show that September was recorded and released as one half of a live album called *London Swings: Live at the Marquee Club*. The other side of the album was given to soul/ska band Jimmy James and the Vagabonds, who were also Marquee regulars. Helliwell remembers the recording process as rough and ready. 'It was just like a gig, maybe a little bit more time in-between the two bands in order to set up the microphones, but it was really a case of, get out there on stage and do it, no second chance. In the weeks leading up to the recording we'd be playing up and down the country and telling people about it, so a lot of our fans turned up on the night, the same with Jimmy, and you can clearly hear the enthusiasm of the audience on the record.'

The Alan Bown Set continued to appear at the Marquee for the remainder of the year and into 1967. By 1969 the band was in crisis when soulful lead singer Jess Roden decided to leave. Auditions were held for a replacement and one aspiring singer who turned up was future Yes front man Jon Anderson. In the end, Bown chose another rising star, the young Robert Palmer. 'You do get some real characters at these auditions, though,' says Helliwell (a future member of Supertramp). 'There was this one chap who arrived and sat around very quietly waiting for his turn, then he leapt up to the mike and stuck one finger up his nose and it remained there all the time he was singing. He didn't get the gig.'

It was not only London that was swinging. Down on the south coast, in Bognor Regis, the Shoreline Club was a strange mix between a youth hostel and musical kibbutz on the sea front – a hotel for teenagers run by teenagers. It was launched by a local entrepreneur named Eric St John Foti in early 1965, and weekends featured sets by local bands in the ballroom. By 1966, more nationally recognised groups were appearing at the club.

However by summer, the hotel was facing sex and drugs charges, and Foti decided to sell up. Harold and Barbara were the buyers. They launched the 'Marquee at the Bognor Regis Shoreline' on Saturday 29 October 1966 with the Action, Long John Baldry, Bluesology and David Bowie and the Buzz. The hotel continued operating as a weekend 'Marquee on Sea' through 1967, with acts including the Who, Pink Floyd, Jimmy James and the Vagabonds, the Herd, the Alan Bown Set and John Mayall's Bluesbreakers. It closed in 1968.

Among the other artists making Marquee debuts in the second half of 1966, two of the more interesting were Episode Six and Neat Change. Episode Six had earned their dues performing eight-hour sets at clubs in Cologne and Frankfurt. By the time they reached the Marquee they had a polished repertoire of R&B and blues covers. They played every other week until the end of the year at which point financial pressures sent them off to work a long Christmas season in Beirut. They never played the Marquee again, and the band fell apart soon after singer Ian Gillan and bassist Roger Glover left in 1969 to join Deep Purple.

Neat Change have been described as London's first skinhead group, with their uniform of Levi jeans with half-inch turn ups, Fell boots, Ben Shermans, braces and cropped hair. Formed in late 1966, and led by art student and singer Jimmy Edwards, the band had only been together a month or so, playing Motown and American soul covers, when they auditioned for the Marquee and were asked to fill in as support to Manfred Mann the following week – when John Gee introduced them as a 'brilliant find'. After they came off stage he took them out for a curry. They did three more support slots that December before they were given their own Saturday night residency starting in January 1967. The club was the making of the band – 'If you played the Marquee, it was easy to be booked anywhere else. It was the rubber stamp of approval,' says guitarist Brian Sprackling. As they toured around Britain, the billing announced them as, 'Coming directly from London's Marquee'. The association with the club almost ended as abruptly as it started. Like the Move before them, Neat Change pushed it too far with the stage pyrotechnics, and John Gee was furious and sacked the band. He did eventually allow them back but they only played the club a few more times before splitting up.

Steve Nardelli was fourteen years old the first time he walked into the Marquee. He was there to see the Yardbirds. The experience inspired him to form his own band. They were the High Court, then they were the Syn. In a merger with another amateur band they gained a very capable bassist called Chris Squire. Eventually they landed an audition at the Marquee. 'It was terrifying,' Nardelli remembers. 'This was the Mecca of all venues for a group in those days. It had an aura about it and a very demanding audience. People didn't go there to dance, they went there to listen to the music.' They played two numbers after which John Gee strolled over and said, 'You'll do'. Their first gig at the club was in September 1966, opening for Gary Farr and the T-Bones. Over the next few months they shared the bill with some of the club's top acts including the Action, the Move, Jimmy James and the Vagabonds, Eric Burdon and the Animals, the Spencer Davis Group and the Pink Floyd. 'The Marquee was like a second home to us,' says Nardelli. 'We got to know everybody there and we recorded a few of our singles at the studio.' They continued at the Marquee through 1967 as the band's sound underwent a radical high-speed evolution from Who-inspired R&B covers to full-blown psychedelia and rock operatics, not least with a track called 'Flowerman', performed live with costumes and gardening props. The reasons for the radical shift in styles may well owe their inspiration to another landmark night at the Marquee, when the Syn played support to a guitarist who would change the way so many bands would approach music in the future.

JIMI HENDRIX

The Syn | Jimi Hendrix | Cat Stevens | Marmalade | The Bonzo Dog Doo-Dah Band | Family

The Syn had played the Marquee at least a dozen times before their appearance on 24 January 1967, so they were hardly novices. But when Steve Nardelli walked onto the stage that night he was quaking. 'Sitting in the four seats literally right in front of me were the Beatles. Next to them were the Rolling Stones. The Who were there and Eric Clapton. Everybody on the London scene was in the audience. It was unbelievable.' None of them were there to see the Syn, they were there for the headliner, the guy everybody was talking about: Jimi Hendrix.

The previous September, as a struggling backing musician who was getting nowhere at home in the US, Hendrix had boarded a plane for London. He'd been persuaded to make the journey by Chas Chandler, former bassist with the Animals, now in management. Soon after his arrival, Chandler took Hendrix to the London Polytechnic on Regent Street to see Cream. He was introduced to the band before and asked Eric Clapton if he could jam with them. Halfway through the set he got up and performed a version of a Howlin' Wolf song. Clapton has said that after that night his life was never the same again.

Hendrix's Marquee debut.

Chandler suggested to John Gee that he book Hendrix. He'd already played a bunch of small clubs in and around London but the Marquee was a bigger gig. Jack Barrie recalls, 'John asked me if I'd ever heard of this guitarist, because he wasn't too impressed with the demo Chas had played him.' Gee ended up saying he'd give the American a shot. 'He wasn't that well known at the time,' says Barbara, 'and we were stunned by the number of people who turned up.' He may not have been widely known, but everybody who had heard about Hendrix wanted to check him out.

At the front of the queue was seventeen-year-old Les Mitchell. He'd been a regular at the club for the past couple of years. That night, Barbara came out asking for help hanging a banner inside the club and Mitchell volunteered. When the job was finished, Barbara said, 'You're in now, you might as well stay.'

Musician and journalist Mick Farren had read in the press that Hendrix was playing the Marquee and knew he had to see him. He arrived early but already the queue was far enough down Wardour Street to fill the club twice over. He decided to see if there was anyone at the Ship who might be able to help. And there was Jimi Hendrix himself, in the pub, with the hair, the scarves, the hussar's jacket, an attractive blonde and a protective circle of roadies. It happened that Farren knew one of the roadies, and he was waved over to meet Jimi. 'Are you coming to see the show tonight?' asked Hendrix. 'That's why I came down here, but…' said Farren, with a shrug. Hendrix said to leave it to him. Farren ended up with a ringside seat.

A teenage Phil Collins wasn't so lucky; in his autobiography he writes about how he was first in line in the queue for tickets and grabbed himself a front-row seat, only to have to leave before Hendrix came on to catch the last train home.

Jack Barrie squeezed in around 1,400 punters that night. There were people fainting because of the heat and the crush who had to be carried outside. 'We laid them in the mews round the back while they recovered,' remembers Harold. Barrie was reprimanded the following day and there would never be that many people in the club again.

The normal schedule was for the support act to open, followed by the main act playing two sets with an interval, filled by the reappearance of the support act. Hendrix insisted he only wanted to do one set, so the Syn did two sets one after the other with a short interval between. (Soon after it became the norm at the club to have a single set from the opening act followed by a single set from the headliner.) When the Syn finished their second set bassist Chris Squire couldn't get back into the dressing room because it was so rammed. Peter Banks did squeeze in and remembers how nervous Hendrix appeared at the thought of performing in front of all the top guitarists in Britain. 'Who's out there?' he kept asking. Later, Squire sat on the grand piano at the side of the stage and watched Hendrix from there. The performance included 'Hey Joe', 'Like a Rolling Stone' and 'Wild Thing'. 'I saw Eric Clapton with his jaw dropping,' recalled Squire, 'as if to register, "I'm not God anymore".'

'Rock history was made that night,' says Steve Nardelli. 'All those great musicians were there and Hendrix changed the way they all played guitar.'

100

Jimi Hendrix at the Marquee, playing for German TV on 2 March 1967.

Hendrix played a further two gigs at the Marquee: in March, in a private performance for the German television show *Beat Club*, with a set list that included 'Hey Joe' and 'Purple Haze', and again in October. Before each gig Hendrix and the band came in like most others to rehearse in the afternoons. There were frequently complaints from the people living in Richmond Mews behind the club about the noise; none more so than on the day that Hendrix rehearsed. Laurie Coombs took the angry phone calls and had to go into the club, interrupt the rehearsal and ask Hendrix to turn it down. 'He was such a lovely man, very polite and quietly spoken – he just said, "Sure thing ma'am." Not many people have asked Jimi Hendrix to turn the sound down!'

Gee hesitated over Hendrix, but he could spot talent – particularly if it was an attractive young man. At one of the Wednesday folk nights, which usually featured several artists and gave opportunities to new faces, Gee was taken by a young singer/songwriter with a gentle voice, strong self-penned compositions and a charisma that marked him out as something special. His name was Steven Georgiou and he lived above his family's cafe on nearby Shaftesbury Avenue. Gee took him out for coffee and explained what the Marquee could do for him – management, booking, festival spots. Georgiou said he'd think about it. The next time they met it was to tell Gee that he'd signed with Decca, who'd promised to take him straight into the recording studio. He was happy to play the Marquee again, though. Gee booked him to make his headline debut on 21 February 1967, by which time the singer had changed his name to Cat Stevens and had a single to promote, 'Matthew and Son', and an album of the same name out in a fortnight. Both were hits and after just the one appearance, Stevens outgrew the Marquee and never performed there again. (He returned in November but in the role of producer, using the club to rehearse Birmingham band Zeus, who debuted at the club in December, opening for the Nice.)

Another of Gee's favourites were melodic Scottish rockers Marmalade. Their first appearance at the Marquee, in January 1967, was supporting Pink Floyd; their second was opening for the Action. 'We did better than them both,' recalls drummer Alan Whitehead. 'I remember John Gee saying, "Boys, if you can displace two top groups like that you deserve your own night."' Landing their own Marquee residency, says Whitehead, was like receiving the keys to the city. He recalls that the band would meet beforehand for a few drinks at La Chasse, and watch as the queue outside the club got longer. They'd regularly spot other musicians in the audience, and Whitehead remembers Hendrix dropping into their dressing room. 'It was a remarkable time. We did about nine months solid at the Marquee and we became so tight – it was like the musical equivalent of going to the gym every day.' They were so confident that when record label CBS suggested they record a song called 'Everlasting Love' they turned it down because they only wanted to do their own material. It was recorded instead by Love Affair – who regularly supported Marmalade at the Marquee – who took the song to No.1 in the UK charts.

Marmalade played monthly through until autumn 1969, by which time they'd had a No.1 of their own with a cover of the Beatles' 'Ob-la-di, Ob-la-da'. The band made their last Marquee appearance in 1973. 'It's a great accolade to the band that we were able to do it for that long and still pack it out,' says Whitehead, 'because John Gee was ruthless. If we weren't pulling them in, he'd have pulled the plug on us.'

Other bands debuting at the club in 1967 included the Bonzo Dog Doo-Dah Band. They'd been around for five years playing London pubs and Northern working-men's clubs with an act that parodied trad jazz and 1920s-style popular music. But around this time they were shifting to something closer to rock, although still full of the whimsy, artiness and outright anarchy that had always characterised their performances. For one of their Marquee shows (of which there were six, all between February '67 and March '68), drummer 'Legs' Larry Smith festooned the stage with the severed limbs, lungs and livers of animals destined for recycling as pet food. He also placed some seafood in the awning above the stage, which got overlooked in the clean up afterwards and lingered until Marquee staff finally figured out where the terrible smell was coming from.

Psychedelic pop band Timebox came from the same small seaside town as Harold, Southport, near Liverpool. Like Harold, they relocated to London, where they found themselves an agent and worked solidly on package tours with the Kinks, Small Faces and others. They landed a Wednesday night residency at London's Whisky a Go Go club, which was in the same Wardour Street building as the Flamingo, before landing their first Marquee appearance in early 1967. Over the next three years they would rack up over forty appearances at the club, mostly in support slots, although they did eventually progress to headliners. In 1970, founder member Chris Holmes left and the remaining four musicians carried on as Patto, playing a further twenty-two gigs at the Marquee. When Patto split, guitarist Ollie Halsall and drummer John Halsey would link up with the Bonzo's Neil Innes in the fictional Beatles parody band the Rutles (Halsey would also play on Lou Reed's *Transformer*).

There was also a first appearance, in 1967, for Leicester's Family, who, along with the likes of Pink Floyd, Soft Machine and the Move, were part of the burgeoning psychedelic scene – although their music also took in influences from R&B, soul, rock and jazz. Along with lead vocalist Roger Chapman's strangulated vibrato – not to mention the use of multiple saxophones, violin and cello – the other thing that marked them out was Charlie Whitney's distinctive double-neck Gibson guitar. Supposedly on the band's Marquee debut, which was in support of Cream (not an easy gig) on 21 March 1967, Clapton was so impressed with the guitar he asked Whitney if he could buy it. Whitney said no, but allowed Clapton to borrow it for Cream's set.

TEN YEARS AFTER

1-2-3 | The Jeff Beck Band | The Creation | Terry Reid | Ten Years After

Midway through the second half of the Sixties bands were swapping styles like kids with a dressing up box. What shall we play today? Take the Premiers, for example, a six-piece from Edinburgh knocking out soul and Motown. Then, all of a sudden, they found themselves three members down, which included the loss of both their guitarists, so they reconfigured themselves as a three-piece – bass, drums and organ – gave themselves a new name, 1-2-3, and relocated to London, where they might just have invented progressive rock.

It was their road manager, blessed with the gift of the gab, who persuaded John Gee to give them a listen. 'Unbeknown to us, John was something of a snob about pop music and a huge jazz fan,' says Billy Ritchie, the band's keyboard player. With no guitars, Ritchie's Hammond organ was worked overtime to fill out 1-2-3's sound, with no chord unfrilled, no keyboard run unflourished. 'When Gee heard us, he thought he'd found the missing link, a pop band that played like a jazz band. He put us straight on as headliners, no support spots.'

The band's first Marquee show was Saturday 11 March 1967, with gigs on the next two Saturdays, followed by a run of Fridays. Sets featured some of their own compositions along with covers, including versions of Simon and Garfunkel's as yet unreleased 'America' and 'The Sound of Silence', performed with changes in time signature, classical and improvisational interludes, and a disregard for verse-chorus-verse-chorus song structure – many of the ingredients that would later become identified with prog rock. Until now, keyboard players were positioned off to the side or at the back, but Ritchie and his keyboard were up front, centre stage under the spotlight – and he played standing up. 'I think I was jealous of guitarists,' he says. 'They seemed to have a lot of the limelight. I wanted to be as up front and in-your-face as they were. I think I tried to think like a guitarist, not a keyboard player.'

A witness to 1-2-3's second Saturday show described how the band completely split the audience: half loved it, half hated it and shouted abuse. A fight almost broke out. It got so bad that an irate John Gee went on stage to take on the hecklers: 'If you want to hear boring R&B, I suggest you fuck off to the 100 Club.' Gee doubled-down on his patronage: he had a life-size cardboard cut-out of the band placed in the club's foyer. The buzz built and the likes of Pete Townshend, Robert Fripp, Greg Lake, Jon Anderson, Chris Squire and Keith Emerson came down to see what all the fuss was about. 'Some of them came into the dressing room to meet us,' says Ritchie. One fellow artist who lent his vocal support was David Bowie, who at this point was working up to the release of his debut album; in an interview for *Record Mirror* he described 1-2-3 as, 'Three thistle-and-haggis-voiced bairns who had the audacity to face a mob of self-opinioned hippies with a brand of unique pop music, which, because of its intolerance of mediocrity, floated as would a Hogarth cartoon in the *Beano*.' On at least one occasion, Bowie helped carry the band's equipment into the Marquee and hung out with them at the Ship.

1-2-3's residency drew interest from the industry and no less a figure than Beatles manager Brian Epstein signed the band, acquiring them for his management company, NEMS. But he didn't appear to know what to do with them: 'He dressed us in pinstripe suits with cravats,' says Ritchie. 'We looked like the Jam only a decade or so earlier. His explanation was, "Sophisticated music must be clothed in sophisticated attire".' When Epstein died unexpectedly in August 1967, 1-2-3 were left in limbo.

In April, Jeff Beck, last seen in these parts with the Yardbirds, introduced the Marquee to his new five-piece Jeff Beck Band with Rod Stewart on vocals, Ronnie Wood on second guitar, Dave Ambrose (later of Fleetwood Mac) on bass and Rod Coombes on drums. It's pretty certain that wedding reception singalong 'Hi Ho Silver Lining' would have been in the set, having just been released the previous month.

The Mark Four were a beat group from Hertfordshire playing covers of the Beatles, the Shadows and American R&B until the loss of two band members heralded a change of direction from which they emerged as the Creation – a name thought up by their new manager Tony Stratton Smith, who we'll hear a lot more of very shortly. The Creation dressed like mods and, in terms of look and sound, the closest comparison would be to the Who. Like Pete Townshend, Phillips pushed the limits of what could be done with a guitar, playing around with feedback like Townshend, sliding random objects up and down the strings, reputedly including frozen meat pies, to create strange skittering sounds. At some point, he dropped the pies in favour of playing the strings with a violin bow – a technique later made famous by Jimmy Page.

The Creation played their first Marquee date in July 1966, supporting the Action. There was a break before they returned in May 1967 to play a handful of headliners. The set highlight and closer was 'Painter Man', the nearest thing they ever had to a hit single. For live performances the band would bring out a ten-foot canvas that vocalist Kenny Pickett would spray with multicoloured aerosols while he sang. Then he'd set it on fire. John Gee can't have approved. Maybe that's why, despite a devoted following, the Creation only headlined the Marquee four times.

The same month that the Creation began their brief headlining run, eighteen-year-old Terry Reid made his Marquee debut as a solo headliner. He was already a veteran of three years, largely spent fronting beat group Peter Jay and the Jaywalkers, who'd provided support to the Rolling Stones on a UK tour in September and October 1966. Handling guitar and raspy vocals, Reid was now backed by a streamlined outfit of an organist (who also played pedal bass) and drummer, who between them packed a huge bluesy-rock wallop. They quickly became crowd favourites and Reid (who would, in 1968, famously turn down the job of fronting Jimmy Page's new band, recommending instead Robert Plant) would go on to make over twenty appearances at the Marquee over the next few years.

That summer also saw the first of what would be almost thirty appearances at the Marquee for raw, jazzy, blues-rock band Ten Years After. The band was built around the pairing of Alvin Lee, once dubbed 'the fastest guitar player in Britain,' and bassist Leo Lyons, who had been playing around the Nottingham area since 1960. The dream was to move to London and make it big, and there were several failed attempts before the break came in the form of an introduction to Jack Barrie, which elicited the promise of an audition, just as soon as John Gee returned from his holidays. A few days later, however, Lyons received a call from a desperate Barrie – the support band for the coming Sunday had let him down, could they fill in? 'We actually supported the Bonzo Dog Doo-Dah Band,' recalls Lyons, 'which made for an unusual combination.' More support slots followed, including one for the Syn. Steve Nardelli remembers it well: 'They blew us off stage. It was very rare for a support band at the Marquee to get such an ovation that they returned for an encore, but that happened with Ten Years After. Alvin Lee was an unbelievable guitar player.' The reception at the club got them boosted onto the bill for the National Blues and Jazz Festival at Windsor that August. 'Playing in front of something like 10,000 people, for us at that time in our career was unbelievable,' says Lyons. 'We felt like we'd gone on stage unknown and come off famous.'

Ten Years After continued to appear at the Marquee up until they left for America early in 1969, where they played a career-defining spot at Woodstock. But the Marquee always remained special for Lyons. 'I've played all kinds of places, the Royal Albert Hall, Woodstock, Madison Square Gardens, the Budokan in Tokyo – I think the Marquee was on par with all those. Playing the Marquee was the first time I thought, after all these years we're starting to get somewhere. I loved it.'

WINDSOR'S SUMMER OF LOVE

7th Jazz and Blues Festival, Windsor 1967 | Peter Green's Fleetwood Mac | The Nice

For many who attended the seventh National Jazz and Blues Festival, held at Windsor for a second year, it was an unforgettable weekend. How could it not be? This was, after all, the summer of love. People showed up in multicoloured clothes, kaftans and beads. Joss sticks were lit and flowers were genuinely worn in hair. Singer PP Arnold released doves at the end of her set. Unfortunately, it was also memorable for a lot of the wrong reasons, including breakdowns, blow-ups, arguments, fights and fire.

The line-up was terrific. Advance publicity promised the Small Faces, the Move, Marmalade, the Pink Floyd, Donovan, the Jeff Beck Group with Rod Stewart, and Cream, among others. By this time, the facilities were much improved on past festivals, with on-site toilets, food stalls, medical facilities and a camping ground. There was also a radically new stage. Harold had been approached by designer and artist Keith Albarn (father of future Blur frontman, Damon), who had an idea for a ground-breaking Cubist stage design. Harold told Albarn to build it. It was unveiled at Windsor and looked like some sort of giant polyhedron sliced in half and opened up. It proved impractical: there was too little stage space for the musicians and their gear, and no shelter from the rain. Part way through one performance, it started collapsing. 'We had to crawl underneath and put in scaffolding poles to hold it up,' recalls Harold.

The festival was also plagued by PA problems for the entire weekend. The Move had the power cut out just as they were reaching the climax of their set. The Small Faces were only half way through when the same happened to them. 'You bastards!' yelled Steve Marriott.

An already restive crowd were further provoked when an announcement came over the PA that the Pink Floyd would no longer be appearing and, instead, here was Paul Jones. 'Do you like soul music?' he inquired, and was met by a barrage of boos that continued all through 'Do Wah Diddy' and 'Pretty Flamingo'. The star of Saturday night was Arthur Brown, he of the 'Crazy World of'. Although it wouldn't be released as a single until the following year, the pulsing, organ-heavy 'Fire' was already a huge live hit. At Windsor, the song was going to kick off with Brown descending from above onto the stage wearing a flaming helmet. He was strapped into his harness, the bowl of lighter fluid on top of his headpiece was lit and the crane began to lift him when he must have tilted his head spilling the flaming liquid over his shoulders. Lawrence Coombs was present and with the presence of mind befitting a recently retired chief fire officer, he

Poster for the 7th National Jazz and Blues festival, at Windsor in 1967.

tipped his pint over the singer and extinguished the flames. The stunt was abandoned. There was fire, though. An element in the crowd set a rubbish tip alight. When a fire engine came to put it out, the firemen were pelted with bottles. Other festival-goers clashed with security and attacked a BBC TV reporter.

There were bright spots: according to *Melody Maker's* Chris Welch, Tomorrow, who appeared with painted faces and freaky dancer Suzie Creamcheese, were excellent and benefitted from great sound on numbers including recent hit 'My White Bicycle'. Another big success were the Nice, who played on the festival's second stage, housed in a large marquee. The core of the group came from the T-Bones, in the form of keyboardist Keith Emerson and bassist Lee Jackson, who'd been left behind by lead singer Gary Farr when he launched an ill-fated solo career. Recruiting guitarist David O'List and Ian Hague on drums, the Nice were principally the backing band for American soul singer PP Arnold. Playing the festival was the band's first major break. 'When we were due to start,' recalls Lee Jackson, 'Pentangle were playing on the main stage a hundred yards away – pitter patter pitter patter of tiny little folky feet, and we came in! Boom! There must have been four people in the tent watching us, and two of those were Davey O'List's sisters, but by the end it was full.'

Also appearing on the second stage were blues-rockers Chicken Shack, led by guitarist Stan Webb, and recently back in the UK from a residency in Hamburg. They stood out from most other acts by virtue of having a woman in the line-up: performing backing vocals and on keyboards was Christine Perfect. By coincidence, making their debut on the main stage at Windsor that weekend were the band Perfect would join three years later, Fleetwood Mac. They had come together only a few weeks previously when guitarist Peter Green, who'd replaced Eric Clapton in John Mayall's Bluesbreakers, also decided to go his own way. He took with him the Bluesbreakers' drummer Mick Fleetwood but couldn't pry away bassist John McVie, who was comfortable earning a good wage. Nevertheless, Green named the group after his favourite rhythm section of Fleetwood and 'Mac' McVie. Green also recruited slide guitarist Jeremy Spencer and hired bassist Bob Brunning, temporarily, until he could get McVie. At Windsor, their first gig, Mick Fleetwood was petrified and Bob Brunning was so nervous that when he stepped up to the mic to announce the first song he forgot what it was. But then Spencer blasted out the first lick to 'Dust My Broom' and the band kicked in, performing a seven-song set that included the recently composed 'Fleetwood Mac'. Andy Powell, a seventeen-year-old budding musician, was in the audience that day: 'I'd never seen Peter Green before and I wasn't sure whether they were going to play an encore or not, so I leapt on stage and grabbed Peter Green round the neck and dragged him back on.' (Two years later, Powell would be up on the festival stage again, this time as a member of Wishbone Ash.) After the gig, the members of Fleetwood Mac saw John McVie backstage, waiting to go on with John Mayall, and they pleaded with him to join their band. Still he refused. He finally capitulated three weeks later.

Peter Green's Fleetwood Mac made their first appearance at 90 Wardour Street just two days after the festival – supported by Chicken Shack. Green and Fleetwood had played the Marquee before with the Bluesbreakers, and Fleetwood had also appeared at the club with the Cheynes and the Bo Street Runners. 'It was there where I went from complete obscurity to learning the tools of my trade,' he once told a journalist. For the Mac, this marked the start of a slog of one-nighters all around the UK, which brought them back to the Marquee on eight occasions over the next three years. The appearance on 29 March 1968, coincided with the release of the band's second single, 'Black Magic Woman', which gave them their first hit as it entered the Top 40 over the next few weeks. However, the band's vulgarity landed them in trouble. They had a running gag involving a large dildo, christened Harold, that Fleetwood always hung on his bass drum. On this night, Harold appeared dangling out of Spencer's trousers. It was too much for John Gee who bounded onto the stage, stopping the music and yelling at them to, 'Bloody well pack it in.' Gee banned them. The Mac wouldn't play the Marquee again until August 1971, when they returned for two consecutive nights. By this time, both Peter Green and Jeremy Spencer were gone, replaced by Bob Welch and Danny Kirwan. Fifth studio album *Future Games* was just about to be released and the band were moving away from the blues and toward the melodic rock for which they'd shortly become famous. These two dates would be the last time Fleetwood Mac played the Marquee.

Following their breakthrough performance at the Windsor festival, the Nice were offered a Sunday night headliner at the Marquee. When that went well, Gee switched them to Mondays. 'And we were off and running,' recalls Lee Jackson. Appearing thirty-two times at the club over the next eight months, the Nice revved up audiences with their theatricality, not least the antics of keyboardist Keith Emerson, determined to show that pyrotechnical techniques weren't only the province of guitarists (the night of 24 October 1967 would have been a tester, as the Nice played support to the Jimi Hendrix Experience). 'One time he was on top of the Hammond, rocking it, and he fell into the audience right in the middle of this group of teenage girls, who loved it,' recalls Jackson. By now, Emerson had discovered his trademark gimmick of stabbing the keyboard with knives. It started with sharp pieces of plastic until a roadie, a twenty-one-year-old called Ian 'Lemmy' Kilmister, gave Emerson a Nazi dagger.

'The Marquee made us,' says Jackson. 'Our drummer, Brian, had this big gong stand and one night he looked over and leaning on the top of it was Jim Morrison. Another time we walked into the dressing room and there was John Lennon and Paul McCartney. They told us, "We've heard about you buggers. You are fucking good, aren't you?"'

The last week of December saw the return to the Marquee of the band formerly known as 1-2-3. Cast into limbo by the death of manager Brian Epstein back in August, they'd decided to strike out on their own and had ended up, in the words of Billy Ritchie, 'Down among the dead men, playing small clubs and pubs.' Then one night, in Ilford, they were seen by record producer Terry Ellis (who would co-found Chrysalis Records in 1969). 'Terry signed us up,' says Ritchie. 'But he said we had to drop the too-clever-by-half material.' He also insisted on a change of name and the band became Clouds. They landed major European and American tours, appearing at the Royal Albert Hall and New York's Fillmore East, and returned to the Marquee on several occasions, but they never ignited audiences in the way they had as 1-2-3. John Gee remained their great champion, telling anyone who asked that they were his favourites. 'John was great,' recalls Ritchie. 'He might at times have been acerbic, pompous and aloof, but he was also kind. It's just hugely ironic that the band he liked best were one of the few from the Marquee that never made it big.'

JETHRO TULL

The Iveys/Badfinger I Taste and Rory Gallagher I Jethro Tull
I Fairport Convention I 10th birthday celebrations I The Who I
Traffic I Joe Cocker

On 25 January 1968, the Iveys, a band, like so many, struggling to make an impression on a crowded London scene, were playing support to Neat Change at the Marquee. This was their tenth appearance at the club, but on this particular night there was someone in the audience who was about to change their lives forever.

Mal Evans had been a roadie for the Beatles since 1963; by 1968, he was their personal assistant. The Iveys' manager Bill Collins knew Evans from his days in Liverpool and when, by chance, he ran into him in Soho, he asked him to drop by the Marquee and see his band. 'We'd built up a respectable following and had a good rapport with the audience,' recalls bassist Ron Griffiths. 'Mal was very impressed and likened it to the way the Fab Four had a similar thing going with the Cavern crowd. Afterwards we were introduced to him, and he came back to our place and spent the next few hours listening to some demos we'd recorded.'

Evans was impressed enough to take the tape back to the office, where he played it to his bosses, Paul McCartney and John Lennon. They weren't overly impressed but over the next few weeks Evans presented more and better demos, until finally McCartney started to hear something he liked. The result was that the Iveys became the first band signed to Apple Records. It was hardly overnight success: the band had been knocking around for the best part of a decade, since forming in Swansea in 1961. Relocating to London in the summer of 1966, they landed their first Marquee spot that November as support for Brian Auger and Julie Driscoll. 'At first it was daunting playing there by virtue of the reputation the venue had,' recalls Griffiths. 'But we came across well and the nerves vanished. One gig we supported Pink Floyd. Everyone was raving about them. After our set a couple of us stood and watched their first few songs, which were, quite frankly, poor covers of rhythm and blues stuff. We looked at each other, shrugged our shoulders and adjourned to the bar.'

While Evans was pressing their case with the Beatles, the Iveys continued gigging, including a handful more dates at the Marquee, the last of which was 13 July 1968. Ten days later they joined Apple and started on their debut album, which was co-produced by Tony Visconti. They were then asked to record several songs for a new Peter Sellers film called *The Magic Christian*, including the McCartney-penned 'Come and Get It'. However, before they released what would prove to be their international breakthrough hit, making the Top 10 in both the UK and US singles chart, Apple thought they ought to dump their name and come up with something cooler. They went with a suggestion put forward by Apple Corps' Neil Aspinall – Badfinger.

Early 1968 saw Marquee debuts for two bands from Ireland. Taste were formed by songwriter and guitar virtuoso Rory Gallagher, who had seen Van Morrison and his band Them make a name for themselves in London and was eager to follow in their footsteps. They found an appreciative audience on Wardour Street and would play the club two or three times a month through the rest of the year, and the next. One night John Lennon turned up to see them. Queen's Brian May was another fan; after one gig he hid in the toilets until everyone else had been thrown out then found Gallagher to ask him how he got his guitar sound (he was told it was a Vox AC30 amp and a Rangemaster treble booster, which became May's set-up ever after). Promoter Paul Charles says that out of the many acts he saw at the Marquee over the years no one ever matched Rory Gallagher and Taste: 'They were a true sight and sound to behold. Rory knew that the secret to a great gig is not playing to the audience but playing with them. You'd wander out into Wardour Street after a Rory show and you'd still be buzzing with it the whole way home and through to the next day, when all you'd want to do would be to plan your next visit to the Marquee.' The last time Taste played the club was in July 1970, shortly before they appeared at the Isle of Wight Festival, on a bill with Jimi Hendrix, the Who and Leonard Cohen. They split soon after.

Granny's Intentions were formed in 1965 by a bunch of Limerick school friends. Relocating to London in 1967, they landed a recording deal with Deram and had already released a first single by the time they debuted at the Marquee in January 1968. John Gee liked the look of them.

'When we eventually broke away from our manager, John Gee took us over and gave us a residency,' recalls singer Johnny Duhan. 'And he used his influence to get us gigs in some of the big clubs in Germany.' Being looked after by Gee brought its own special requirements. 'He used to inspect us for cleanliness before we went on stage,' says Duhan. 'His heart was in the big band era, so he expected us to look well-groomed and presentable before going before an audience. He also started inviting us back to his pad for games of Monopoly after our gigs. He took a particular shine to our drummer, Pat Nash, but Paddy wasn't having any of it.'

Gee also saw something in Putney psychedelicists the Open Mind, but he thought they needed a proper singer. He took them to Ronnie Scott's to check an American vocal band and tried fixing them up with Jon Anderson, but that didn't work out. 'That was indicative of what went on at the Marquee,' says the former Open Mind bassist Timothy du Feu. 'They wanted you to develop as an artist. In that way the Marquee was like a university for music – they helped you and gave you guidance.' Another beneficiary of Gee's interest were a four-piece, originally formed in Blackpool, who, in early 1968, were new to London. They were landing gigs but struggling to get repeat bookings, so they took to changing their name frequently – one week they were Navy Blue, another Ian Henderson's Bag o' Nails, then Candy Coloured Rain. On 2 February they were playing the Marquee under yet another name, this time supplied by their booking agent, a history enthusiast with a knowledge of 18th-century agriculturists. 'It was probably the fourth time we played there,' says the group's frontman Ian Anderson, 'and we just seemed to click. Not necessarily click with the audience, so much as click with John Gee. He decided he liked us. And that was the break we so desperately needed.' The band decided to stick with the name that had worked for them that night, which was Jethro Tull.

'John was a fairly immediate supporter,' says Anderson, 'because we had a little bit of a jazzy swing thing in the music.' There were support slots for the Bonzo Dog Doo-Dah Band and Fleetwood Mac, and, by May, they had their own Friday-night residency. Powered by Anderson's jazz-informed flute and Mick Abrahams' bluesy guitar, the group picked up regular gigs elsewhere in the capital, including Klooks Kleek up in

West Hampstead, the Speakeasy and Cromwellian, but for Anderson the Marquee was key to the evolution of Jethro Tull. 'It was a bit like being thrown into a swimming pool and having to learn to swim. It was a very energised environment where you really had to learn quickly because you would be ridiculed and booed off stage if you were rubbish. You had to find not only the musical substance but you also had to find that stage craft, the beginnings of establishing a rapport with the audience.' It was at the Marquee that Anderson's stage persona evolved. At first it started almost unconsciously, the raising of one leg as he played, but music journalists latched on to it fast. 'I felt, I'm going to have to live up to my new reputation and it became something of a trademark for the band from there on in.'

Tull's time at the Marquee lasted nine months, from debut support gig in February to a final headliner in November – nineteen appearances in total. But by the end of the period, they had released debut album *This Was*, with a single, 'My Sunday Feeling', that made the playlist on John Peel's BBC radio show and won the band a legion of fans. As a gesture of thanks to the man who gave the group their big break, when Jethro Tull released their second single that September, 'A Song for Jeffrey', the B-side was a jazzy instrumental titled 'One for John Gee'.

Making their Marquee debut the same week in February as Jethro Tull were Fairport Convention. Made up of guitarists Richard Thompson and Simon Nicol, singers Ian MacDonald and Judy Dyble, bassist Ashley Hutchings and drummer Martin Lamble, Fairport had been performing their American-influenced folk rock for eight months at underground venues such as UFO on Tottenham Court Road and the Electric Garden in Covent Garden. They'd already recorded a first album, although it wouldn't be released for a few months yet. Nicol remembers the gigs at the Marquee: 'It was hot, deafeningly loud, airless, smoky and as packed as a tube train. There wasn't much room on stage either!' After two appearances, there was a gap of five months before Fairport returned to the Marquee. In the intervening time, they'd replaced Judy Dyble with Sandy Denny, who had previously appeared a handful of times at the Marquee as a solo artist on folk nights. 'Sandy was all the things others have said about her,' recalls Nicol. 'Shy yet forceful, hilarious yet sometimes blue, fierce yet

John Gee, Keith Moon and Barbara Pendleton celebrate ten years of the Marquee.

withdrawn, confident but vulnerable. She brought colour and depth to us, and the power and class that took us up to another level altogether.'

April sparked a month-long jamboree, as the Marquee celebrated its first ten years in business. For a club to have survived that long, especially during a period of such revolutionary changes in musical styles and fashions, was no small achievement. An article in the American music trade paper *Billboard* reported that the Marquee could claim two million customers passing through its door since first opening back in April 1958. At a star-packed party, the highlight of the evening was the arrival of a specially baked cake, which was cut by Keith Moon and Barbara. 'Keith always behaved himself with us,' says Barbara.

The calendar that month featured some of the club's favourite acts, including the Nice, Ten Years After, Jeff Beck, the Crazy World of Arthur Brown, the Bonzo Dog Doo-Dah Band, Jethro Tull, John Mayall's Bluesbreakers, Marmalade, Al Stewart, Long John Baldry and, as a nod to the Marquee's origins in jazz, the National Youth Jazz Orchestra. The highlight was Tuesday 23 April, when Moon and his bandmates took to the stage for a triumphant one-off gig. Townshend found it strange to be back in the cramped confines of 90 Wardour Street after playing to over 2,500 at the Fillmore East in New York earlier that month and admitted to being scared beforehand that it was all going to go wrong. For Who fan Dermot Bassett, it's a night he's never forgotten. He'd seen the band live a few times before, but never anywhere as intimate as the Marquee. There were two support bands, the Gun, featuring on keyboard and vocals Jon Anderson, and Jethro Tull. Then the Who came on. 'The sheer power and volume was extraordinary,' recalls Bassett. 'Third number in, 'Summertime Blues', Pete spins his guitar up into the air, doesn't catch it properly and the head hits the stage. It makes it to the end of the number and Pete says, "I think I've broke me guitar already," hits the neck a couple of times and it falls off. He picks up another guitar which is still in its cardboard wrapping.' Townshend wrecked two guitars that night, including a Gibson that retailed at £200. 'I can't put it down to tax,' he told the press, 'because when I say I use seventy guitars a year, they don't believe me.'

To mark the anniversary, John Gee was interviewed by *Melody Maker*. Typically, he began not by talking about the music but by emphasising how orderly the club was. 'I am proud to say that [the Marquee] has never once been raided by the police in ten years, and has a completely clean record.' He went on to say that the leader of the House of Lords, Lord Longford, had visited the club and personally congratulated him on how well it was run. How very rock'n'roll.

The celebrations went on into May, with returns for Manfred Mann and saxophonist Dick Morrissey, who'd been a mainstay of the club in the early years – this would be the last of Morrissey's sixty-three appearances at the Marquee as a band leader, although he'd be back in the early 1970s as part of the line-up of jazz fusionists If. Also returning was ex-Spencer Davis Group alumni Steve Winwood, appearing with his new band Traffic.

Making his Marquee debut two days after Traffic was a vocalist who would score a hit in 1969 with a Traffic-penned song ('Feelin' Alright?' – released by Traffic in September 1968, but failing to chart in either the UK or US). A native of Sheffield, Joe Cocker honed his chops working the Steel City pubs, which is where he came to the attention of Denny Cordell, producer of Georgie Fame, the Moody Blues and Procol Harum. Cordell arranged the gig at the Marquee, which was followed by a second the following month, then a Wednesday night residency starting in July. Ray Bennett, future bassist for prog rockers Flash, caught one of Cocker's earliest Marquee performances: 'He was playing to a very small audience of about fifty or so people. I was sitting about two rows back with him straight in front of me, dodging his spit flying about. People weren't quite sure if there was actually something wrong with him physically because of the way he was flailing his arms about. He was good though, with a nice backing band that really cooked behind him.' Audience numbers would have ballooned later in the year as Cocker's version of the Beatles' 'With a Little Help from My Friends' went to No.1 in the UK in November. Cocker continued to play the Marquee through into January 1969, even as he was now packing out far larger places around the country.

SUNBURY

8th National Jazz and Blues Festival, Sunbury 1968 I Entec

Joe Cocker and Traffic both made it onto the bill of that year's National Jazz and Blues Festival, held over the weekend of 9–11 August 1968. This eighth edition took place at the new location of Kempton Park racecourse at Sunbury, on the north bank of the Thames in Surrey. The reason for the move was that the festival had been kicked out of Windsor.

Along with the disastrous new stage, another of Harold's innovations at the previous year's festival had been a prototype sound system. Until now, the sound at outdoor concerts was poor going on atrocious. The technology wasn't up to carrying quality sound over far distances. Enter

Charlie Watkins, audio engineer and pioneer in music technology. Through a colleague who worked security at the Marquee, John Thompson, he'd made a proposition to Harold that he could put together a festival PA system that was louder than anything else in existence. 'Pendleton, being no fool, screwed me down to doing it for nothing and warned me that if it went wrong it was going to be entirely my fault,' Watkins recalled in an interview given shortly before he died in 2015. What Watkins came up with was a system that delivered a seemingly impossible 1000 watts – 100 watts being the norm at the time. It is an achievement that has been described as the audio-engineering equivalent of breaking the four-minute mile. Ten times the wattage does not mean ten times as loud, but even so, nobody had ever heard anything like it. Which was fantastic until, seated at his soundboard beneath the stage, Watkins felt a hand on his shoulder and heard the words, 'I must ask you to accompany me to the station, sir.'

Watkins' system was far too powerful for the denizens of Windsor and there had been complaints about the noise from as far away as Eton, across the river. The festival was only allowed to continue because the last thing the authorities wanted was 40,000 unhappy rock fans taking out their frustrations on the town, but the organisers were told to 'turn it down'.

In the aftermath, an enraged Windsor Council sought an injunction banning the festival from returning. Summonses were issued to both Marquee Promotions and Watkins Electric Music to appear before magistrates at Reading County Court. To fight his corner Harold called on Lord Hailsham, the formidable barrister Quintin Hogg, a former Conservative Party chairman. As a figure of some celebrity, he drew an excited crowd to the courtroom, and as a barrister of some ability he succeeded in getting the case dismissed. Windsor Council fell back on plan B, which was to threaten the racecourse's owner, Jack Knight, with losing his licence unless he got rid of the festival. Knight gave in.

It would have been little consolation to Harold, but Watkins' success would prove critical to the future of outdoor festivals. More powerful sound systems opened the floodgates to an explosion of future mega outdoor events, such as the Isle of Wight and Bath festivals, the Stones at Hyde Park and the first Glastonbury.

He couldn't host Harold again, but Jack Knight did make the suggestion that Harold ring Henry Hythe, the owner of Kempton Park racecourse in Sunbury. Hythe was delighted to welcome the festival: 'It will drive them mad,' he said.

'Drive who mad?' asked Harold.

'All those bastards in the housing estate who complain about the racing.'

Sure enough, it did drive them mad, and they made sure that the 1968 festival was the first and last music festival at Sunbury – but, at least, it was a good one. Friday kicked off with a couple of Marquee regulars in Taste and Timebox, followed by a special guest, American rocker Jerry Lee Lewis. His rock'n'roll set, which included the likes of 'Blue Suede Shoes' and 'Whole Lotta Shakin' Goin' On', got the Teds in the audience a little over-excited, and one stage assistant lost four teeth in a ruckus. The following act, Marmalade, were showered with pennies for not being Jerry Lee Lewis, and a scaffolding pole was launched through the bass drum belonging to headliners the Herd, who then refused to go on.

Saturday afternoon was given over to jazz, followed by an interval allowing all beatniks and mods to clear the area prior to the arrival of Deep Purple – although at this early stage, even though keyboardist Jon Lord, drummer Ian Paice and guitarist Ritchie Blackmore were already in place, they were far from the heavy beast they would become. Instead, they offered a few self-penned songs and a bunch of rocking-ish covers from their debut album, *Shades of Deep Purple*, and were met with general indifference. Not so, Joe Cocker. He already had fans among the audience who'd seen him at the Marquee, and he had plenty more by the time he was done at Sunbury.

Acts had little time in which to win over an audience. With eight artists appearing between 7pm and lights out at 11.25pm, they had half an hour each. The festival policy was don't worry if you don't like this lot, there'll be another group along shortly. After Cocker came Tyrannosaurus Rex promoting just released debut disc *My People Were Fair and Had Sky in Their Hair...*, followed by Ten Years After, followed by Jeff Beck, followed by the Nice, followed by Ginger Baker, and climaxing with Arthur Brown. Beck had Ronnie Wood on bass and Rod Stewart up front, engaging in vocal duelling with both Beck's guitar and a bunch of Geordie hecklers down the front casting aspersions on the singer's sexuality. When the Geordies took to pelting him with beer cans he had to take refuge behind the protective wall of amps, from where he continued singing. The Nice's Keith Emerson battered his keyboard within an inch of its life and also burned the US flag as a protest against America's war in Vietnam. Ginger Baker's set had him duel with top jazz drummer Phil Seaman; twenty minutes in, a shadowy figure strolled on stage, plugged in a guitar and revealed himself as Eric Clapton.

What had been an incredible evening of music ended in disaster. As luck would have it, it involved Arthur Brown again. Kempton Park had its own railway station with an elevated walkway linking it to the racecourse. A couple of hundred people had clambered onto the walkway's roof to watch the bands. According to press reports, Brown and his band had just launched into their first number when the walkway collapsed. Unaware, the band carried on until a panicked John Gee rushed on stage to announce there had been a terrible accident. 'Oh shit,' said Brown and walked off stage. Luckily, nobody was killed but dozens were injured and had to be taken to hospital. Later, Arthur Brown re-emerged on stage to play a shortened and subdued set, with fans distracted by the blue flashing lights of arriving and departing ambulances.

Sunday went ahead as planned. The afternoon was given over to folk, with appearances by Al Stewart, Fairport Convention and the Incredible String Band. The evening line-up included John Mayall, Chicken Shack, Spencer Davis and Traffic, all of whom were put in the shade by Jethro Tull. This was the first time the band had played anything other than small clubs but, by the end of the set, the audience were on their feet. 'John Gee went on stage to try and announce the next act but was shouted down and booed by the audience,' recalls Ian Anderson. 'So, we were pulled out to do an encore.'

'Sunbury was one of the biggest days in my life as it was the day when we knew we were going to make it,' recalls Tull bassist Glenn Cornick.

Summer 1968 also saw a significant evolution in the Marquee's business interests. Ahead of the festival, Pat Chapman, who traded under the name of Crab Nebula Lights, had approached Harold with the suggestion of using his lighting services to add something new to the festival staging.

Harold gave the go-ahead and was sufficiently impressed with the results to set up Crab Nebula – named after an exploding star – with a workshop in the Marquee's basement. Harold also agreed to become Chapman's backer. 'Like most of the innovators I supported, their idea of backing was that they lost the money and I paid the bills,' he recalls. Nevertheless, the company, now trading as Entertainment Technicians Ltd, grew, providing both light and sound, and moving to new premises at Shepperton Film Studios – where it continued to lose money. 'After a while I got fed up,' recalls Harold. 'I told them that there'd be no more money unless I was given some control.' He was given a majority stake. A further row over money led to Chapman resigning, at which point Harold changed the company name to Entec and it became part of the Marquee group of companies. In future, Entec, operating as an independent concern, would lease PA systems to the bands playing the Marquee.

YES

Mabel Greer's Toyshop I Yes I Free

Around 1967–68, one of the more whimsically named bands appearing at the Marquee were Mabel Greer's Toyshop. They were formed by guitarist/vocalist Clive Bayley and drummer Robert Hagger, who came together over a shared passion for US West Coast bands. Bayley and Hagger were joined by guitarist Peter Banks and bassist Chris Squire of the Syn, who, for a time, played in both bands. Hagger had been going to the Marquee since he was sixteen. 'I remember one night being blown away by Steve Winwood doing Ray Charles's 'Georgia'. This kid my age from Birmingham, England, sounding like he was sixty and from Birmingham, Alabama.'

'It was always a great place to play,' says Hagger. 'Very professionally managed. We knew exactly what to expect from the time we loaded in to the time we left. And there was such a buzz about the way people queued at the door. Whether you were playing or in the audience, you could feel the excitement building.'

Jazz-fan Gee liked Mabel's free-form style of playing, but assistant manager Jack Barrie thought they were lacking something. He thought he had the solution. Jon Anderson was a twenty-four-year-old singer from Accrington, currently between bands, who Barrie had hired as a barman at La Chasse, where he also sometimes slept, dreaming of playing the Marquee. He had his first shot with a band called Gun. 'We opened for the Who. I agreed to us playing for no money just to be on the same bill.' His bandmates didn't appreciate playing for free and kicked Anderson out. 'It was Jack Barrie, bless him, that introduced me to Chris Squire one rainy Friday in the bar.'

'Jon's voice made the band much more listenable,' says Hagger. Which is magnanimous of him given that Anderson's arrival precipitated a change in the band's direction that saw Bayley and Hagger edged out, replaced by precocious teenage jazzy drummer Bill Bruford and classically trained keyboardist Tony Kaye. Anderson also decided the group needed a less ridiculous name – they settled on the supremely positive Yes. As the new five-piece began rehearsals in the basement of a nearby Shaftesbury Avenue cafe, Barrie provided a modest amount of financial support. 'I think we're only talking a couple of hundred pounds on a few occasions, but that money was an absolute lifeline,' says Bruford. 'We could continue for another month on that.'

Yes made their first appearance at the Marquee on Monday 5 August 1968, supporting Bournemouth's Nite People. It was their second ever gig, the first being two days earlier at East Mersea youth camp in Essex. Sets were made up of covers of songs by artists including the Beatles and Traffic. There were more support slots, for Joe Cocker and the Nice, among others, before Yes gained their first headliner, in November. Starting in January 1969, the band played most Wednesday nights for the rest of the year. Even so, they were barely getting by. 'For years it cost us more to do the gig than we were getting paid,' recalls Bruford, 'and Jack Barrie and our manager, Roy Flynn, kept us afloat.'

The drummer remembers the period as an important learning curve for the band. 'It was when you learnt what you were about, on a rainy mid-week night with more people on stage than in the audience.' Yes probably hold the record for one of the lowest club attendances. It was New Year's

Day and London had suffered heavy snowfall. Peter Banks recalled they played for sixteen people. Persistence paid off. 'The Marquee was the place where we found the sound of Yes,' says Bruford. 'Our own little patch of the musical cosmos.' It was during their residency at the club that they signed a deal with Atlantic Records and, in July 1969, released their eponymous debut album, full of harmonic vocals, bubbling organ and rumbling bass, a prototype for the rising tide of prog that was shortly to inundate the scene.

Early Yes gigs at the Marquee might have been poorly supported but sixteen was a crowd compared to the number who showed up on 21 June 1968 for the debut performance of Free, playing support to Taste. 'Our first night I believe we had six people there, and three of those were girlfriends,' recalls drummer Simon Kirke. The band had only formed a few weeks earlier and with just a few rehearsals in a Battersea pub, the Marquee support slot was their first ever gig.

Kirke came down to London from Shropshire fresh out of school and took up residence in a one-room flat in Twickenham.

Yes begin their Wednesday residency.

He heard about the Marquee and became a regular in the audience. He particularly remembers seeing Ten Years After: 'They were just stunning. I saw them quite a few times. The Nice, too. The standard of musicianship was so high that after a few visits there I became thoroughly discouraged and felt like going back to Shropshire.' He was on the point of quitting, when he went to watch a band called Black Cat Bones (Marquee regulars), got talking to the guitarist, Paul Kossoff, and discovered they were looking for a new drummer. He played with them for six months before he and Kossoff hooked up with vocalist Paul Rodgers, and the trio recruited fifteen-year-old bassist Andy Fraser, thanks to a tip off from Alexis Korner, who was still acting as a one-man support and introduction service for fledgling blues musicians. It was also Korner who persuaded John Gee to give Free a try out. 'John was an irascible character,' says Kirke. 'I'm sure that we passed the audition on our musical merits alone, but I had a feeling that our pretty-boy looks and bums encased in tight bell bottoms might have tipped the balance.'

The applause from the six friends in the audience must have been thunderous because on the back of their debut support slot, Free were granted a Monday night residency, starting in October. This continued through to the end of the year, including one night on which they shared the bill with genuine blues legend Muddy Waters. Another night, Muff Winwood was in the audience. He'd left the Spencer Davis Group to become an A&R man at Island Records, and the Marquee was one of the places he went to check out new talent: 'I used to go down there as often as I went into the office,' he recalls. He was impressed by Free and talked them up to his boss, Chris Blackwell. 'We got a six-month contract from that gig and never looked back,' says Kirke. The last three months of 1968, while the band performed at small clubs by night, they recorded by day, putting down on tape the songs that comprised their live set. Free's debut album, *Tons of Sobs*, came out in March 1969, by which time they'd already played their last gig at the Marquee and were well on their way to bigger stages.

LED ZEPPELIN

The New Yardbirds | Led Zeppelin

Art student and part-time manager of the Marquee coffee bar Les Mitchell regularly made his way to work the same way: from St Martin's College of Art on Charing Cross Road along Manette Street into Soho, then via Greek and Bateman Streets to Dean Street, and down an alley to Richmond Mews and the back entrance of the Marquee. Approaching the club one afternoon he was met halfway by a deep thudding boom: 'As I got closer, it grew louder and louder, until I opened the back door and this wall of noise just hit me.' It was a new band doing a soundcheck. Mitchell had walked in on the gestation of Led Zeppelin.

Four-and-a-half years ago, the Yardbirds had played at the opening night of 90 Wardour Street. Since then, they'd undergone dramatic changes. There'd been the replacement of Eric Clapton with Jeff Beck, then original bassist Paul Samwell-Smith had left and been replaced by session player Jimmy Page. Painfully aware that Page was wasted on bass, rhythm guitarist Chris Dreja switched down to four strings, giving the Yardbirds a front line of Beck and Page on lead guitars. This fantastical arrangement lasted only a short time before Beck jumped ship. At the end of a lengthy and exhausting tour of America, the remaining three original members, Relf, McCarty and Dreja, also decided to call it a day, leaving Page as the sole Yardbird, with a list of contracted gigs to fulfil.

Led Zeppelin's Marquee debut.

Page's search for a new singer led him to Robert Plant, who made the suggestion that his friend John Bonham come in as drummer. Session-man John Paul Jones heard Page was looking for a bassist and offered his services. Still billed as the Yardbirds, the quartet played a run of Scandinavian shows in September 1968 before making their UK debut at Newcastle's Mayfair Ballroom on 4 October. Their second-ever UK gig was two weeks later, on 18 October, at the Marquee. The club's ad in *Melody Maker* announced 'the British debut of the Yardbirds', which was confusing, to say the least.

Page knew the Marquee well. Back when the club was on Oxford Street he used to take part in the jams that filled the intervals between Cyril Davies and the All-Stars' sets. He was also in the line-up of the Yardbirds when they played their last gig at the Marquee in June 1966. Robert Plant had also played the club before, on two dates in February

1968, fronting West Bromwich outfit the Band of Joy, a group that also featured Zep drummer John Bonham.

Ed Bicknell was only in London for a few days. As chairman of Hull University entertainments committee, he was doing the rounds of agencies, looking for bands to book when he heard about the gig. When he arrived at the Marquee about 7.30pm there was a line already stretching along Wardour Street. 'There must have been four or five hundred people in that line,' recalls Bicknell. 'I joined the end of it and managed to get in. It was the first time I'd ever been in the place. I remember they played an early and rather crude version of "Dazed and Confused". It was blitzkrieg loud.' The group returned to the club on 10 December 1968, this time performing under their new name of Led Zeppelin – although a review of the performance in *Melody Maker* still referred to them as the 're-grouped Yardbirds'. The write-up mentions Page's use of a violin bow on his guitar and Bonham's forceful drumming – 'perhaps too much so' – and ends by suggesting the band cut down on volume a bit. A sentiment seconded by John Gee, who thought they were overpoweringly loud.

Zeppelin's second appearance.

A little over three months later, they were back again, on 28 March 1969. In the intervening time, they'd recorded their first album, which had been released in the US in January and would hit the UK market the same week as the gig. A journalist from *Record Mirror* was there that night and described Jimmy Page, 'bent over his guitar and straining for unknown notes, listening hard because he's right there in the middle of that Led Zeppelin wall of sound, sweat oozing torrential down his face, and dripping off the ends of that long wavy hair down onto the guitar and one expects that guitar to fizz and steam because it's so near boiling point.' Another press report claimed there were 1,800 in the audience that night, which is a wild exaggeration because the Marquee couldn't accommodate anywhere near that number of people, but Zeppelin were hot and the place was rammed.

When the band's next Marquee appearance was announced, two years later, in March 1971, it was as part of a Back to the Clubs tour. Zeppelin's last London gig before this had been at the Lyceum, with a capacity in the thousands rather than the Marquee's hundreds. 'The phones haven't stopped ringing since the news came out,' Jack Barrie told a reporter. Tickets were limited to one per Marquee club member. One fan remembers that the queue for tickets started the night before the morning they went on sale and that the management allowed fans to spend the night inside the club rather than outside on the Soho street.

Those lucky enough to get in were witness to peak Zeppelin: the band played a set that opened with 'Immigrant Song' and showcased three tracks from the forthcoming fourth album, including 'Black Dog' and 'Stairway to Heaven', which was being played for the first time on this short tour. Jim Bradshaw, who'd slept on the pavement outside the Marquee to secure a ticket, swears 'the ceiling nearly caved in with the applause'. With 'Whole Lotta Love' closing the set and an encore of 'Communication Breakdown', the band were on stage for more than two and a half hours, but 'God, it seemed short to us,' wrote a French journalist. 'The Marquee in its long and colourful history, has probably never had a night like it,' judged *Melody Maker*.

ROCK AND ROLL CIRCUS

Village | Shotgun Express | Love Sculpture | East of Eden | Colosseum | The Rolling Stones | The Who

In October 1968, a young bass guitarist called Bruce Thomas was hanging around Ted Wallace's amplifier workshop, just off Soho Square, when Jimmy Page strolled in to collect a new amp. Bruce had no idea who Page was, but overhearing that his new band was playing that night at the

Marquee he offered to carry the amp over to the club. As a thank you, Page let the twenty-year-old sit front and centre for the gig. Thomas recalls thinking they sounded a bit like the Jeff Beck Band, but not as good. Thomas had already discovered how easy it was to get into the Marquee without paying by wandering round the back whenever equipment was being loaded and hiding in the toilets for an hour or two until he heard other people coming in. He claims he saw dozens of bands that way, of which his favourite – a band he would even pay to see – was Peter Green's Fleetwood Mac. In Green, Bruce saw not only the best guitarist he'd ever heard, but the most gloriously inspiring musician, little realising that he would soon be sharing the very same stage with him.

It came about through a group called Village. This was the brainchild of Pete Bardens, a keyboard player who, back in 1963, frequently played the old Marquee as leader of jazz outfit the Peter Bardens Trio, then, in 1964, as part of R&B outfit the Cheynes. Following a spell with Belfast's Them, he formed a band called Peter B's Looners, which eventually morphed into Shotgun Express, a soul outfit featuring old Cheynes bandmate Mick Fleetwood, along with Peter Green and Rod Stewart. Shotgun Express played one date at the Marquee in June 1966 but split up in early 1967 after Stewart left to join the Jeff Beck Group, and Fleetwood and Green signed up with John Mayall's Bluesbreakers. With Village, Bardens wanted an organ trio in the same mould as the Nice. For his rhythm section, he hired drummer Bill Porter and, on bass, Bruce Thomas. The band sat somewhere between jazzy R&B and prog rock, playing material by the likes of Jimmy Smith and Miles Davis, generously padded with lengthy improvisations. Unsurprisingly, John Gee liked them and, starting in October 1968, he gave them a run of support slots, opening for the likes of Family, Joe Cocker, Terry Reid, Yes and the Nice.

In July 1969, Village finally landed their own Marquee residency, a good one, on Saturdays. One of the features was that Bardens would call in favours from old friends to do a guest spot. So it was that one night Peter Green came bounding on stage to stand alongside Thomas. It's a moment he's never forgotten. 'Shuffle in A,' announced Green, recalls Thomas, and then leaning his head towards the bassist, he whispered, 'Nothing fancy,' and started playing. 'Neither before, nor since, have I heard anyone play with such tenderness, passion, purpose, precision, intelligence, lyricism, tone, taste, soul and power,' says Thomas. There were other benefits to being in Village. Bardens was quite a cool guy, recalls Thomas: 'He used to date Liza Minnelli and drive around in a Jag. He and I used to meet Rod Stewart for lunch in a cafe just up the road from the Marquee, or Stewart would come to our gigs. And Mick Fleetwood would pop round Pete's house when Fleetwood Mac were just breaking in the States. I was enthralled by it all.'

Village didn't last much more than a year and played their last Marquee date in September 1969. Pete Bardens would go on to co-found Camel, while Thomas moved on to soft-rock band Quiver, then the Sutherland Brothers, before joining Elvis Costello and the Attractions, with who he spent a decade touring and recorded nine albums.

As 1968 drew to a close, highlights at the Marquee included the likes of Love Sculpture, a Welsh blues rock band featuring Dave Edmunds, and East of Eden, a jazz-oriented prog-rock band, who had a Top 10 hit in the UK in 1970 with the single 'Jig-a-jig'. Colosseum were a prog-oriented jazz band, formed in the spring of 1968 by drummer Jon Hiseman; they made their Marquee debut on 1 November that year. Back in 1965, Hiseman had played with the New Jazz Orchestra at the last of the National Jazz and Blues Festivals to be held at Richmond, where, much to his surprise, he won the musician of the weekend award. Later he joined the Graham Bond Organisation, replacing Ginger Baker, and had only been in the band for a few gigs when he made his first Marquee appearance. Baker was famous for his long drum solos and Bond insisted that Hiseman do the same, despite the fact it wasn't his style of playing. 'Suddenly, after a few choruses of "When Johnny Comes Marching Home", a Graham Bond inspired fantasy with a vaguely military feel, I was cut loose. Thrashing about as best I could for as long as I could, I finished up rolling around on the two bass drums whilst hitting out at the cymbals. Suddenly, Graham's deepest voice came over the PA: "Two bass drums, ladies and gentlemen, and he's only twenty-two." That moment will stay with me for life.' Having already appeared at the Marquee with the likes of Graham Bond, Georgie Fame and John Mayall, Hiseman had enough credibility to pull in a decent crowd from the off with Colosseum. A successful debut album early in 1969 ensured interest and the band played the club regularly over the next twelve months. 'I liked playing the Marquee but it was very cramped because I played a big drum kit and the stage was relatively small,' recalls Hiseman. 'There was almost no backstage area, and if you were in the audience at a successful gig it got very congested. I doubt that health and safety had any say in the number of people they rammed in. God knows what would have happened if someone had shouted, "Fire!"' After four albums, Colosseum split in 1971; Hiseman would return to the Marquee with new outfit Tempest in 1973, and with Colosseum II in 1976.

Before 1968 was done, there were two special events at the club. On 6 December the Marquee hosted a rehearsal and camera tests for *The Rock and Roll Circus*. Always looking to keep up with the Beatles, the Rolling Stones wanted a television special to rival the previous Christmas's Fab Four-led *Magical Mystery Tour*. The idea was to mix music with performers hired from Sir Robert Fossett's circus. The line-up of guests included actual Beatle John Lennon, as well as Eric Clapton, Jethro Tull, Marianne Faithfull, the Who, drummer Mitch Mitchell and blues singer Taj Mahal (also invited to perform were Traffic and Cream, but both groups split up just before filming took place). The Marquee was one of three venues used for rehearsals, while the actual filmed performance took place five days later at studios in Wembley. The show was not released commercially until October 1996.

Then, on 17 December, the Who appeared at a special Christmas party. This would be the last time they played the club. Once again, Who fan Dermot Bassett was there. Support came from Yes. Then on came the Who, with Roger Daltrey sporting long curly hair and the fringed clothes which were to become his stage persona for most of the 1970s. 'The club had hung Christmas decorations around the canopy above the stage,' remembers Dermot. 'But the first swing of Roger's mic split through them, leaving them dangling down and very quickly ripped off! The set ended with Pete knocking over his stack, which narrowly missed Yes bass player Chris Squire, who had sneaked on to the back of the stage to watch. Then it was time to wander out into the night. I've seen the Who many, many times since, but none of us would ever see them at the Marquee again.'

KING CRIMSON

Earth/Black Sabbath I Caravan I King Crimson I John Surman
Octet I Circus I Audience I Gilbert and George I Hardin and York

Alongside the established acts kicking off 1969 at the Marquee (Yes, John
Mayall's Bluesbreakers, Jon Hiseman's Colosseum) was a band new to the
club, called Earth. They were four guys from Birmingham playing heavy
blues-tinged rock. They were managed by a guy called Jim Simpson,
who was also manager for the bands Locomotive, Bakerloo, and Tea &
Symphony, and Earth shared the bill with one or more of these bands on
three subsequent Marquee appearances. Later in the year, while touring
England, they discovered there was another group called Earth and, given
the lead singer was never a fan of the name, anyway, they decided to
change it. The story goes that a cinema across the street from the band's
rehearsal room was showing an old Boris Karloff horror movie with a
title that seemed appropriate to the sort of more ominous, darker music
the group was writing, so they nicked it. By the time they returned to
the Marquee in November they were Black Sabbath. 'We didn't go down
very well with John Gee,' guitarist Tony Iommi recalls in his memoirs. 'He
probably thought we were really scruffy. Well, we were.' Ozzy Osborne
took to the stage wearing a striped pyjama top and a water tap tied around
his neck on a piece of string. Gee supposedly told them if they wanted to
play the Marquee again, they all had to have a bath first.

Supporting Yes on the first Wednesday in February, and making their
Marquee debut, were Canterbury prog pilgrims Caravan. However, it was
the band's second Marquee gig, which took place just under two weeks
later, on Tuesday 18 February, playing support to Jon Anderson's former
outfit Gun, that has gone down in Caravan history. That night as Caravan's
Pye Hastings came on stage and took hold of the mic 240 volts shot
through his body. 'There were some flashes and multicolour happenings,'
recalls keyboardist Dave Sinclair, 'and I'm sure the audience thought it
was part of the stage act. Our drummer Richard tried to pull Pye away
from the mic but he was thrown to the floor. Luckily, I remembered where
one of the main socket boards was and I dived across the stage and ripped

out all the plugs.' Sinclair remembers they dragged the guitarist backstage. 'He was still breathing, but looking in a bad way.' An ambulance was called and Hastings was rushed off to hospital. Amazingly, he recovered enough to make it back to the club in time for the band's second set, although he didn't join them on stage. (The same thing would happen to Kippington Lodge's bassist Nick Lowe at the Marquee five months later, in July.)

April 1969 saw a debut for Harmony Grass, an Essex outfit who, until the previous year, had traded as Tony Rivers and the Castaways, gaining a reputation as England's Beach Boys. As Harmony Grass they had a single, 'Move in a Little Closer', that made No.24 on the UK chart. At the Marquee, where they appeared seven times, they became part of the club's folklore. 'Their roadies would stick Harmony Grass labels on every bit of equipment they could find at every gig,' recalls Barbara. 'For the next twenty years, whenever any gear went missing we'd say it had been Harmony Grassed.'

In the club's May 1969 newsletter, Gee announced the launch of a series of sessions advertised as 'New Paths': 'There has been considerable discussion of late about merger of jazz and popular music,' he wrote. 'The Marquee is most interested in this form of development and proud to introduce a magnificent discovery called King Crimson.' Led by guitarist Robert Fripp, the group had first convened in the basement of a cafe on Fulham Palace Road that January. Along with Fripp were Ian McDonald on woodwinds and keyboards, Michael Giles on drums, Greg Lake on bass and vocals, and Peter Sinfield on lyrics and lighting. Almost as soon as the group started playing their first proper gigs in April they picked up a lot of word-of-mouth buzz and enthusiastic press. This was in no small part down to the track they invariably opened sets with, including at the Marquee: '21st Century Schizoid Man', a number that *Rolling Stone* magazine has called progressive rock's Big Bang, the track that launched a whole genre.

Crimson's Marquee debut was on Friday 16 May. They opened for American band Steppenwolf, who were over in Britain for two weeks of TV and sundry promotional appearances, plus a handful of live dates, of which the Marquee was their only London gig. It was the only time they would play the club. Crimson returned just nine days later as headliners.

They played most Sundays through June, July and August. Almost immediately, the band created a huge stir on the London scene. So much so, that on Saturday 5 July 1969, when the Rolling Stones played their famous free gig at Hyde Park, Crimson were one of the support acts. According to the *NME* journalist and Stones fan Nick Kent, Crimson were 'just fucking amazing' and 'blew the Rolling Stones off the stage'. The very next evening they were back at the Marquee, a gig that Peter Sinfield regarded as infinitely superior to Hyde Park: 'The Marquee the next night. NOW that was a humdinger!' he wrote in his diary. The gig was captured by a member of the audience and given an official release in 1998.

Other New Paths artists included the John Surman Octet, a progressive jazz outfit that regularly played support to Crimson, with whom they shared a similar spirit of adventure and experimentation. Then there were Circus, a British psychedelic jazz-rock band that supported Crimson on at least one Sunday, and who Gee subsequently gave a Wednesday-night residency of their own. At first saxophonist Mel Collins was a little apprehensive about performing at the Marquee, wondering whether his playing was up to the mark: 'My mind was put at rest by a very drunk Stan Webb [of Chicken Shack], who we met in La Chasse before the show. Stan insisted that he was going to sit in with us and came on stage half way through our set and literally grabbed the guitar from our guitarist. The strings instantly went out of tune and the very drunk Stanley Webb lurched forward to the microphone to tell the world that he was as "fucking drunk as a lord". The audience loved him. They cheered him as he played some sort of blues completely out of tune. I was speechless.' In 1970, Collins was invited to join King Crimson, beginning an on-off relationship with the band that continues until this day.

Audience were a London-based group, who supported Crimson on a couple of occasions during their Sunday night residency. The music they played was described at the time as 'art-rock' – mixing acoustic with electric, along with flutes, saxes and oboes. Singer Howard Werth remembers turning up at the Marquee for their audition. Waiting in the van round the back of the club, in Richmond Mews, he saw two odd looking blokes pass by, dressed in identical tweed suits with their faces and hands painted metallic bronze. They were there for an audition as well, which Werth got to watch: 'It consisted of the two men sitting at a table facing each other with one listening intently, elbow on knee, fist under chin, whilst the other one told these macabre little stories, one of which involved a dwarf committing suicide.' Werth later found out that the pair were budding conceptual artists about to graduate from St Martin's College of Art, and they were called Gilbert and George. They appeared at that August's National Jazz and Blues Festival as Singing Sculptures, performing 'Underneath the Arches' for hours at a time.

Audience went on to secure their own headline slots, playing the club over twenty times between summer 1969 and August 1972. In that time, they released four albums and played on the soundtrack to cult skinhead film *Bronco Bullfrog*, before splitting up – at which point, Howard Werth was asked to become Jim Morrison's replacement in the Doors.

Also under the banner of New Paths, Gee gave an opportunity to Hardin and York. They were keyboardist/vocalist Eddie Hardin and drummer Pete York, blending hard rock, soul, prog and jazz. York had previously played the Marquee as part of the Spencer Davis Group. 'The crowds were still incredible and during the summer months it would get very hot indeed. One night I was so dripping with sweat that every stitch I had on was soaking wet. I sloshed along to the Ship where people cleared a space for me – I must have looked like the creature from 20,000 fathoms. The Marquee was something very special and to have played there so often makes me proud. I even used to sing a couple of George Formby songs at the end of our show. The Marquee was that kind of place.'

Hardin and York also featured in another new venture for the Marquee, which was a series of Sunday all-nighters at the Lyceum, launched in 1969 and promoted as the 'Midnight Court'. The West End theatre, just off the Strand, was an established major music venue, and the Marquee made use of its all-night licence to run a series of ambitious multi-artist gigs hosted by John Peel with lighting by Crab Nebula and sound by WEM. As well as Hardin and York, other artists featured included the Nice, the Jeff Beck Group, Family, Soft Machine and King Crimson. On 14 November, a short-lived band called Flaming Youth gave the first public performance of their debut concept album, *Ark II*, with full orchestra and choir; on drums and backing vocals was an eighteen-year-old Phil Collins

PLUMPTON

9th National Jazz and Blues Festival, Plumpton 1969 |
Renaissance | Black Sabbath | Hawkwind

As expected, the Marquee was informed that they would not be welcomed back for a second year at Kempton. Alternative plans were made to move to West Drayton in Middlesex, until the local council scuppered them by refusing permission. Instead, Windsor racecourse owner Henry Hythe suggested that they go and see his good friend Izzy Kertzman at Plumpton racecourse, down in East Sussex. It turned out, to nobody's surprise, that Kertzman was at war with his local council and, once again, the festival was being used for political ends. Still, it was a useable site, and in the run-up to the second weekend in August workers laid out a mini village of tents that were transformed into fashion boutiques, record and book shops, a coffee shop, dairy, souvenir store, camping equipment supermarket and disco. The first fans arrived on site four days before the festival. Among them were two Dutch nurses from Maastricht and five Swedish students who came provisioned with twenty-five economy size cans of meatballs.

The ninth National Jazz and Blues Festival kicked off on Friday 8 August 1969 with a line-up of Village, Junior's Eyes, the Keith Tippett Jazz Group, Blossom Toes, East of Eden, Soft Machine and Pink Floyd, each group playing for a tightly abbreviated thirty minutes. As in previous years, there were problems with both the sound and the power. The electricity cut out just six minutes into Soft Machine's set. It was temporarily put right, but when the group resumed it was only for thirty seconds before the electricity failed again. Robert Wyatt kicked over his drums and left the stage in tears. A long delay followed before the Floyd could get on stage, which resulted in them playing into the early hours of Saturday morning – a set that opened with 'Set the Controls for the Heart of the Sun' and finished with 'Interstellar Overdrive', played under a star-filled sky, deep in the English countryside.

The weather that weekend was hot. The festival ran out of water at one point, with the pipes supplying the site running dry. Hundreds of parched music fans descended on Plumpton village in search of something to drink.

Residents responded by putting buckets of water and cups outside their houses. Eventually, the Mid Sussex Water Company sent out engineers to open a valve at a nearby reservoir, and water was restored to the festival ground. The racecourse took on a holiday atmosphere, with thousands of fans sunning themselves on the grass, boys in shorts, girls in bikinis, waiting for the music to begin. A security force that included mini skirted 'dolly-girls' communicating via walkie-talkies kept the crowd in check. An afternoon session was capped by the Bonzo Dog Doo-Dah Band, while the evening line-up featured no less than twelve bands, including the Groundhogs, Aynsley Dunbar, King Crimson, Yes and Chicken Shack, with Stan Webb appearing in full fox-hunting regalia. PA problems tested Webb's patience during Chicken Shack's set and when the next band came on, headliners the Who, Pete Townshend strolled over to the mic to say, 'Before we start, Stan Webb would like you to know the PA's fucking rubbish.' They then proceeded to play most of *Tommy* – almost the same set they would be playing a week later in up-state New York at Woodstock.

Sunday afternoon was a gentle procession of folk and blues, headlined by Pentangle, while the evening session was very much a mixed bag with Chris Barber, a lone artist flying the flag for jazz, along with Blodwyn Pig (led by former Jethro Tull guitarist Mick Abrahams), Keef Hartley (who, like the Who, would be at Woodstock the following week), Family (at the end of their set the crowd demanded an encore and when compere John Gee said there wasn't time, they pelted him with beer cans) and the London cast of *Hair*, which included Marsha Hunt and Paul Nicholas, and who were shouted down as 'plastic hippies' and booed off stage. The weekend ended with the Nice, who were accompanied by an extravaganza of a forty-piece symphony orchestra, along with thirteen pipers, all conducted by Joseph Eger, founder of the New York Symphony. They aired some of the tracks that would be on their soon-to-be-released third album, including their twelve-minute take on Bob Dylan's 'She Belongs to Me'.

Elements of the audience decided to mark the close of a successful weekend of fine music by piling up rubbish and setting it alight, creating bonfires faster than the security teams could put them out. One of the marquees nearly went up in flames and there was a call to the fire brigade to ask them to stand by. The site was eventually cleared without major incident – if you discount Aynsley Dunbar's bassist having his £400 instrument nicked. The local press was unhappy, too: the *Plumpton Evening Post* reported, '…the toilet facilities provided were grossly inadequate to deal with the numbers present, with the result that many cases of public urination were observed.'

The Monday following the festival, saw the Wardour Street debut of Renaissance. Another group to emerge from the ashes of the Yardbirds, this one was formed around the nucleus of singer Keith Relf and drummer Jim McCarty. 'We wanted to do something different,' says McCarty, 'something not so heavy, a bit more folky.' With the addition of bassist Louis Cennamo, pianist John Hawken, and Relf's sister Jane as an additional vocalist, Renaissance were born. Their first album, simply called *Renaissance*, was released in October 1969, and produced by fellow former Yardbird Paul Samwell-Smith. 'We used to get much more of a listening crowd at our Marquee gigs, rather than a bopping and jumping around one,' recalls McCarty. 'They'd be sitting on the floor with the waft of marijuana in the air.' They played the club around fifteen times, with the last appearance in August 1972; by this time, both McCarty and Relf were long gone, and the group was now fronted by Annie Haslam, singer on the group's one-and-only-hit, 1978's 'Northern Lights'.

The headliners advertised for Tuesday 9 September were an act new to the club: Deep Purple. However, for reasons now forgotten they never played the gig. In fact, they never played the Marquee at all. Fellow proto-heavy metallers Black Sabbath were back, though. It was Alvin Lee from Ten Years After who persuaded John Gee to give them another go. Sabbath played in November. By that time, there was a buzz building around them, and managers and agents were keen to check them out. One of the most controversial agents in the country was Don Arden, who handled the Move and the Small Faces. He was in the audience that night, accompanied by his eighteen-year-old daughter Sharon. It was her first trip to the Marquee and she wasn't especially impressed, as she explained in her autobiography: 'It struck me as very seedy for somewhere with that kind of reputation. Your feet stuck to the floor and you could barely breathe for the fug and stink of cigarettes and crammed-together bodies, and where sweat was running down the walls.' Following the performance

Arden was determined to sign the band and introduced himself in the dressing room with the line, 'You are superstars and I am going to make you a million dollars.' A meeting was set up in his office and Sharon did the meet and greets, coming face to face with her future husband for the very first time. Sabbath would return to the Marquee for a further four performances the following year.

Hawkwind Zoo had only been gigging for a couple of months, mainly around Notting Hill where they were formed, before making their Marquee debut, in November 1969. Founded by former London busker Dave Brock, their unique sound fused blues, folk and rock – or in Brock's own words, 'basically freak-out music.' Or, as one-time member Lemmy once described the band: '*Star Trek* with long hair... and drugs.' There is a legendary story to the effect that prior to that first gig at the Marquee, Brock busked for the queue outside and earned more money than the band. It would be another fourteen months before they touched down again on Wardour Street, by which time they'd dropped the 'Zoo'. Surprisingly, that would be it – they only played the Marquee twice.

CHARISMA

Rare Bird | Van der Graaf Generator | Genesis | Amazing Blondel | Daddy Longlegs | Lindisfarne

After twelve years of battling, Harold's persistence paid off and, in January 1970, in the face of opposition from every pub in the area, the Marquee was granted a public licence to serve alcohol. A sort of antechamber, between the entrance corridor and the performance room, was carved out as the new bar area, separated from the main room by a soundproofed screen of wire mesh-strengthened glass. You could see the bands from the bar but at vastly reduced noise levels that still allowed for conversation. Immediately, the bar became a hang out for managers, agents and musicians. From now on, there would always be the suspicion that reviews of Marquee gigs were composed on a bar stool, separated from the band by an inch of soundproofing. About twelve months later, a second bar was added at the back of the main room.

One character who could reliably be found making good use of the Marquee's new facilities was the Orson Welles-like figure of Tony Stratton Smith – or Strat, as everybody called him. Born in Birmingham in 1933, Strat trained as a reporter and during the 1950s became the youngest sports editor in the industry while working for the *Daily Sketch*. He narrowly missed the plane that crashed and killed most of the Manchester United team in 1958, and played a role in facilitating the transfer of Jimmy Greaves from Chelsea to AC Milan. He also loved the horses. However, a chance meeting with Brian Epstein persuaded Strat he should get into music publishing and he took a one-room office at 31 Wardour Street. He bought the rights to a lot of what turned out to be worthless songs and hired musicians to make demos of them in a Denmark Street studio. From there, it was a small step into management. His first band was Paddy, Klaus & Gibson – Klaus being Klaus Voorman, who would later provide the cover for the Beatles album *Revolver* and join John Lennon's Plastic Ono Band. He lost the band to Epstein. Strat's second group was the Koobas, a Liverpool group that had supported the Beatles on their final British tour in December 1965. The following year Strat also took charge of the Mark Four, who, soon after, at his suggestion, changed their name to the Creation.

Strat's links to the Marquee began when he woke one morning on a sofa in an unfamiliar apartment. The place belonged to Jack Barrie and the two subsequently became the best of friends. When Keith Emerson of the Nice, despairing of the group's ever-diminishing earnings and increasing debts, contacted Barrie asking if he wanted to manage them, he pointed the group in the direction of Strat. Strat took them on and used the Marquee Agency to book their gigs and tours – by now, it was actually the Marquee-Martin Agency, since John Martin had become head of the operation, with Chris Barber, John Toogood and Simon White as directors. Around the same time, Strat also took on the Bonzo Dog Band (who had recently dropped the 'Doo-dah' part of the name).

Strat took a paternalistic interest in the artists under his charge – the Nice used to refer to him as 'mother', hence the US title of their third album, *Everything as Nice as Mother Makes It* – and exasperated by the shabby practices of the record companies, he decided to form his own label. This was Charisma, which Strat launched in October 1969. The early history of the label is intimately linked with the Marquee. Although Strat had a Wardour Street office, La Chasse was where most of Charisma's work got done. Strat was more often than not to be found at the end of the bar in the company of a large vodka and tonic in a pint glass filled with ice cubes, scribbling down ideas on the back of a packet of Silk Cut. His mode of operating was characterised as seldom sober, but rarely drunk. His policy for Charisma was simple: 'Anything good'. The first album release was the self-titled debut by keyboard-led UK prog-quartet Rare Bird, which was supported by gigs at, among other venues, the Marquee, starting in December 1969 and running through the following year. The group also brought Charisma its first taste of commercial success with a single 'Sympathy', which did nothing in the UK but hit the top spot across Europe and eventually sold a million. To celebrate, a gold disc reception party was held at the Marquee. 'The spread of food and champagne was amazing and must have cost a fortune,' recalls Rare Bird's founder and keyboardist Graham Field. 'But the thirty or so radio DJs who were there took no notice of the band and didn't speak to any of us.' The band were also in for a shock six months later when a statement arrived and they learned that the cost of the party had been deducted from their royalties.

Another early Charisma signing were baroque prog rockers Van Der Graaf Generator. They were known at the Marquee, having debuted at the club back in November 1968, opening for Yes. The following year they landed their own first headline spot. The band's singer/drummer Chris Judge Smith was a big fan of the club: 'My stand-out evenings include King Crimson's first ever gig and the pre-America version of Fleetwood Mac – and much later the Rezillos. I also remember an evening when a young couple in the audience began ballroom dancing. They were obviously serious dancers, and the crowd parted to give them space and started applauding wildly. I also remember that the entrance lobby became slick with water whenever it rained and I slipped over – not drunk – and put my shoulder out. It still rattles a bit to this day.' Soon after signing with

Charisma, the group recorded an album (their second, but their first with Charisma) called *The Least We Can Do is Wave to Each Other*, which was showcased extensively at the Marquee throughout 1970.

When Audience signed to Charisma, they were sent out on tour with a bunch of other artists from the label, along with three roadies that Strat liked to say had four lungs, five eyes and no brains between them. 'I don't know about the brains,' says Howard Werth of Audience, 'but two of them definitely had one lung each and one certainly had one eye.' Another story has the Nice due to leave for Dover at six am for a series of European dates and everyone was on the tour bus except Strat. At the last minute, he turned up in a tuxedo holding a vodka and tonic, straight out of the club where he'd spent the night drinking.

Supporting Rare Bird on 19 February, playing only their second Marquee date (their first had been fifteen days earlier, opening for Keef Hartley), was a bunch of public schoolboys from Surrey. These were their first forays onto the Wardour Street stage, but some of the group were already familiar with the club. At the approach of dusk, and careful not to be seen, the young Michael Rutherford would climb out of the window of his chambers at Charterhouse boarding school, in Surrey, and make his way to Godalming station to catch a train to central London. His goal was the Marquee – 'The home of everything that meant anything to me back then,' he says. It's where he saw Cream, the Herd, the Nice and the Syn. 'The volume was mind-blowing and the heat was amazing,' he recalls in his memoirs. 'The Marquee was on ground level but you felt underground as everything was dark and dripping with sweat.' Afterwards, Rutherford returned on the milk train at five-thirty in the morning, clambering back through the window of his study, careful not to disturb his fellow schoolboys. While always anxious that his nocturnal adventures didn't reach the ears of his masters, the excitement of escaping to London, 'of feeling part of the scene,' far outweighed the risks. 'By the time I left school, the pinnacle of my ambition was to play the Marquee. I thought that if you could play there, you really were somebody.'

At least two other Charterhouse pupils were also making their own occasional pilgrimages to the Marquee: Peter Gabriel and Anthony Banks. One night they saw the Nice, an event Banks later described as having a profound effect. Gabriel and Banks were in a school band called the Garden Wall. Rutherford, along with his friend, guitarist Anthony Phillips, was in another Charterhouse group, called Anon. The two groups merged to form Genesis. By the time they first played the Marquee, they'd already released an album, which flopped badly. Nevertheless, Rutherford saw the gig as a breakthrough, 'and the realisation of my dreams'. Strat heard about this new band through Rare Bird and went to check them out upstairs at Ronnie Scott's, where they had a midweek residency. (Perhaps taking note of the success of the Marquee, Ronnie Scott's had started to put on regular rock nights of its own under the imaginative banner of Upstairs

Genesis make their Marquee debut.

at Ronnie's.) 'It was one of our better nights,' recalls Rutherford. 'There must have been at least eleven people in the audience.' Before the evening was over, Strat had signed Genesis to Charisma. That was March, and Genesis returned to play another couple of gigs at the Marquee – now with the weight of Strat behind them, as headliners. Then in July, the group took a break from gigging to rehearse new material for their second album (the first with Charisma), which was *Trespass*, recorded at Trident Studios, round the corner from the Marquee. They were back at the Marquee on 4 October, only now with a slightly different line-up, featuring a new drummer, a bloke named Phil Collins.

This would be Collins' playing debut at the club (and only his third outing with Genesis), but like his new bandmates, he'd been haunting Wardour Street for years. He'd been a big fan of mod band the Action and, through 1966 and '67, he tried to see them every time they played at what he considered 'London's best venue', the Marquee. In *Not Dead Yet: The Autobiography*, he writes that as a teenager he was at the Marquee at least twice a week, heading for Soho straight from school in west London.

John Gee, he says, used to let him in for free in return for sweeping floors, setting out chairs and enduring his harmless advances. He saw Jeff Beck's Marquee debut with the Yardbirds, as well as the first appearance at the Marquee of the Yardbirds with Jimmy Page on bass, and the first show of the group that would become Led Zeppelin. He was also there for a bunch of Who shows and several early performances by Yes. 'I used to go and see Yes pretty regularly, and when Bill Bruford was going back to Leeds University before their first album they were looking for a drummer to replace him. I went backstage to see Jon Anderson, he said, "Give me a call Tuesday." I never called him and I often wonder how my life would have been different had I gone for that and got it.' Instead, in early summer of 1970, Collins saw an ad in *Melody Maker* placed by Tony Stratton Smith looking for a drummer and a guitarist. Collins knew Strat and cornered him at the Marquee, telling him, 'I want that gig with your new band.' Strat said it wasn't up to him, but he could at least make sure the drummer got an early audition. Collins did the rest.

October 4th, the date of Genesis's return to the Marquee stage, was a Sunday. Such was Strat's influence that he'd managed to persuade John Gee to hand over the club's Sunday night slot as a showcase for mainly Charisma acts. Under the banner 'Marquee Sunday Specials', Strat served up regular helpings of Genesis, Van der Graaf Generator and Audience, as well as former Bonzo Dog Roger Ruskin Spear with his Giant Kinetic Wardrobe, and Amazing Blondel. The latter were a three-piece trading in medieval folk-rock, playing recorders, crumhorns, lutes, dulcimers, harpsichords and tabors. They looked like Elizabethan court minstrels, sang madrigals and ballads about Lincoln cathedral and Saxon damsels, and were not averse to the odd bit of Latin. They gained a loyal following, which included schoolboy and future Tourist and Eurythmic Dave Stewart, who, when they played his hometown of Sunderland, stowed away in the band's van and it wasn't until they'd travelled almost a hundred miles that anyone realised he was there. 'He stayed on with the band for several days and picked up a few tips musically,' recalls Blondel Eddie Baird. 'I wonder what ever happened to him?' Amazing Blondel did okay, too – they were never signed by Strat but instead landed up on Chris Blackwell's Island Records.

On Sunday 31 May 1970, the Stratton Smith offering was Daddy Longlegs, four Americans dodging the draft in Britain and entertaining the natives with Haight Ashbury-tinged psychedelic backwoods country rock. Support came from Alan Hull and Brethren, a band with a solid following in their native Northeast England, who were now looking to break into the London scene. They'd managed to get a demo tape into Strat's hands and on the strength of what he heard, Strat persuaded Jack Barrie to put them on for one night. The band drove down the A1 in a Transit van and arrived at the Marquee brimming with excitement. 'The Marquee was seen as the ultimate place to play,' recalls drummer Ray Laidlaw. 'Most of our boyhood heroes had played there and some of them still did. It was much smaller, scruffier and more downmarket than we imagined. We had better-looking gigs in Newcastle. However, what it lacked in decor it more than made up for in atmosphere.' Despite few in the audience knowing who they were, the first gig went down well and, most crucially, Strat was sufficiently impressed to offer the band a home at Charisma. It was also around this time that the band changed their name to Lindisfarne.

Strat organised more Marquee shows for his latest signing, including a slot opening for Ginger Baker's jazz-rock supergroup Air Force (which featured Steve Winwood, Denny Laine, Graham Bond and two additional drummers in the shape of Alan White and Phil Seamen). Again, the band set off to drive all the way down from Newcastle. In the meantime, the bloody-minded Baker informed the Marquee that he, 'Didn't want a fucking warm-up band.' Strat's assistant Gail Colson was given the task of taking the just-arrived Geordies to the Ship to break the news. 'I told them that one day they would be headlining the Marquee and that they would be bigger than Ginger Baker,' recalls Colson. 'They then went on their way back to Newcastle, poor buggers. But it did turn out that I was right.'

Ray Jackson (vocals, mandolin and harmonica) describes playing the Marquee: 'Our performances were mixed from the front row by the roadie, the stage being very small and only able to accommodate the performers and their gear. We had no monitor wedges for vocals in those days and everything you heard came back at you from the wall behind the audience. This was no hardship, as it was what you were used to at the time and your ears adjusted to the acoustics very quickly. The more you drank, the better it sounded!' Long John Baldry was in the audience one night and, as a result, asked Jackson to guest on an album he was recording (1971's *It Ain't Easy*), which was being co-produced by Elton John and Rod Stewart. This led to Stewart asking Jackson to play on his own album, *Every Picture Tells a Story*, including on 'Maggie May' and 'Mandolin Wind'. Jackson was never credited by name on the album sleeve, instead Rod wrote: 'The mandolin was played by the mandolin player in Lindisfarne. The name slips my mind.'

Lindisfarne went on to play the Marquee many more times. 'After a while the Marquee felt like ours,' recalls Ray Laidlaw. 'We were cocky, confident and beginning to build up a head of steam with regular appearances in the heart of the music scene. We were having a ball after years of refining our music without much return.' The Marquee bar became the band's regular haunt in London, along with the Ship and La Chasse. Manager of La Chasse, Roger Nickson, recalls Lindisfarne practically living there. Most of the Charisma bands were regulars. Nickson says Phil Collins borrowed a tenner most Mondays. 'Gail Colson would come in on a Friday and say, "Go on then, hit me," and I'd get out all the credit notes,' recalls Nickson. 'That one's a tenner, there's another tenner, and Strat's bill for the week, a hundred and ten pounds, and she'd settle up with me.'

The Charisma offices seemed to move every few months, but they never strayed far from the Marquee. And at the centre of the scene was Strat, always surrounded, remembers Ray Laidlaw, by a jolly band of camp followers made up of music journalists, sports writers, musicians, roadies and young ladies. 'It was all extremely good fun and I loved it.' There was one night, says Laidlaw, the band were with a singer-songwriter pal who over indulged and they had to carry him out to the tour bus: 'We eventually got him to his seat but he was still shouting,' recalls Ray. 'We couldn't understand what he was on about, then I realised that his teeth were missing. I went back into the club and found the seat where he'd been sitting and there, in a warm pile of puke, I found his teeth. Fortunately, my Mam always encouraged me to carry a hankie so I wrapped his gnashers up and took them back to the bus, where he was asleep, and put his teeth in his pocket.'

SOUNDS OF THE SEVENTIES

Slade I Status Quo I Wishbone Ash I Uriah Heep I Elton
John I Fat Mattress I Atomic Rooster I Blossom Toes
I Writing on the Wall

At least two members of 1970s chart-monsters Slade had made their acquaintance with the Marquee as far back as 1965. Drummer Don Powell and guitarist Dave Hill, both of Wolverhampton, were in a band called the 'N Betweens. Having just turned professional, their promoter organised an audition for them at the Marquee in front of a bunch of German club owners who were in London to book British bands. They played one song and were hired. 'We played a month in Dortmund for £14 a week each, cash,' recalls Powell. On the ferry over, the pair bumped into a singer from the Midlands called Noddy Holder, on his way to Frankfurt as part of another group. Not long after, back in Wolverhampton, the three would team up, add bassist Jim Lea, and make a name for themselves on the local live circuit. By 1969, they had a record deal and a new name, Ambrose Slade, soon to be shortened to just Slade.

Whenever Slade were down in London they'd drop into the Marquee. 'I remember thinking then, it would be great to have a residency here,' says Powell. When the band signed a management deal with Chas Chandler, their wish came true. In March 1970, they debuted at the club as support for the Crazy World of Arthur Brown. The following month they were opening for Yes. 'I don't know who thought that billing up,' says Powell. 'We were skinheads at the time and they were hippies. A total mismatch.' After that, Slade were given their own headline slot, playing once a month through the rest of the year. 'It was at the Marquee where we started to involve the audience in our show,' says Powell. 'As we were there regularly, we needed to do something different each time, and involving the audience was it.' For Holder, playing the Marquee was special because the first gig he ever saw in London was the Who at the Marquee. 'They were just breaking through,' he wrote in his memoirs. 'But the real buzz for me was going to the Marquee. I had read all about it in the music press. I was expecting it to be this great, glamorous venue full of rock stars just standing around, and it turned out to be this grotty little club – but what a fantastic atmosphere. Bands didn't earn much from the Marquee. You played it for the prestige.'

Status Quo were another band who, under a succession of different names – and playing in a succession of different styles – paid their dues in the Sixties before achieving fame in the following decade. In fact, they'd had a UK Top 10 hit with 1968's psychedelic-tinged 'Pictures of Matchstick Men' but by the time of their Marquee debut – straight in as headliners on 25 April 1970 – they had already ditched the modish Carnaby Street threads in favour of a more rockin' look. Prog-folk band Heron supported Quo at the Marquee and their guitarist Gerald Moore recalls seeing one of them arrive in a suit carrying an attaché case, and then change into his stage gear of jeans and T-shirt. 'They were very friendly and there was none of the airs and graces you got from some bands. After our set, we stepped back into the dressing room to watch Status Quo building up steam for their set with a couple of crates of beer and several black-hash joints. Someone said, "Nice gig man," and then they stepped through the door onto the stage. Their first number was so loud we couldn't hear each other talk, so we went to the bar.'

According to Bob Young, who started as a roadie, but went on to play with Quo and write for them, appearing at the Marquee was an important step. 'We were knocked out when they let us play there. If you can put markers in the ground in the history of Quo, then the Marquee was the first stake in the ground, when everybody felt we were definitely on the right track.' The Marquee also became one of Quo's favourite watering holes: drummer John Coghlan recalls that he and Rick Parfitt often used to meet there for a beer, and if they didn't like the band, they'd move on to the Ship or La Chasse. Parfitt always used to say that La Chasse was one of those places where you remembered going up the stairs but could never recall coming back down again.

Later, when Harold began to sublet office space on the first floor of 90 Wardour Street, Status Quo's management took an office there. Other rooms were later taken by Billy Gaff, who was Rod Stewart's manager, and, inevitably, by Tony Stratton Smith and Charisma. Harold kept the biggest office, at the front, overlooking Wardour Street, for himself.

For musicians like Andy Powell, guitarist with Wishbone Ash, playing the Marquee was all about being acknowledged by your peers: 'When we were schlepping up and down the M1, playing the provinces, I think the goal for all of us was to be playing the Marquee.' They got there on 8 May 1970, opening for Slade. 'Because it was a musician's club,' says Powell, 'and the fans were so knowledgeable, if you could deliver the goods on such an important stage as that, it was a real achievement.' The group played the club fourteen times and among those dates were some of their most memorable gigs, notably New Year's Eve 1971, which also doubled as Powell's stag night. 'The management made us a cake which was brought up onto the stage, along with champagne.' There was also a low-key gig in October 1977, played for fun a couple of nights before they appeared at Wembley Empire Pool as part of the Front Page News tour. Tracks from this Marquee date have appeared on various Wishbone Ash live albums.

May also saw a first appearance for Uriah Heep, playing support to Hardin and York. The band were no strangers to the Marquee: under their previous name, Spice, they'd played the club more than a dozen times during 1968–69. But they'd recently added a keyboard player/guitarist, Ken Hensley, and this had taken the band's sound in new directions, so they'd decided on a change of name. Their sets at this time would have featured tracks that would appear on their first album, ...Very 'Eavy... Very 'Umble, released in the UK in June.

In June, former Bluesology pianist turned solo artist, Elton John, included a date at the Marquee on his first ever tour. It was in support of his impressive second album, *Elton John*, so the setlist would almost certainly have included 'Your Song', 'Border Song' and the blistering 'Burn Down the Mission'. On the second leg of this tour, kicking off in August, the band flew to the US, where they played the six nights at LA's Troubador that effectively launched Elton John's career. This would be his only solo Marquee appearance.

Other additions to the programme around this time included Fat Mattress, a folk-rock band formed by ex-Jimi Hendrix Experience alumnus Noel Redding, hard-edged prog rockers Atomic Rooster, formed in the summer of 1969 by organist Vincent Crane and drummer Carl Palmer (shortly to depart to become one-third of ELP), and Blossom Toes, a psychedelic rock band, signed to Giorgio Gomelsky's Marmalade label.

Although obscure today, Writing on the Wall held two residencies at the Marquee, racking up over forty appearances, until in 1973 all the band's equipment was stolen and they broke up. 'They were five very nice but very gruff and hairy Scotsmen,' recalls their agent at the time, Ed Bicknell. Although they only ever released one album, these prog rockers had one stage gimmick that Bicknell never forgot. 'They had a bass player called Jake who would wear baby's nappies and hobnailed boots and nothing else. As they got to the last number in the set, and it was kind of like a ritual, Jake would climb up onto the PA stack and work himself up into such a frenzy that he'd piss himself.'

1970 was also the year the Marquee introduced Saturday night disco dances. Starting in April, the DJ sessions took the place of the support band. The DJs occupied a small booth to the side of the stage; 'The equipment in the booth was dangerous, more or less in bits, mostly covered by the gaffer tape that was holding parts of it together,' recalls Bob Harris, who spun disks at the club in addition to his regular duties on BBC Radio 1 hosting its popular *Sounds of the Seventies* programme. Other regular DJs were Ian Fleming, Jerry Floyd and Gerry Collins, who was the lead engineer at the studios, and who would later co-found Bang, London's first gay disco, in the basement of the Astoria on Charing Cross Road.

GOODBYE, JOHN GEE

Medicine Head I Pink Fairies I Supertramp I Stackridge I
10th National Jazz and Blues Festival, Plumpton 1970
I Derek and the Dominoes I The Faces I Mott the Hoople I
Lifetime I Ginger Baker's Air Force

In summer 1970, as the Marquee geared up for its annual summer festival, a further clutch of new bands arrived to see if they could cut it at the club, including Medicine Head, a blues-folk-pop duo who cut three highly regarded albums for DJ John Peel's legendary Dandelion label,

Ladbroke Grove anarchists the Pink Fairies and Supertramp, who had just released their debut album to general indifference and were only just starting on the road to *Breakfast in America*. There was also Stackridge, a Bristol-based rock act managed by Mike Tobin. Tobin had been involved with local music in Bristol for years before being recruited by Tony Hall Enterprises in London. Now based in offices in Noel Street, Tobin was immediately plunged into the Soho scene. 'Inevitably I started doing what everybody else in the music business was doing, which was after you'd finished for the day you stayed in Soho, even though you might live in Fulham or Ladbroke Grove, or wherever. Usually you'd go to the Ship first and then on to the Marquee, almost every night of the week, regardless who was playing. Because we were in the biz we all got in free and it was another meeting place for us all to do what's now known as networking.'

It was at the Marquee that Tobin met manager Ed Bicknell and was asked to join John Sherry Enterprises. Sherry looked after a lot of up-and-coming bands for whom gigs at the Marquee were crucial. 'The Marquee used to advertise in the music press every week,' says Tobin, 'and it was important that a band's name was seen as often as possible. Being a regular act at the Marquee helped to get your band other bookings around the country. And there was always the chance if you had a good following, then you would probably get a slot at the festival.'

The festival this year was back at Plumpton for a second year. For the first (and only) time it was expanded to four days, kicking off on the evening of Thursday 6 August and running through until Sunday night. The opening night was billed as a showcase for local bands and, as such, attracted a limited audience. Although it was still billed as a 'jazz, blues & pop' festival, Chris Barber was the only jazz artist on the bill, and the Chicago Climax Blues Band and Peter Green (who had just left Fleetwood Mac) were the only blues purists. Instead, the line-up for the other three days was slanted toward folk (Cat Stevens, Strawbs, Magna Carta, Incredible String Band), prog (Rare Bird, Yes, Family, Van der Graaf Generator) and heavy rock: Saturday night featured Black Sabbath, whose breakthrough single 'Paranoid' had been released just the previous day. Sunday had Wishbone Ash, who were shortly to begin recording their self-titled debut album, and, as headliners, Deep Purple. They were showcasing the recently released *In Rock* album, featuring the classic line-up of Ritchie Blackmore, Ian Gillan, Roger Glover, Jon Lord and Ian Paice. They reinforced their heavy rock credentials by setting fire to their stage monitors.

The line-up was a very British affair with virtually no visitors from overseas. Compared to previous years, it was also light on big names. Part of the problem was that the success of the festival had inspired others and in summer 1970 there was fierce competition for music fans' money. The Bath Festival, held in June, featured the Byrds, Canned Heat, Donovan, Dr John, Led Zeppelin, Pink Floyd, Santana, Steppenwolf, Frank Zappa, Fairport Convention and Maynard Ferguson. The Isle of Wight Festival, at the end of August, boasted Joan Baez, Leonard Cohen, Miles Davis, the Doors, Emerson Lake and Palmer, Gilberto Gil, Jethro Tull, Jimi Hendrix, Joni Mitchell, Procul Harum, Sly and the Family Stone, and the Who. Plumpton's offerings were meagre by comparison and attendance was correspondingly low.

Stackridge, who had just made their Marquee debut a month before, did not play Plumpton; instead they created history by being the opening act at the Pilton Pop, Blues & Folk Festival held that September, the first such event to take place at Worthy Farm organised by Michael Eavis – the following year it would be renamed the Glastonbury Fayre festival.

The Tuesday following Plumpton, one big name was back at the club. Eric Clapton and his new outfit, Derek and the Dominos, had made their celebrated debut at London's Lyceum theatre in June. In August they undertook a tour of small clubs around the UK that included the Marquee. The sets were made up largely of numbers from Clapton's debut solo album, released that same month, as well as a handful of covers, notably Hendrix's 'Little Wing'.

In September, Rod Stewart was also back, now fronting the Faces, the good-time band formed from the remnants of the Small Faces, plus former Jeff Beck Group guitarist Ronnie Wood and Stewart. This would be the first of four gigs at the Marquee, all in the space of five months – one of them, on Sunday 7 December, would be filmed for German TV. The setlists were made up predominantly of covers, including Paul McCartney's 'Maybe I'm Amazed' and Rod Stewart's 'Gasoline Alley'.

Also in September, Mott the Hoople made the first of their two Marquee performances (the second was in January 1971). They had just released their second album, *Mad Shadows*, which, sales-wise, would underperform even compared to their largely ignored debut effort. Be that as it may, the Hoople were one of the UK's finest and most in-demand live acts, to the extent, claimed journalist Roy Carr in the *NME*, that bands refused to work with them for fear of being upstaged. Performances were as much party as gig, with audiences encouraged to get up on stage and dance, and lead singer Ian Hunter passing the mic around.

Following former Cream mate Clapton back onto the Marquee stage was Jack Bruce, who, in October, appeared with Lifetime, the band put together by former Miles Davis drummer Tony Williams, which included John McLaughlin on guitar and Larry Young on organ. They were a jazz-rock fusion outfit who failed to find favour with either jazz or rock critics. Their polyrhythmic sound – which has been described as like a burning car thrown down a lift shaft – was a template for future jazz-rock experiments, including Miles Davis's *Bitches Brew* (which featured Larry Young) and McLaughlin's own Mahavishnu Orchestra. Lifetime played few gigs, so for this rare London outing every muso in town showed up: as *Melody Maker*'s Raver column commented, 'If someone had dropped a bomb on the Marquee last Tuesday, half the thinking musicians in London would've been wiped out'. Three weeks later, on Tuesday 27 October, the third former Cream member was also back, as Ginger Baker led jazz-fusion outfit Air Force onto the Marquee stage.

On Sunday 9 December, Tony Stratton Smith took over the Marquee for a private Charisma party. It had been a very good first year for the record label, which had even made a small profit. Present were members of Rare Bird, Van der Graaf Generator, Lindisfarne, the Bonzos and all of Genesis, who provided the music. Nice frontman Keith Emerson dropped in en route to a gig with his new outfit, Emerson, Lake and Palmer, who were playing the Lyceum that night. The party made headlines in the *Melody Maker* when somebody used the cover provided by a power cut to make off with the birthday cake. A search party was sent out and the cake was found a couple of streets away. Party-guest Keith Moon was the chief suspect.

One major change at the Marquee also occurred in 1970. John Gee had been finding it increasingly difficult coming to terms with changes in the musical landscape. The emergence of heavy rock bands, with their long hair, unkempt appearances and deafening volumes, was the final straw for a man whose idea of a big sound was a ten-piece horn section. 'He used to moan and moan about the new music and the bands we were putting on,' recalls Harold. 'He drove me mad.' Eventually, Gee couldn't stand it any longer and resigned. Jack Barrie, who had been Gee's assistant for the last few years, was asked to take over. Rather than lose Gee completely, Harold transferred him to a music publishing company he was running in conjunction with Radio Luxembourg. Gee remained working at their London offices until he retired in 1992.

STICKY FINGERS

UFO | Led Zeppelin | The Rolling Stones | Gilberto Gil | Fela Kuti | Queen | Thin Lizzy | Stray

From the age of thirteen, Pete Way and friends would catch the train from the north London borough of Enfield down into town to visit the Marquee most Saturday nights. 'We were really just school kids hanging around the West End, but it was so exciting,' he recalls. Watching the likes of Hendrix and the Small Faces developed his taste for rock. But the defining moment came, aged eighteen, when he caught one of Led Zeppelin's early Marquee appearances. 'That really made me focus on wanting to achieve something with music.' In 1968, Way, along with vocalist Phil Mogg, guitarist Mick Bolton and drummer Andy Parker, formed their own band, which they first called Hocus Pocus and then UFO, after the London club they were playing when they landed their first record deal. In February 1971, the band played their first Marquee date – and over the course of the next six years they would rack up close to fifty shows at the club – many of these with Michael Schenker on guitar, after he joined in 1973. 'It was the place to play in London at the time,' recalls Andy Parker. 'On a good night, the sweat would literally be dripping from the ceiling. And they always treated us fairly. Even when an idiot crew guy set off some smoke bombs and cleared the club, they didn't hold a grudge. And I remember the dressing room walls were a who's who of artists.'

By this time, the dressing room had become a place of infamy. It was reached via a door tucked off to the side of the bar. This led through to a small area with a toilet and sink, and doors that led directly onto the back of the stage and into the dressing room itself. This was a narrow space with a sloping ceiling, a cross between a corridor and an under-stair cupboard, with a bench along one wall. And it was small: 'Barely enough room for four people,' recalls Jethro Tull's Ian Anderson. 'Let alone change or swing a guitar.' Bands amused themselves while waiting to go on by defacing the place. Graffiti was scrawled, scratched and spray-painted onto every surface. For years, there was a prominent drawing of the Who's guitarist with the words, 'Pete Townshend's nose is a Rickenbacker on legs', as well as the original Yes logo from the band's first album until both were gradually buried under new additions.

No money was ever spent on the dressing room, but the main hall received a makeover of sorts early in 1971. Out went the carnival striping and green walls in favour of all-over matt black, which, it was thought, would combine better with the lighting. On the back wall behind the stage, the decorators added a large Marquee logo in yellow that in future would appear in nearly every shot of a performance at the club. The logo was designed by Harold himself, who had a fascination with graphic design and typography. In the early days he used to do the layouts for *Jazz News* and he designed the club's newsletters, with liberal use of the theatrical Playbill typeface. He would also design and draw the maps for the annual festival programmes. The new logo was created the year after the move to Wardour Street; it was designed to mimic the vertical striping on the awning that covered the stage: the width of the upstrokes on the extended-height letters are the same as the spaces separating them. All the letters are lower case except for the R, which is in upper case, because it works better that way. It is a beautiful piece of work – Harold was very proud of it – and the logo was first introduced in the weekly press ads in January 1966.

A month after UFO's debut, the group that first inspired Pete Way, Led Zeppelin, were back on Wardour Street for a one-off date as part of their Back to the Clubs tour – as described previously. The gig was booked for Tuesday 23 March, however there was the problem of the stage being too small even for the limited amount of equipment they were using for this pared-down tour. The problem was solved thanks to the Rolling Stones.

Three nights after Led Zeppelin were appearing at the Marquee, the world's greatest rock band were returning to the club where it all first began. The Stones were booked in at the club to shoot a TV special promoting the imminent release of their new album, *Sticky Fingers* – after which they'd be fleeing the UK to become tax exiles in the South of France. British Lion, who were doing the filming, had called Jack Barrie to ask if they could come into the club the night before to rig up extra lighting and set dressing, and enlarge the stage. Barrie told them the club couldn't allow late-night working because the noise would disturb the neighbours. But they could come in the Saturday before, he said – three days before Zeppelin were due to play – and do the work during the day, which is what happened. 'One stage enlargement for two great bands and at no cost to the Marquee,' recalls Barrie.

According to *Melody Maker*, the Stones gig on Friday 26 March took place before a 'small but elite audience' that included Eric Clapton, Jimmy Page and the Stones' old manager Andrew Loog Oldham. The performance showcased four of the new album's nine tracks, as well as 'Live with Me' and 'Midnight Rambler' from *Let It Bleed*, and the inevitable 'Satisfaction'. The set closer was new number 'Brown Sugar'. It would be two years before the band would play a concert in Britain again.

The performance made the front page of *Melody Maker* – thanks to a row between Jagger and Harold. The shoot had been going on for five hours when Harold came down from his office to see how things were going. 'I found that the film crew had rigged a curtain across the back of the stage covering up the large "Marquee" lettering.' The Stones' road manager, Chip Monck, said it was interfering with colour values. Unconvinced, Harold stepped in front of the cameras to stop the filming, at which point Jagger called him 'a bitch' and Keith Richards rushed forward and swung his guitar at Harold's head. Les Mitchell was a witness: 'If he'd hit Harold, he could have done serious damage.' The event was also notable for being the first time the famous lips-and-tongue logo made its appearance. Designed by John Pasche, a student at the Royal College of Art in London, the logo was used on VIP passes for the show.

One of the more surprising bookings in the first half of 1971 was Brazilian singer-songwriter and future minister of culture Gilberto Gil. Gil and his musical collaborator Caetano Veloso were two of Brazil's biggest pop stars, now exotic fixtures on London's underground scene having fled a military dictatorship back home. They caught the Stones at the Roundhouse and hung out with counter-cultural figures, including anarchic journalist and singer Mick Farren, and members of Hawkwind. Gil made multiple appearances at the club through 1971.

There was more world music on 19 July, on what must have been an extraordinary evening, a one-off appearance by Nigerian Afro-beat legend Fela Kuti. He'd been brought to London by EMI to record at Abbey Road (the resulting album was *Fela's London Scene*) and took the opportunity to play a handful of gigs. Drumming with Kuti that night – and billed as the supporting act – was Ginger Baker, who earlier in 1971 had driven from London to Nigeria in a Land Rover to immerse himself in African rhythms. Kuti, singing and playing keyboards, acted as bandleader, directing the crowd of musicians crammed onto the Marquee's tiny stage. Like a James Brown soul revue, their sound was reportedly funky, tight and precise, with percussive grooves and interlocking rhythms, over which soloists, Baker included, traded leads.

There was an early one-off gig, too, in the first months of 1971 for Thin Lizzy. The group was far from the finished article and their landmark Marquee nights were still a way in the future. One rock band that already seemed destined for big things were Stray. They were a west London outfit that had been around since the mid 1960s, but it was only in the early 1970s, after signing to Transatlantic Records, that the hours motoring up and down the M1 started to pay off. They were immensely popular at the Marquee, where they made close on fifty appearances – although success on Wardour Street didn't necessarily translate to success elsewhere. In later years they gained a degree of notoriety when they were briefly managed by Charlie Kray, brother of Ronnie and Reggie, fresh out of jail for having helped to dispose of the body of Jack 'the Hat' McVitie. Bookings for the band practically dried up overnight, as guitarist Del Bromham recalled to *Classic Rock* magazine in November 2016: 'We were booked to play the Marquee and the support band wouldn't even come into the dressing room. When we invited them in, they sat there shaking, terrified. On the upside, we no longer had trouble getting paid for live work – promoters thought they'd get their legs broken.'

READING

11th National Jazz and Blues Festival, Reading 1971
I King Crimson I Fleetwood Mac I Vinegar Joe I
Fusion Orchestra I Nazareth

The Marquee's annual jaunt out into the countryside came earlier than usual in 1971, thanks to a problem-solving bit of good fortune. Just as happened at Richmond, Windsor and Sunbury, Plumpton decided that having 20,000 beer-necking, urinating rock fans gate-crashing their summer wasn't for them after all. A Tory MP threatened an injunction to prevent the event from returning for a third year. Then, out of the blue, Harold was approached by an advertising agency that had been tasked with organising a festival in Reading marking the 850th anniversary of the town's historic abbey. 'Reading was known in our business as a graveyard,' says Harold. 'Nothing ever worked there because it was the apathy capital of the UK.' Still, Harold went to take a look.

Representatives from the local council took him down to the banks of the Thames, to the site earmarked for the festival. Harold pointed out that because of the way the field sloped down to the water the optimum place for the stage was occupied by the river. However, over on the other side was a large flat field that seemed perfect: it turned out to be the recently grassed-over local tip. Harold suggested holding the festival there and the councillors said, why not? The dates were determined by the need to fit in with other events on the Reading cultural calendar that summer. This meant the festival was to take place 25–27 June, six weeks earlier than the previous year, with a correspondingly higher risk of rain. Sure enough, the weeks leading up to the festival saw torrential downpours. It now became clear that the site occupied a flood plain. 'I went down there a few days before we were due to start setting up and it was a sea of water,' recalls Harold. Undeterred, he got in touch with a company called Trackway, who provided temporary road surfaces, without which it would have been impossible to get the equipment on site.

When the festival weekend arrived, the Reading site brought to mind the Somme. Savvy operators were selling sheets of plastic for exorbitant sums for people to drape over their shoulders or sit on. Agent Ed Bicknell was there with Wishbone Ash: 'My lasting memory was seeing earth-moving trucks pulling articulated lorries out of the mud and thinking, this is a fucking shambles. I'm going home.'

The efforts of the weekend's line-up – which included East of Eden, Van der Graaf Generator, Lindisfarne, Wishbone Ash, Ralph McTell, Colosseum, Rory Gallagher and Arthur Brown – to entertain the crowds were severely undermined by the lashing rain, not to mention the heavy-handed actions of the Thames Valley Police. Festival-goers were stopped and searched on their arrival in town. An estimated 2,000 people were subjected to the attentions of the police, of whom 115 were arrested for possession. The paranoia extended to many residents and businesses in Reading, which in the weeks before the festival had been bracing themselves for a long-haired and denim-clad invasion. Speaking in the local paper, the manager of the Caversham Bridge Hotel explained how any customer giving off a whiff of hippie would not be served.

Some amusement was provided by Del Bromham, guitarist with Stray, who had a suit of mirrors made for the show. The problem was that he couldn't bend his legs and it took three roadies to lift him onto the stage.

Despite everything, the festival made a profit, Reading wasn't flooded with dope and everyone concerned deemed the event to have been enough of a success to make it worthwhile doing again next year. The Reading era had begun.

The summer of '71 at the Marquee saw the return of King Crimson for two consecutive nights. This booking of a band to play consecutive nights was an experiment that Jack Barrie was trying out, intended to woo back bands that had outgrown the club – the thinking being that two nights at the Marquee equalled one at the Lyceum in terms of the size of the audience. The Crimson gigs previewed much of the material that would make up the *Islands* album, which they were shortly to go into the studio to record. Rounding out the month, was another two-nighter, this time with Fleetwood Mac. They were now without both founder Peter Green and second guitarist Jeremy Spencer, who, while on tour in February, had said he was just going out to 'get a magazine' and never returned (after days of searching, the band discovered he'd joined a religious cult).

At the end of September, fans turning up to see folk-rockers Renaissance were harangued with demands to get up off their arses and boogie by support act Vinegar Joe, who were making their club debut. Vinegar Joe were notable for being fronted by two contrasting but equally impressive lead singers: Elkie Brooks and Robert Palmer. Both were already familiar with the Marquee, having previously played the club on a handful of occasions as part of a jazz-fusion outfit called Dada – Vinegar Joe was essentially Dada minus a few members. They were signed to Island Records, with whom they would release three albums, none of which would sell in significant numbers. Live, they were a different proposition, an electrifying, good-time, full-on rocking blues band, with Brooks providing high-powered raunchy vocals and the debonair Palmer all smooth and laid back.

Other debutants from around this time included Fusion Orchestra, who melded jazz with rock and Celtic rhythms. The lead vocalist was sixteen-year-old Jill Saward, who lied about her age at her audition in case the other members thought she was too young. The band's first gig at the Marquee, in early September 1971, was one of Saward's most memorable. Nerves got the better of her and she was intimidated by the audience. In the bar that night was Mott the Hoople's Ian Hunter, who, after the show, gave Saward a little stage presentation help: 'Let go of the fucking mic stand!' She got better fast. 'I learnt everything from those Marquee gigs,' says Saward. 'How to stop a fight. How to give the same crap back to whoever was dealing it in the audience. How to command a stage. Everything.' It was also at the Marquee that the Fusion Orchestra were seen one night by an EMI executive, which led to the offer of a record deal, along with the chance to work at Abbey Road Studios. After the band split in 1974, Saward would find success as lead singer of Eighties jazz-funksters Shakatak.

Nazareth were a gritty hard rock band that emerged out of the 1960s Scottish beat scene. Playing in local pubs and clubs but getting nowhere, they switched to a harder sound and moved down to London in the summer of 1971. Their first official gig outside of Scotland was at the Marquee. While in Soho, the band had a set of publicity photographs taken at the Nell Gwynne Club, a strip joint at 69 Dean Street, just round the corner from the Marquee. Several more dates on Wardour Street followed, but it would be another two years before Nazareth broke through, when *Melody Maker* readers voted them 'Brightest Hope'.

ART POP

Alex Harvey I JSD Band I Gary Moore I Flash I Camel I Mahatma Kane Jeeves I Fumble I David Essex I Roxy Music I Reading 1972 I Sparks I Queen

February 1972 saw the welcome return, after an absence of seven years, of Alex Harvey. Back in 1965, Harvey and his Soul Band had been Marquee regulars. Raised in the Gorbals in Glasgow, the some-time carpenter, dodgem-car attendant, navvy and tombstone carver apprenticed in skiffle bands as a teenager before graduating to R&B. Looking like Norman Wisdom with a broken nose, Harvey toured ceaselessly but never got the break his talent and ambition merited – although the singer-guitarist did get to meet the girl who would become his wife at one of his Marquee gigs. The band split and Harvey spent four years playing in the pit for hippie musical *Hair*. Now he was back, with the modestly titled Sensational Alex Harvey Band, which included guitarist Zal Cleminson, whose trademark was to perform in white-faced Pierrot make up. SAHB were all about getting a reaction: they were usually preceded on stage by a pair of bagpipers, and the band's own smash 'n' bash rockers were peppered with a bizarre choice of covers, from Sly and the Family Stone's 'Dance to the Music' to Irving Berlin's 'Cheek to Cheek', accompanied by a pair of dancing girls in cocktail dresses with the backs completely cut away to reveal the ladies' bare bottoms.

'Playing the Marquee always had a special buzz,' says Cleminson. 'It was also intimidating. We knew the great bands who'd played there and that we were on hallowed ground. And that dressing room had an atmosphere that oozed into you and propelled you on stage.'

Also hailing from north of the border were the JSD Band, Marquee regulars through 1972. They were an electrified folk-rock outfit that cut their teeth as part of the thriving Glasgow/Edinburgh folk scene of the late 1960s, alongside the likes of Billy Connolly and Gerry Rafferty. Relocating to London, they found a champion in John Peel after he saw them perform at the Marquee. Peel rated the band highly enough to write the sleevenotes for their 1972 album release, the same year they were invited to open for David Bowie on his Ziggy Stardust tour.

February also saw a solo debut for Belfast-born guitarist Gary Moore, who'd previously played the club with blues rockers Skid Row, but had recently left them to pursue a solo career. There was also a debut that same month for a short-lived outfit called Flash. They were a progressive rock group formed by ex-Yes guitarist Peter Banks, who recruited bassist Ray Bennett, along with vocalist Colin Carter and drummer Mike Hough. Bennett used to hang around with Yes and recalls how one afternoon during a rehearsal at the Marquee a couple of guys walked up to the stage and took away Chris Squire's purple-painted Marshall stack. He had apparently failed to make his HP payments. 'I don't recall how he managed to scrounge a bass rig for the night's gig, but he did somehow.'

In April, veteran R&B keyboardist Pete Bardens was back with his new group, Camel, who played the first of two Marquee support slots opening for Vinegar Joe; their Marquee year would be 1974, when they would play a monthly residency at the club. The same month saw a Marquee debut for Mahatma Kane Jeeves, a prog-rock outfit whose drummer was formally of Clouds and whose guitarist was Alan Murphy, who would go on to tour and record with Kate Bush, play sessions for Rod Stewart and David

Bowie, and join Level 42. They were looked after by Marquee Artists, which perhaps explains why they appeared at the Marquee more often than any other band in 1972, a total of twenty-two times.

May saw a Marquee debut for Fumble, a rock'n'roll revival band who would also rack up over twenty appearances at the Marquee over the next few years (during which time they'd also open for David Bowie on the US leg of his Ziggy Stardust tour). For vocalist and bassist Des Henly, the big deal about playing the Marquee was that it almost guaranteed exposure in the music press: 'It could be a tiny review on page fifty-two, but after playing the Marquee the music press couldn't really ignore you. It got the ball rolling. It was massively important in that respect.'

May boasted two further intriguing Marquee debuts. On Sunday 28th the headline act was David Essex. Essex had history with the Marquee. As a teenage blues fan, he'd been a regular attendee at the club around the time it relocated to Wardour Street. Then, in October 1966, he auditioned at the club for a band called Mood Indigo, which he subsequently joined – although there's no record of Mood Indigo ever actually performing at the Marquee. When Essex did finally take to the club's stage in 1972, it was his one and only appearance. Three nights later was another first and only appearance, on this occasion for pop avant-gardists Roxy Music. It was the third date on a UK tour to promote their self-titled first album, which would be released in two-and-a-half weeks' time. They were opening for UFO – God knows what the crowd, who'd turned up for a night of hard rock, made of Bryan Ferry and friends' arch mash-up of dressing-up box glam, camp vocals and Arts Lab-inspired synthetic pop. An appearance on *Top of the Pops* propelled first single 'Virginia Plain' into the national Top 5 and, before that first tour was over, Roxy Music had already left the Marquee far behind.

In August, the Marquee's annual festival was held for the second year at Reading. Genesis were the stars of Friday night, as much for Peter Gabriel's between-numbers storytelling as for the music; they left the stage to a full five minutes of cheering and applause. The acts that followed – Mungo Jerry and Curved Air (with future Police drummer Stewart Copeland) – received a more muted reception. Headliners on Saturday were Birmingham's Electric Light Orchestra, only four months old and already having to make rapid adjustments following the loss of frontman Roy Wood, and then the Faces. Roy Wood showed up Sunday with his new outfit, Wizzard. Also performing that day were Stackridge, Vinegar Joe, Status Quo, Stray, Ten Years After and Quintessence. John Peel was the weekend's compere and DJ.

A big innovation this year was the introduction of two stages, enabling a faster turnover between acts. The idea was prompted by the demands of Reading Council. 'They were always looking for an excuse to fine us and make more money,' recalls Harold. 'They said, if you go past eleven o'clock you'll be fined. I didn't like paying fines, so I started thinking of ways I could speed things up.' Previously, there would be a lag between one band finishing and the next starting, while the roadies cleared one lot of gear and brought on the next. It was getting worse as bands were using ever more and bigger pieces of equipment. 'The delays drove me mad,' says Harold. 'In the end, I thought, twin stages! One band could set up while another was playing.' With fine weather all weekend, the only dampener on proceedings was a repeat of the previous year's heavy-handed approach by Thames Valley Police. Once again, festival-goers were targeted and subjected to random searches by almost 500 officers pulled in from Reading and neighbouring towns. Police helicopters circled above the site. Some 130 people were arrested over the weekend, mostly for drug offences, but it was a very large sum of money and deployment of resources targeted against a largely inoffensive crowd.

Growing up in Los Angeles, brothers Ron and Russell Mael started their musical career as Halfnelson in 1968. With disappointing record sales, their label suggested a catchier name and Sparks were born. Sparks were freakish in appearance and uncompromisingly odd in their music and its presentation (brother Russell knocked himself unconscious with a giant wooden hammer onstage in Texas). They were too weird for West Coast America and so in October 1972 they did a series of dates at Max's Kansas City in New York and then flew to London, birthplace of some of the Mael's favourite acts, including the Kinks and the Who. Initially they based themselves in Beckenham, where the Maels' parents were living at the time, but then they moved to South Kensington and took up residence in the basement of a house belonging to theatre critic Kenneth Tynan.

That December Sparks played a weekly residency at the Marquee where, to everyone's surprise, they had punters queuing down Wardour Street. It helped that the press was comparing the American newcomers to T-Rex. Although there had been no hit singles at this point, the band did have a couple of albums of largely original material to draw on, plus their own unique take on *Sound of Music* fave 'Do-Re-Mi', performed with blizzards of confetti. The Marquee gigs led to an appearance on the *Old Grey Whistle Test*, which brought them to the attention of Muff Winwood and a deal with Island Records. Not long after, the Maels moved permanently to the UK to record breakthrough album *Kimono My House*.

EMI introduce Queen to the press.

Playing support to Sparks on 21 December was a band making their Marquee debut. Two of the members, guitarist Brian May and drummer Roger Taylor, had played the club on one previous occasion, back in December 1969, when, along with bassist and singer Tim Staffell, they were in a band called Smile. Since then, Smile had disintegrated and May and Taylor had hooked up with an aspiring singer called Farrokh Bulsara, who, shortly after, changed his name by deed poll to Freddie Mercury. With the addition of bass player John Deacon, the band – now called Queen – rehearsed, played a few small gigs and recorded some demos. After a break from playing live that lasted eight months, the Sparks support spot was one of two gigs, the other being at the Pheasantry on the Kings Road the previous month, intended to showcase the band and their new material. This pair of shows was followed by a further break, during which Queen would record their first session for the BBC. They taped four songs: 'Keep Yourself Alive', 'My Fairy King', 'Doing All Right' and 'Liar'. The session was broadcast ten days later and on the strength of it, the band landed themselves a record deal.

Monday 9 April 1973 was the night that EMI launched Queen as the label's great new signing and it took place at the Marquee. The music press turned out in force and variously described what they witnessed as 'glam rock with guts' and 'Britain's very own New York Dolls – but better'. Jac Holzman, founder and president of Elektra Records in the US, was present, famously saying afterward, 'I have seen the future of pop music and it is a band called Queen.' Friend of the band Doug Puddifoot was also there with a camera and one of his shots, of Freddie Mercury caught in a spotlight, ended up being the basis for the artwork used for the cover of Queen's debut album, released that July.

Queen were back at the Marquee the month of the album's release, opening for Mahatma (formerly Mahatma Kane Jeeves). It was to be their last appearance at the club: 1974 was their breakthrough year with the release of *Queen II* in March, which reached No.5 on the British album chart and spawned hit single 'Seven Seas of Rhye' (No.10 in the UK singles chart). After that, the Hammersmith Odeon beckoned. May and Taylor, however, would play the Marquee again in 1992, when the drummer's band, the Cross, played two Queen fan club Christmas concerts at the club. On the second night Taylor was joined on stage during the encore by May and Tim Staffell for a Smile reunion.

THE 1980 FLOOR SHOW

King Crimson | Average White Band | Robin Trower | Ace | Strider | Reading 1973 | David Bowie | Gryphon | Magma | Babe Ruth | The Sharks | Heavy Metal Kids

In February 1973, King Crimson returned for two consecutive nights, with a largely new line-up, now including drummer Bill Bruford (formerly of Yes), bassist John Wetton (formerly of Uriah Heep), violinist David Cross and percussionist Jamie Muir. The band presented the album Larks' Tongues in Aspic, which would be released a month later. These were the last shows that Crimson would play at the Marquee, although

Robert Fripp and John Wetton would both return to the club performing with other musicians in other bands.

The Average White Band were a Scottish funk and R&B seven-piece riding the transatlantic soul renaissance. Their February 1973 Marquee headliner was the first of about a half dozen appearances at the club this year. One night, in particular, stands out for bassist Alan Gorrie: 'Robbie McIntosh, our drummer, had been having a libation or five with Scots blues singer Frankie Miller at lunchtime and our manager Robin Turner had to literally prop him up on the drum stool for the gig.' When the band bounded back on stage for an encore, there was no McIntosh. 'The dressing room door opened,' recalls Gorrie, 'and he momentarily appeared in silhouette then tumbled backwards.' Fortunately, a drummer friend in the audience jumped on stage to fill in. Tragically, just over eighteen months later, after a concert at the Troubadour in LA, McIntosh died when he accidentally took heroin at a party thinking it was cocaine. Back in London, AWB played a benefit gig at the Marquee to raise funds for his family, which included a guest appearance by Elton John.

Other notable artists appearing at the club around this time included ex-Procol Harum guitarist Robin Trower, now fronting his own power trio, and Ace, a rock band later to become famous for their hit single 'How Long'. Right now, they were knocking out mainly soul covers sung with three part harmonies – one of those voices belonging to keyboardist Paul Carrack, later lead vocalist with Mike + the Mechanics.

April 1973 marked the club's fifteenth anniversary, although there were no special celebrations. The group playing the club on the Marquee's birthday were Strider, a hard-edged blues/rock outfit in the Deep Purple mould, who would make two largely ignored albums before splitting.

That August's Reading festival featured Greenslade, Rory Gallagher, Lindisfarne, Alex Harvey, Strider, Status Quo, the Faces, John Martyn, Stackridge, Spencer Davis and Genesis, among others. Dave Lawson of Greenslade retains vivid memories of the weekend: 'Reading was like most festivals – appalling sound, badly organised, caravans as dressing rooms, gear problems, roadies wandering off crumpet hunting, dodgy burgers, poor toilet facilities and the heavy smell of grass hanging in the air. Just great!'

Highlights included Rod Stewart arriving on site in a white Rolls-Royce and taking to the stage in a yellow satin suit. John Martyn led the festival crowd in an acapella version of 'Singin' in the Rain' – although this year the weather was so gloriously hot that the organisers were warning people not to drop matches in case they set the tinder-dry grass on fire. Genesis closed the festival with Peter Gabriel emerging from a white sarcophagus in the centre of the stage and exiting dressed as a flower. One of the surprises of the weekend turned out to be the re-emergence of jazz, with Chris Barber and George Melly both receiving enthusiastic receptions. Backstage there were a number of familiar faces, too, with Keith Moon and George Harrison amongst the VIPs. Harrison was acting as Melly's roadie. Myra Hickey, who was the Marquee's festival director, recalls getting a call from Terry Doran, Harrison's personal assistant, saying George wanted to come down to the festival and would like a hospitality caravan in the backstage area for drinks and entertaining over the weekend. 'I duly sent an invoice for provision of said caravan and asked for a budget for drinks,' recalls Hickey. 'I got the invoice back with a huge FUCK OFF stamped in red all over it. Terry said the stamp was the most used piece of Apple's office equipment.'

There were problems this year with security. Since the early days of the festival, there had always been a small number of people who tried to get in without a ticket. Harold ended up employing some of the more persistent of them to work in security, on the theory that the best person to catch a poacher is another poacher. 'There was one chap that had a chain round his neck with a battered Harpic can hanging off it. He was known as Harry Harpic. He used to regularly smuggle himself in. I used to find him backstage and say, "Oh you got in again then". A bigger concern were the Hell's Angels. 'They started to be a nuisance,' recalls Harold. 'They would arrive on their motorbikes demanding to be let in.' The police were no help. 'They wouldn't lift a finger. It would be, "That's your problem, it's not our job". Harold had to create his own force to deal with the gate crashers. Nicknamed the 'Beasts', this makeshift security outfit was made up of serious muscle with some serious charge sheets. Years later, Harold was watching TV one evening when the news came on about the abduction of the notorious Great Train Robber Ronnie Biggs from

Brazil. Harold recognised the leader of the abduction gang, John Miller (aka John McKillip), as one of his former Beasts.

That July, at the Hammersmith Odeon, at the height of Ziggymania, Bowie had announced that this was to be the last show. 'Bowie Quits,' wailed the headlines. What he really meant was that he was moving on and leaving Ziggy behind. He'd be back in less than twelve months with *Diamond Dogs*. Meanwhile, he had another album to promote. Released on 19 October, *Pin Ups* was Bowie's reworking of some of his favourite songs from the years he spent paying his dues fronting a succession of small-time R&B outfits on the London club scene. It's a tip of the chapeau to the people and places that made Ziggy, and includes tracks by 'all those bands I used to go and hear play down the Marquee between 1964–1967,' as he writes on the back of the album sleeve. So, it made sense that when American channel NBC wanted to film Bowie for a sixty-minute *Midnight Special* TV spectacular, he would choose to stage it back at the Marquee. The club was booked for 18–20 October, a Thursday, Friday and Saturday. The concept was a highly theatrical cabaret extravaganza called the '1980 Floor Show'.

With strange logic, having chosen the Marquee for its associations and atmosphere, the TV crew removed all the club's identifiable features and built a new stage with an anonymous backdrop, much to the chagrin of Jack Barrie. There were three 'shows' – one on Friday night and two on Saturday, with a different audience of 200 souls for each, drawn by ballot from Marquee club and Bowie fan club members. Mingling with the audience were friendly neighbourhood New York drag queen Wayne County, Angie Bowie with baby Zowie, Lionel Bart, Dana Gillespie and Mary Hopkin (former Apple Records artist and now wife of Bowie-collaborator Tony Visconti). A queue of fans without tickets straggled down a drizzly Wardour Street for most of the three days, remaining remarkably peaceful despite never getting in.

Bowie was backed by Spiders Mick Ronson and Trevor Bolder, but no Woody Woodmansey – instead Aynsley Dunbar, ex of John Mayall's Bluesbreakers and Frank Zappa, was behind the drum kit. Mike Garson was on keyboards and there were the Astronettes, a trio of backing vocalists. Musical guests over the three shows included Marianne Faithfull, the Troggs and Carmen, an Anglo-American flamenco-rock group who were never heard of again, as well as the statuesque model Amanda Lear, who had just appeared on the cover of Roxy Music's album *For Your Pleasure*. The setlist featured tracks from *Pin Ups*, *Aladdin Sane* and new material from the forthcoming *Diamond Dogs* – the shows featured the first ever live performances of '1984/Dodo'. 'One thing has always stuck in my mind,' recalls Robin Mayhew, who was the show's sound engineer. 'I had set up the sound system and was checking out the piano mics, playing the intro of David's "Lady Stardust" from the Ziggy album. He came over to me and said, "That's yesterday's music".'

Because the club was so small there was only room for two cameras, which meant each song had to be performed multiple times with the cameras in different positions. The Marquee's studio served as the dressing room for Bowie's numerous costume changes. The TV company was particularly scared by Bowie's outfits. One was a fishnet body-stocking adorned with disembodied golden hands clutching his chest and groin – the hand on the groin had to go. Another was open down the front, so low you could see his pubic hair. After a first wearing, NBC had it sewn up and insisted Bowie do another take. And then there was Marianne Faithfull's backless nun's habit and another bare bottom on the Marquee stage. These performances – Bowie's final appearances at the club – were him bidding a farewell to Ziggy Stardust and Aladdin Sane, and to the Spiders: this would be the last ever full gig with guitarist and close collaborator Mick Ronson, who he first met up the stairs at La Chasse.

As 1973 drew to a close, the Bowie shows might not even be the oddest performances to grace the Marquee stage. In mid-November, Gryphon played their first headliner at the club. They took to the stage armed with crumhorns and recorders dressed in attire that was half King's Road, half court jester. Their music mixed Elizabethan jigs with Beatles tunes. *Melody Maker* dubbed them the '13th-century Slade'. Still, they connected with audiences and Gryphon would notch up a double-figure tally of appearances at the Marquee between then and 1977.

The Marquee hadn't quite seen anything like Magma, prog-rockers from France making two appearances at the club, the first of which was on 5 December 1973. The black-clad band advertised their music as extra-terrestrial, which presented itself on stage as throbbing bass, swirling twin keyboards, Horsemen of the Apocalypse drumming and vocals screamed in a made-up language of the band's own devising called Kobaïan. The band had crossed the Channel in support of their third album, *Mekanik Destructiw Kommandoh*, the first to be released in Britain. It was produced by former Rolling Stones and Yardbirds manager Giorgio Gomelsky, who had quit England for France in 1970 and was now heavily involved in the Continental prog and experimental rock scene. Magma would be back at the Marquee three months later playing a set that would eventually be issued as a live album, *AKT XVIII - Marquee - Londres 17 mars 1974*, in 2018.

Seeing out the year, December had headlining nights from a handful of Marquee favourites of the time, including Babe Ruth, rockers with a bluesy, guitar-led sound and powerful vocals by Jennie Hahn. They started life in 1971 as Shacklock and were spotted one night playing a support slot at the Marquee by an A&R man from EMI's Harvest label and promptly signed up. Changing their name to Babe Ruth, after the US baseball legend, they went into Abbey Road studio to record their debut album (Pink Floyd were at work on *Dark Side of the Moon* in the studio next door) and, in late 1972, played the first of twenty-four headliners at the Marquee, most of which were in 1973–74.

Sharks were a similarly bluesy-rock outfit, formed in 1972 by former Free bassist Andy Fraser, and signed to Island Records. Fraser quit in mid 1973 to be replaced by Busta Jones, and the band was fronted by vocalist Steve Parsons and guitarist Chris Spedding. In the early days, they travelled to gigs in a Pontiac Le Mans with a fibreglass shark's fin on the roof and shark's teeth on the grille – until it was written off after being driven into a tree. There was also the second of what would eventually be seventeen appearances for purveyors of Faces-style bar-room boogie, the Heavy Metal Kids. Their charismatic Artful Dodger of a front man, Gary Holton, brought a sense of absurd theatricality to his stage antics, including blowing up a dummy of himself. A former child actor, Holton returned to acting in the 1980s as Wayne, the womanising cockney carpenter in TVs *Auf Wiedersehen, Pet* – until he died of a drugs overdose while filming the second series.

THE MARQUEE ROCKS

Judas Priest I Bearded Lady I Be-Bop Deluxe I Rory Gallagher
I Thin Lizzy I Reading 1974

The Marquee had been rocked thunderously before. Led Zeppelin had been loud. Black Sabbath had been loud. Until now, though, such nights were still occasional spikes into the red, in a general sonic landscape of blues, purplish prog and white soul. But come 1974, the volume was increasing all round. It was all getting heavy.

The year got off to a loud start with the first of several appearances that year by Judas Priest. In one form or another, the group had been knocking around their hometown of Birmingham since 1969. They travelled down to London for a one-off early gig at the Marquee in October 1972, opening for Mahatma Kane Jeeves. 'The first time we all walked through the doors it was disbelief,' says guitarist Kenny 'KK' Downing. 'We're actually playing the Marquee.' Downing was always confident Priest could compete with anybody: 'As a live act we packed a punch and I always felt that in Rob Halford we had the greatest singer that we could possibly get.' It would be another sixteen months before they returned, in February 1974, opening for Cardiff rockers Budgie (who were making their third appearance at the club). Without a record deal, Priest's manager invited David Howells, who ran an offshoot of Decca called Gull Records, to see the band perform that night. 'As an up-and-coming band, that's what we wanted, this kind of showcase gig,' says Downing. 'If it went right, then you could win big time.' At the end of the night, Priest joined Budgie onstage for a full-throttle encore, and it was largely because of the wild reaction from the audience that Howells agreed to sign them. (Budgie's performance that night, complete with encore, was recorded and released, in 2018, as *Budgie Live at the Marquee 1974*.) Priest stayed with Gull for two albums before being snapped up by CBS and going on to score huge international success, emerging as one of the most influential of all British metal bands. Their relationship with the Marquee stretched to a total of eleven gigs, with the last being in November 1975, just before they went into the studio to record their breakthrough second album, *Sad Wings of Destiny*.

As Judas Priest snagged a recording deal on the Monday, another group of hopefuls took their first steps onto the Marquee stage on the Thursday. Bearded Lady were rock with a glam sheen, epitomised by the stage appearance of guitarist and lead singer Johnny Warman, who sported a sparkly bowler hat and shirt, and boots sprayed different colours. Their first two appearances at the club were opening for a now forgotten act called Quadrille, but Bearded Lady would return in late 1975 to begin a one-Saturday-a-month residency at the club that would run through into 1977. 'I loved the whole ambience of the Marquee,' says Warman. 'The smell, the sodden sopping wet carpet, the stage, the tiny changing room and the staff, but most of all the audiences. I had great nights there especially when people like Phil Lynott and Lemmy turned up to see us, and even Chuck Berry.'

There was some respite from the volume merchants. Mid-January saw the first of a handful of Marquee appearances for Bill Nelson's art-rock project Be-Bop Deluxe, with a second spot five weeks later – both times opening for String Driven Thing. Be-Bop landed their first headline spot in March and then, following the release of first album *Axe Attack* that summer, they were back in October for what would be their final gig at the club. May saw the long-awaited return of Rory Gallagher, a guitarist who could count Clapton, Hendrix and Bob Dylan among his admirers. Since his former band Taste had split a few years before, Gallagher had played the Marquee on several occasions under his own name. He'd also recorded his 1973 album *Blueprint* at Marquee Studios, and was often to be found propping up the club's bar.

In July, another Irish band performed a showcase set. Thin Lizzy had first played the Marquee back in 1971, when they'd opened for Status Quo (a memorable gig for unfortunate reasons: much of the band's gear was stolen from their van while it was parked in the mews behind the club and they had to perform with borrowed instruments). Since then, Lizzy had toured the UK with Slade and Suzi Quatro, had a hit single with 'Whiskey in the Jar' and appeared on *Top of the Pops*. But guitarist Eric Bell had left and been replaced by Gary Moore, who'd then also quit. Then the group's drummer and co-founder, Brian Downey, quit, too. That left bass guitarist and vocalist Phil Lynott on his own, a one-man band. Album sales were poor, the group, such as it was, was £30,000 in debt, and a recording deal with Decca was coming to an end and wasn't going to be renewed. It looked like Thin Lizzy were over. But Lynott persuaded Downey to return and together they set about rejuvenating the band. They recruited two new guitarists, Scott Gorham and Brian Robertson, and the new line-up played their first gig in July. They had two more warm-ups to settle in before, on Tuesday 9 July, they had a headliner at the Marquee in front of representatives from Phonogram. It was so hot that night that all the guitars went out of tune, but the band performed well enough that they landed the deal that kept them in business.

Lizzy also earned themselves a slot at that year's Reading. This was the fourth year at the site, and Harold was petitioning the local council for some permanent infrastructure, including proper roads and water mains. 'I finally talked the council into it, because they were earning good money off me. Every year they increased my licence fee until it was outrageous, despite the fact the festival was a good earner for the local economy. The police charge went up every year, too. They all regarded me as a cash cow.' Once again, the line-up drew heavily on Marquee favourites, including the Sensational Alex Harvey Band, Camel, Hustler, Greenslade, Heavy Metal Kids, Barclay James Harvest, Gryphon and Strider. There were some surprises, notably top-of-the-bill appearances from 10cc (who opened with new single 'Silly Love' and closed with previous hit 'Rubber Bullets'), Dutch prog band Focus and Traffic, who were making their last ever UK appearance.

Possibly due to the overbearing presence in the past of the Thames Valley Police, or possibly just due to changing habits, there was little evidence of drug use this year. Instead, festival-goers got tanked up on booze and indulged in what would become the new scourge of the festival, can-throwing. One of the main targets was a fish and chip van. Punters took offence at the exorbitant prices and the fact that the vendor wouldn't sell chips on their own. They expressed their anger with a barrage of thrown cans and then a group attempted to rock the vehicle over onto its side. The owner managed to get the vehicle's engine started and make an escape but spilled chip fat caught fire and the van exited the festival grounds trailing a pall of black smoke.

A novel solution was arrived at this year to a problem that had vexed Harold since the early days of the festival: how to manage people leaving the event and then wanting to come back in later. Until now, punters had either been given a ticket, which they had to retain and show, or they'd had the back of their hand stamped. 'That got us in trouble with the Red Cross,' says Harold, 'because they had a case of somebody who had an allergic reaction to the ink.' One day Harold was talking to one of his security officers, Pete Becket, who ran the main gate at Reading. Beckett had just been in hospital and was still wearing his hospital identification wristband. A bell went off in Harold's head. He contacted the hospital and asked where they got the bands from. 'It was a company in America. I wrote to them and asked if they could send over a box. When they arrived, I removed the strip that was used for the name of the patient, just leaving the band, and tried them out.' It was the perfect solution and Harold ordered more bands. 'At first the company were baffled, but they picked up on what I was doing very quickly and went into the business of wristbands themselves for other festivals.' Today wristbands are standard at festivals the world over. Toilets were another of Harold's festival innovations. Back in the early days of the festival, the original facilities had been something called Elsans, which involved an evil-smelling blue chemical in tin drums with a toilet seat precariously placed on top. 'I thought they were very unpleasant,' recalls Harold. He replaced them with the mobile flushing toilets used by road workers on the motorways that were then under construction across the country. For Harold this was one of the things he enjoyed the most about putting on his festival: facing challenges and finding solutions.

Back at Wardour Street, the club had a new manager. Uli Pritz came from Hamburg, where he used to watch bands at the Star-Club, where the Beatles once had a residency. When he came to London, in late 1971, he got a job as a chef in the City. He eventually made his way to the Marquee, where he began working in the cloakroom three nights a week. From there, he graduated to the coffee bar, and, when they converted that into a licensed bar, Pritz ended up managing it. Because the licence only covered the bar area, one of Pritz's jobs was to stop people taking drinks into the auditorium. 'Jack had to rescue me one time when I stopped some people and they turned out to be Led Zeppelin and their manager Peter Grant. We let them in.' Pritz also worked at the festivals behind the artists' bar. 'I used to go on two weeks holiday straight after Reading to recover and spend the money I'd made. We worked twelve hours a day and I had to sleep on the floor behind the bar with the stock.'

In 1974, Jack Barrie was promoted to director of the Marquee club, and Pritz became manager, which included booking the bands. 'When I took over there was a bit of a lull after the Sixties explosion.' His booking strategy was to make it as difficult as possible for bands to play at the club by turning them down a few times, so when they did finally play, they were appreciative of the opportunity and made more of an effort. 'I turned most bands down many times before I booked them.' He rarely had to ring an agent. 'They would ring me.' Saturday was the night to give new bands a chance as the club would be full no matter who was playing. 'We eventually had people like the Police and the Jam playing the Saturday night slot for just fifty quid before they went on to success.'

PUB ROCK

Alberto Y Lost Trio Paranoias | Brinsley Schwarz | Chilli Willi and the Red Hot Peppers | Dr Feelgood | Ducks Deluxe | Kilburn and the High Roads | Kursaal Flyers | Reading 1975 | Motörhead | The Scorpions

It's rare for a band to show up at the Marquee for an audition and end up as headliners that same evening, but that's what happened to Alberto Y Lost Trios Paranoias, in October 1974. Formed in Manchester the previous year, they were rock satirists in the vein of the Bonzo Dog Doo-Dah Band, very capable musicians, expert at spoofing any and all musical styles. After establishing themselves in the North, the next step was to see if they could get any interest in London. Blackhill Enterprises, run by Peter Jenner and Andrew King, former managers of Pink Floyd, expressed a desire to see the band in action and arranged a try-out slot for them at the Marquee, supporting French prog-rockers Ange. 'We were offered five quid,' recalls the band's vocalist and guitarist CP Lee, 'which wasn't even enough money to cover the petrol.' When the Paranoias arrived to set up, Peter Jenner told them that Ange had been held up at customs and wouldn't make the gig. The Paranoias were now top of the bill. 'So we went from a five-quid support act,' says Lee, 'to you're on stage at nine-thirty – knock 'em dead.' There was a journalist in the audience from *Melody Maker* and he gave the band a front-page mention. 'And that was how we hit London.'

'We didn't do pastiches, like the Barron Knights,' explains Lee. 'We'd take the essence of something and have fun with it.' They spoofed Lou Reed's song 'Heroin' with a number called 'Anadin', targeted Pink Floyd in 'Mandrax Sunset Variations: I, II, III' and lampooned country and western in numbers like, 'If You Don't Leave Me, I'll Find Someone Else Who Will.'

By now, the importance of the Marquee to new acts like the Paranoias was greater than ever. Where in the late 1960s central London had boasted dozens of small venues, numbers had declined rapidly in the first years of the new decade, largely thanks to economic recession. Losses included the Flamingo, Ram Jam Club, Klooks Kleek, the Electric Garden, Tiles and UFO. There were still the colleges but, as an article appearing in *Melody Maker* headlined 'Smaller venues are hard to find for smaller bands' noted, there were otherwise just a handful of places, including the Marquee and the 100 Club, that offered a stage to aspiring new bands. There was no shortage of pubs though – hence a new wave of bands starting to turn up on Wardour Street having first paid their dues in the back rooms of suburban boozers, all part of a scene loosely labelled as pub rock.

Ironically, this London-based scene was started by three American musicians. In 1970, US trio Eggs Over Easy were in London to make a record with Chas Chandler. Holed up in Kentish Town, they started playing at a local jazz pub, the Tally Ho. They went down a storm and were soon playing four nights a week. On 15 June 1971, they appeared at the Marquee, opening for Hardin and York. It was a one-off appearance but in the audience that night was Dave Robinson, manager of Brinsley Schwarz. Robinson was blown away by the Eggs and introduced them to his band. As a consequence, when the Eggs returned to America, Brinsley Schwarz took over their spot at the Tally Ho. This was early 1972. Over the next twelve months, the Brinsleys were joined by several more bands playing a similar brand of raucous, good-time, saloon-bar rock with its roots in R&B and country. It was music to drink, dance and pull birds/ blokes to, played by ungroomed bands who often looked 'like villains on *The Sweeney*,' according to music journalist David Hepworth. Soon there was a recognised scene with an expanding circuit that included pubs like the Kensington in Shepherd's Bush, the Lord Nelson in Holloway Road, and the Hope and Anchor in Islington. These venues gave a wave of new bands the chance to get up and play with the minimum of fuss and equipment. The scene was a reaction to mainstream rock that had got too precious, too showbiz, too up itself. Pub rock became the Next Big Thing.

It reached the Marquee in 1974. The club was never a bastion of pub rock but almost all the major acts on the scene played Wardour Street at some point, many of them returning multiple times. Brinsley Schwarz, the band that kick started the party, had appeared at the Marquee as far back as June 1970, with three more appearances in 1971–72. They were back on 18 March 1975, which turned out to be the band's final ever gig before they split up. Chilli Willi and the Red Hot Peppers, or 'the Willies' as they were known, started as a country-blues outfit, whose line-up included guitarist Martin Stone, formerly of the Savoy Brown Blues Band, the Action and Mighty Baby, and drummer Pete Thomas, who would later become part of Elvis Costello's backing band, the Attractions. The Willies became one of the most entertaining acts on the circuit and played the Marquee half a dozen times during 1974.

October 1974 saw a first Marquee date for Dr Feelgood, the Canvey Island band fronted by singer Lee Brilleaux and guitarist-songwriter Wilko Johnson, the latter memorably described as 'zig-zagging around the stage like a broken Dalek'. The following January, it was the turn of both Ducks Deluxe and Kilburn and the High Roads. The Ducks (who named themselves after a slot machine at the Severn Bridge Service station) played high-intensity R&B and were fronted by abrasive singer-guitarist Sean Tyla – 'Encore? You don't fucking deserve one!' The Kilburns came out of Canterbury College of Art. Student Keith Lucas and his tutor, Ian Dury, formed the band for the end of term dance. Mixing 1950s rock'n'roll with music hall, they started to play the London pubs, including the Tally

Ho, and ended up supporting the Who on their Quadrophenia tour. For guitarist Lucas (who later changed his name to Nick Cash), playing the Marquee was a big deal: 'Ever since I was a young lad, I knew that the Who, Hendrix and the Stones had all played there so it was like a dream come true to play it with the Kilburns. It was a step up from all those pub gigs and we had some really good shows there.' Lucas would return to the Marquee with punk band 999, including an impressive five nights in a row. 'The Marquee was to me the most important club gig in the world.'

The Kursaal Flyers were mates who'd hung out together since the late 1960s, playing in a variety of bands around the Southend-on-Sea area. In late 1973 they were asked to put a group together for a one-off show. 'The gig was a blast,' recalls singer Paul Shuttleworth. 'And we decided to keep the band together, just for fun.' Thanks to friends in Dr Feelgood, they landed a couple of gigs on the London pub circuit and a first gig at the Marquee in March 1975, where Shuttleworth had been a regular audience member for years: 'The Nice and Ten Years After were my favourites, along with bluesman Eddie Boyd, who had Aynsley Dunbar in his backing group. They were all decked out in the regulation worn denim while Eddie was immaculate in a sharp mohair suit and crocodile shoes!' The Kursaals played the club sporadically through into 1977, when they chose to use it as a venue for a live album. In a cheeky nod to an earlier landmark recording, they called it *Five Live Kursaals*. 'We had a firm following at that time,' recalls Shuttleworth. 'And the audience really got it. It was great to be in a fairly intimate atmosphere with them. The band was shit hot too – a great night! One of my all-time favourite gigs.'

Dr Feelgood and the Kursaals, along with Alberto Y Los Trios Paranoias, made the bill for Reading '75. That summer's festival was the biggest to date in terms of attendance (50,000), and boasted one of the strongest line-ups of the decade, despite no-shows by Lou Reed, and Richard and Linda Thompson. The Feelgoods played the Friday night (following UFO, Judas Priest and Joan Armatrading) and were a massive hit, transforming a field in Berkshire into a tiny, sweaty, steaming, Essex R&B club. Hawkwind had the thankless task of following them and closing out the evening. The performance was accompanied by psychedelic lighting provided by Liquid Len and the Lensmen, and the set closed with 'Silver

Machine', but it was cold and even Stacia, the band's Amazonian dancer performing topless in body paint failed to warm up the crowd – *Melody Maker* ungraciously described her as 'stomping around with all the grace of the Statue of Liberty animated by Ray Harryhausen on an off-day' (this would be her last appearance with the band).

The Kursaals and the Paranoias played Saturday. The Paranoias were in the middle of a European tour. 'On the Friday night we'd played a gig in Rotterdam,' recalls CP Lee. 'They put us on a private plane, flew us to Stansted, and then drove us to a hotel in Reading. On Saturday afternoon we lurched into the festival, went on stage, came off stage, went straight to the airport and flew back to Holland.' Also on that night were Thin Lizzy, the Heavy Metal Kids and Supertramp, who'd scored a hit single the previous year with 'Dreamer' and were promoting new album *Crisis? What Crisis?* The evening's headliners were Yes, who boasted an elaborate stage set designed by album-cover artist Roger Dean and the first festival use of lasers (despite objections from the council that they could blind festival-goers and bring down aircraft). Yes were promoting new album *Relayer*, but filled the set with popular favourites including 'I've Seen All Good People', 'And You and I', 'Close to the Edge' and 'Roundabout'. Unfortunately, they had to contend with torrential rain, which put a damper on the whole thing.

On Sunday, the weather was warm and sunny all day, culminating in a blistering afternoon of virtuoso fretwork from John McLaughlin, fronting the Mahavishnu Orchestra, Robin Trower and Wishbone Ash.

Beer-can fights were constant throughout the weekend. Generally, it was groups of fans attacking each other, though on occasion the barrage was directed at a particular band on stage – it happened to a group called Stella, who were forced to run for cover. On Sunday night, as the festival ground emptied, Harold retired to his on-site caravan with a feeling of satisfaction. When he woke the next morning, it was completely dark and the caravan door wouldn't open. During the night, the security teams had buried the caravan in a giant haystack. Harold had to be bailed out.

While Hawkwind played Friday evening at Reading, the previous night in Soho their former bassist was stepping out with his new band on Wardour Street. Lemmy had recently been sacked from Hawkwind after being busted for drugs on the US–Canadian border. He was arrested on possession of cocaine: a felony later downgraded to a fine when it turned out it wasn't coke he was carrying but amphetamine sulphate, which was not then illegal in Canada. Still, the band sacked him. 'The most cosmic band in the cosmos fucking fired me for being busted for the wrong drug,' Lemmy told his biographer Mick Wall. He was back within two months with a new outfit, which was billed as Lemmy's Motörhead. On Thursday 21 August, just a month after their very first engagement, supporting Greenslade at the Roundhouse, they played their first gig at the Marquee. The line-up was Lemmy on clattering bass and scorching vocals, Larry Wallis (formerly of the Pink Fairies) on buzz-saw guitar and Lucas Fox on thundering drums; the set was made up of covers, including Chuck Berry's 'Bye Bye Johnny' and the Yardbirds' 'Train Kept a-Rollin', plus three tracks Lemmy had written with Hawkwind (including 'Motörhead') and some Larry Wallis originals. The reviews were not kind. Writing in the *NME*, Nick Kent described Motörhead as having 'all the panache of a butcher stripping meat from an overripe carcass'. The Marquee loved them and Motörhead were back again in November.

Motörhead's first Marquee gig.

The night before Lemmy and crew's second Marquee date, another hugely influential metal band made their club debut. The Scorpions had been around their native Germany since 1965 but only really broke through in 1974 with their *Fly to the Rainbow* album. It won them a solid fanbase, which they built on with dates around Europe. In November 1975 they played their first UK dates: one night at the Cavern in Liverpool followed by a night at the Marquee. 'It was a huge adventure,' recalls vocalist Klaus Meine. 'To play the Marquee was like rock'n'roll heaven. All of a sudden, we were touching the same ground as Hendrix and the Rolling Stones. At the same time, you are super nervous – can we pull this off? Or will they kill us in the press?' At the soundcheck Gary Moore showed up to wish them good luck. The gig went well and the reviews were a confidence booster. 'We felt we'd accomplished something, and having been influenced by so many British bands, it felt good to prove ourselves in the UK,' says Meine.

The show had even greater significance for the Scorpions' lead guitarist Uli Jon Roth. A Hendrix fanatic, he was thrilled to learn that in the Marquee audience was Monika Dannemann, last girlfriend of the American guitarist – she was with him on the night he died. That night, the band played the Hendrix track 'Red House'. After the show Dannemann and Roth met and, as result, became romantically involved. The Scorpions would return to the Marquee for two more dates, both in 1976.

Otherwise, the back end of 1975 was dominated by middle-of-the-road, deservedly long-forgotten rockers, with occasional outbursts of vigour from the pub rockers. But by now, life was ebbing even from the pub-rock scene. In some ways, its work was already done: bands like Dr Feelgood, Kilburn and the High Roads, and the Kursaal Flyers had cleared the path for their gobby, foul-mouthed, snarling successor – punk.

THE SEX PISTOLS

Eddie and the Hot Rods I The Sex Pistols I The Stranglers I
AC/DC I Reading 1976 I Graham Parker and the Rumour
I Giggles I The Fabulous Poodles I The Enid I Brand X I
John Coghlan's Diesel I Woody Woodmansey's U-Boat

One of the most momentous nights in the Marquee's history started innocuously enough when Jack Barrie and assistant manager Nigel Hutchings went off to a wine-tasting event in the East End. Barrie had decided to take the Marquee's bar offerings up market by adding wine. After the tasting was finished, Barrie and Hutchings headed back to the club where Eddie and the Hot Rods, a pub rock band from Canvey Island, were playing. Not long out of Essex, the Rods had already scored residencies at the Kensington and the Nashville, and this was their Marquee debut. 'As we came in the door,' recalls Hutchings, 'there were all these people in leather and rubber with safety pins all over, and some girl with a rat on her shoulder, and we thought, what the bloody hell's going on here!' They weren't Rods fans, they were there for the support act, the Sex Pistols. 'We walked to the bar,' says Hutchings, 'and started watching this band play and we were absolutely pole-axed by what we were seeing. That was the first punk gig at the Marquee.' The date was 12 February 1976.

At this point the Pistols had played just a handful of gigs, all at colleges. This was their first appearance at a major venue. By chance, the *NME*'s Neil Spencer was there, sent to cover the Rods. 'Hurry up, they're having an orgy on stage,' the guy in the ticket office told him. He missed that – the group cavorting with two dancing girls in plastic thigh boots and bodices – but he did arrive just as the singer hurled a chair, which skidded across the stage and thumped loudly into the PA. Spencer described the band as, 'a quartet of spiky teenage misfits from the wrong end of various London roads.'

maRquee

90 Wardour St., W.1	01-437 6603
Open every night from 7 p.m. to 11 p.m. Reduced admission for Students and Members	
Thurs. 12th Feb. (Adm. 60p) **EDDIE & THE HOTRODS** Plus Support & Ian Fleming	Mon. 16th Feb. (Adm. 80p) The only London date of . . . **SAVOY BROWN** Plus Guests & Jerry Floyd
Fri. 13th Feb. (Adm. 70p) **DANA GILLESPIE** Plus Friends & Ian Fleming	Tues. 17th Feb. (Adm. 75p) **NUTZ** Plus Support & Jerry Floyd
Sat. 14th Feb. (Adm. 70p) Free admission with this ad. before 8 p.m. **ASYLUM** Plus Support & Ian Fleming	Wed. 18th Feb. (Adm. 65p) **KILBURN & THE HIGH ROADS** Plus Support & Jerry Floyd
Sun. 15th Feb. (Adm. 65p) Free admission with this ad. before 8 p.m. **PALMBEACH EXPRESS** Plus Dave Paul & Jerry Floyd	Thurs. 19th Feb. (Adm. 70p) **NATIONAL FLAG** Plus Cock Sparrow & Ian Fleming
Hamburgers and other hot and cold snacks are available	

Support on the 12th were the Sex Pistols.

They played covers of tracks by Dave Berry and the Small Faces, plus Iggy and the Stooges' 'No Fun', as well as several self-penned numbers, including, noted Spencer, 'the moronic "Pretty Vacant"'. The Marquee crowd was not impressed. People were shouting abuse. What was novel was that the band were screaming abuse back. No one asked for an encore but the Pistols did one anyway, announcing, 'We're going to play "Substitute"'. 'You can't play,' someone heckled. 'So what?' replied the bass player. Before they finally quit the stage, the Pistols trashed the Rods' gear.

Backstage, the Pistol's manager Malcolm McLaren was quietly pleased with events and even happier a few days later when Spencer gave his band their first ever write-up in the music press. Looking back, thirty years

The Sex Pistols pose outside 90 Wardour Street.

later, in *The Guardian*, Spencer described that night at the Marquee as a Year Zero moment: 'One of those cusps between before and after; in this case before the Pistols and after the Pistols.' There would be no after at the Marquee for the Pistols, though, because they were never allowed back to perform again – although McLaren did hire the club one afternoon for the filming of the 'God Save the Queen' video.

Jack Barrie was reluctant to book any more punk bands. 'He just didn't like the punk aesthetic,' says Nigel Hutchings. 'All those yobbos with safety pins all over them.' But in March, the Stranglers, one of the handful of bands in the vanguard of punk, supported the Pink Fairies. That went off without any trouble, so the Stranglers were allowed back as headliners in November. That didn't go so well. On this occasion, the Stranglers were eager to prove their punk credentials. From the stage, singer Hugh

Cornwell launched a tirade against the club: 'We'd like to mourn the death of the Marquee. The place is dead. The regulars have grown into the wallpaper, the Marquee don't know what's going on today. Wait till we've finished then smash the place up.' The audience failed to rise to the bait, but bass player Jean-Jacques Burnel did smash his instrument through the window of the DJ box. Hutchings was furious: 'At the end of the night I was cashing up and Jean-Jacques came down to collect the band's money. I told him to piss off and get all their gear out of the club, and that I was going to fine them the cost of damaging the box. He got really nasty but I stood my ground and told them they were never going to play here again.'

Hutchings had joined the Marquee in January 1975. He originally trained as a chef in a hotel on the Isle of Wight. This was in the heyday of the Isle of Wight festivals and he ended up cooking for a lot of bands as they came back in the middle of the night wanting something to eat. Hutchings once found himself in a service lift with Jimi Hendrix – 'I was too scared to talk to him.' Moving to London in the early 1970s and working in a succession of bars, he started visiting the Marquee and got to know Jack Barrie. One day, Barrie mentioned he was looking for a bar manager. It paid less than he was already earning but Hutchings decided the club would be a great place to work. 'When I started at the Marquee the whole rock music scene was in the doldrums,' says Hutchings. 'That's why when the whole punk thing kicked it all up the arse and shook everybody up, it was an absolute godsend for the business.' Hutchings got into the act with his own band, Stormtrooper: 'We did a gig or two and recorded a single called "I'm a Mess", which became quite iconic within the punk movement when Sid Vicious wore a badge saying "I'm a Mess" on his biker's jacket.'

Surviving sharing a stage with the Pistols, Eddie and the Hot Rods returned to the Marquee in April and again on 9 July, a gig for which Island Records hired the Rolling Stones' mobile recording studio. The result was an EP, *Live at the Marquee*, with four tracks – including a rendition of Van Morrison's 'Gloria' that segued into the Stones' 'Satisfaction' – that perfectly captured the raw energy of what was one of the best live bands on the scene. '98% of that recording is real,' says singer Barrie Masters. 'A few guitar overdubs but that's all.' It even entered the national charts. The Rods were a massive hit at the club and were rebooked a number of times that summer. On one date, the police were required to marshal the crowds down Wardour Street, and the band had to perform two shows when shut-out fans wouldn't give up on their attempts to storm the doors.

But there was another new band that summer – new to the Marquee, at least, and new to the UK – who made their debut with two support slots in May before being given a string of headliners and going head-to-head with the Rods to see who could pull the biggest crowd.

In the three years since forming, Australian band AC/DC had released two albums and made it big at home. In spring 1976, they decided to have a crack at the UK. They were booked to play support on a tour by Back Street Crawler, the Anglo-American band formed in 1975 by ex-Free guitarist Paul Kossoff. Two weeks before AC/DC were due to fly, Kossoff died of a heart attack. The Aussies decided to go to the UK anyway. Their management set them up with a few low-key gigs, including at the Red Cow (23 April, their first UK gig) and the Nashville, two key London punk/pub rock venues. On 11-12 May, AC/DC played the Marquee,

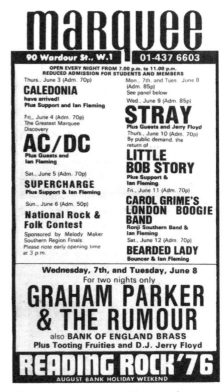

'The Greatest Marquee Discovery.'

supporting Back Street Crawler, who had hastily recruited a replacement guitarist and were breaking him in with these two charity gigs on behalf of the Free Drug Clinic (Kossoff had struggled with addiction for much of his life). The following month, AC/DC were back at the Marquee as headliners. The club programme touted them as the 'Greatest Marquee Discovery', which was a bit rich, given they were also playing half a dozen other London venues. However, on 26 July, the band settled in at the Marquee for a weekly residency that ran for six weeks, culminating in two shows on 7–8 September. By the third show, the queues for AC/DC were forming in the afternoon and reaching all the way up to Oxford Street by the time the club's doors opened at 7pm. The club's capacity was 700 but manager Uli Pritz reckons there were a thousand or more people at each gig. That summer, 1976, was the hottest on record and the sweat literally ran down the walls; steam rose from the crowd and people fainted from heat exhaustion, and had to be lifted and passed over everybody's heads to the waiting paramedics.

Even Caroline Coon, *Melody Maker*'s chief cheerleader for punk, although deriding the band's 'legs astride uncompromisingly male stance', couldn't help but be amazed by the antics of the 'extraordinary, virtuoso' sixteen-year-old guitarist Angus Young, dressed as a schoolboy and looking like a twelve-year-old who'd skipped homework to come out and play. At some point in the set, he would climb onto singer Bon Scott's shoulders and solo as Scott walked through the audience. Because of the heat and exertion, Young would end each show stripped down to just his string Y-fronts. Jack Barrie was telling everybody that AC/DC were the most exciting band he'd seen since Led Zeppelin.

Competition developed between AC/DC and the Rods as to who could top the attendance records. 'It was mental,' recalls the Rods' Barrie Masters. 'One week we'd win, then they would break it, then we would break theirs, and so it went on. I remember the queues and thinking, this is madness, there's no way all these people are gonna get in. But they did.'

No surprise that both AC/DC and Eddie and the Hot Rods were booked to play Reading this year – now rebranded as 'Reading Rock'. Predictably, following six weeks of blistering heat, the festival weekend would be when the weather broke, with torrential downpours bringing at least one set to a premature end. Highlights included the ever-reliable Rory Gallagher, Manfred Mann's Earth Band (who got a rousing reception for new single 'Blinded by the Light') and Roxy Music guitarist Phil Manzanera's new project, which saw him reunite with old bandmate Brian Eno to perform selections from their solo outputs, plus a couple of well-chosen covers – the project would only run to three performances in total, the last of

AC/DC's Angus Young at the Marquee, July 1976.

which, at London's Royal Festival Hall, would be recorded and issued as *801 Live*. As usual, John Peel was festival DJ and enjoyed himself frisbeeing Bay City Roller LPs into the crowd.

Back at the Marquee, there were further adventures in pub rock in the shape of a two-night residency by Graham Parker and the Rumour – members of the Rumour came from Brinsley Schwarz and Ducks Deluxe. There was glam, in the form of Giggles, a four-piece from Chelmsford. Formed in 1973, they signed a deal with EMI the following year. They first played the Marquee in late 1975, and then stormed the club in 1976 with a Saturday night residency in January, a Sunday night residency in May and at least one appearance most other months. In fact, in '76 Giggles played the club more than any other band. They were junk shop glam rockers in the mould of the Sweet, who dressed up in zany outfits and put on a good show. Guitarist Jeff Carpenter remembers the Marquee being packed out with young girls. It didn't pay that well, he recalls – 'You could get treble the money at a college in Leicester' – but it was always a good gig. If Giggles are remembered at all, it's usually as a footnote to the career of their manager Tom Watkins, who would go on to work with the Pet Shop Boys, Bros and East 17.

In August, a band who had played a dozen gigs at the club over the last twelve months as the Poodles, upgraded themselves to the Fabulous Poodles. They combined mature musicianship with juvenile humour. 'I would play "My Generation" on an electric ukulele through a distortion box with a smoke bomb inside,' explains the band's founder, singer/ guitarist Tony de Meur. 'We would also get audience members up on stage to smash spare ukuleles. Golden days.' All this while pianist Bob Suffolk auctioned poodle-print wallpaper and inflatable dolls were battered with ketchup bottles. 'Mary Whitehouse was not our biggest fan,' says de Meur. The Fab Poos would rack up over twenty appearances at the club before calling it a day in 1980.

The Enid were a throwback to the days of high prog. They were formed in 1974 by Royal Academy of Music and Barclay James Harvest alumnus Robert John Godfrey, along with guitarists Francis Lickerish and Steve Stewart. All three had attended Finchden Manor in Tenterden, which was described as a residential experimental educational facility and therapeutic community for adolescents. Led by Godfrey, the Enid wrote and performed extended pieces of music with recurrent themes and motifs – in other words, they played the much-despised classical rock. In spring 1976, the band landed their first Marquee headliner, which roughly coincided with the release of their debut album, *In the Region of the Summer Stars*. It was originally to have had vocals, but this changed when Peter Roberts, the band's singer, killed himself. The Enid would play *Summer Stars* live in full, all ninety minutes of instrumentation, no breaks, no vocals. They would perform this roughly once a month at the club through the rest of the year. They also featured at Reading that summer, when John Peel needled the band by calling their music 'A-level rock'. This was in keeping with the attitude of the press, which generally considered the Enid humourless and a hard slog, and the record companies, who ignored them. But this most determinedly individualistic of bands amassed a fanatical following and regularly won over festival audiences, sending up their own bombast by ending sets with the 'Dam Busters March' – a tribute to roadie Matin Wallis, grandson of bouncing bomb inventor Barnes Wallis – and 'Land of Hope and Glory', alongside covers of 'Wild Thing' and 'Pretty Vacant'. Performances had a Last Night of the Proms air about them. Over the years, they would play the Marquee close to forty times, and gigs had the feel of family gatherings or meetings of long lost friends. The circle of initiates was extended in the early 1980s when prog came back into fashion.

Phil Collins was back in 1976, too, but without his pals in Genesis – he was moonlighting with jazz fusionists Brand X, who played the club twice this year. Status Quo drummer John Coghlan launched his off-shoot band, Diesel, at the Marquee in October ('Just to play a bit of blues and rock'n'roll, to get up there and enjoy it,' says Coghlan), while former Spiders from Mars drummer Woody Woodmansey was also back, fronting his new band, U-Boat. They made a first appearance in September, followed by a Sunday night residency the following month. That was thanks to former Marquee employee Carl Leighton-Pope. Since leaving the club, Leighton-Pope had ventured into the music business as the manager of Sassafras, a rock band from South Wales (they played the Marquee a dozen times between 1973 and 1978). Leighton-Pope poured every penny he had into

Sassafras, but despite appearances on the *Old Grey Whistle Test* and a US tour, success proved elusive. On his financial uppers, and with four children to support, Leighton-Pope was thrown a lifeline by John Sherry who asked him to join his booking agency. The first act he was given was Woody Woodmansey's U-Boat. The band comprised a crew of relative unknowns besides Woodmansey. Their style was light rock, not unlike Queen, but without the memorable tunes. 'I thought, what am I going to do with this? So, I called Jack Barrie and I said, "You've got to get me out of jail here. You've got to give me a night at the Marquee." Jack came through. He even added them to the bill for the next summer's Reading but by summer 1977 music was on the cusp of a 'new wave' and bands like U-Boat were sunk.

NEW WAVE

Motörhead | The Jam | Ultravox! | The Only Ones | The Motors | Generation X | The Vibrators | X-Ray Spex | Wayne County and the Electric Chairs | The Police | The Lurkers | Squeeze | The Boomtown Rats | Chelsea | The Damned | The Adverts | Penetration | The Buzzcocks | Wire

By this time, it was obvious that however distasteful Jack Barrie or Uli Pritz found the likes of the Sex Pistols, the Stranglers and punk bands in general, they didn't have much of a choice but to book them. 'In the end I had to say it was good for business,' says Pritz. 'But I'd rather go home and listen to the Eagles or something.' Harold had also stopped going into the club by now because he didn't like the audiences punk was attracting: 'It was the spitting,' he said. 'It was very unpleasant. So was the music.'

The Marquee was never a major punk venue. It was left to that other Oxford Street basement bastion of jazz, the 100 Club, to host the game-changing 'Punk Special', featuring eight punk bands over two days in September 1976. The punk scene then found its gob-stained home at first the Roxy on Neal Street in Covent Garden, then the Vortex, just up the road from the Marquee at 203 Wardour Street – two venues that exploded into life with punk and just as quickly burned out. But bar the Clash, and Siouxsie and the Banshees, almost every band that played the Roxy and Vortex also played the Marquee. When the Roxy and Vortex closed in 1978, the Marquee continued to embrace the new wave of artists inspired by punk. Before then, punk ensured that 1977 at the Marquee was an extraordinary year, maybe one of the most exciting since the heyday of the Stones, the Yardbirds and the Who. It saw first gigs at the Marquee for the Jam, Ultravox!, the Only Ones, the Motors, Generation X, the Vibrators, X-Ray Spex, the Police, Squeeze, the Boomtown Rats, John Otway and Wild Willy Barrett, the Damned, the Buzzcocks, Wire, Tom Robinson, Japan, Sham 69, Adam and the Ants, and XTC, all in the same year. At the same time, the club retained its commitment to a catholic booking policy, so the programming could still accommodate appearances by influential folkster Bert Jansch, the reformed Pink Fairies, medieval progsters Gryphon, the old school rock of Edgar Broughton and Wishbone Ash, and a nostalgic two-nighter in the company of Georgie Fame and the Blue Flames. Not to mention what was supposed to be the farewell concert by Motörhead.

By the time Motörhead returned for a third gig at the Marquee, in November 1976 (a year on from their second), it was with a new line-up of Lemmy, 'Fast' Eddie Clarke on guitar and Phil 'Philthy Animal' Taylor on drums. The reviews were no kinder than before. By the start of 1977, things were starting to look bleak. The band were living in squats and surviving on a diet of porridge and speed. Lemmy was for stubbornly carrying on but Clarke and Taylor had had enough. It was agreed the band would bow out with one final gig, honouring a date they had coming up at the Marquee, on Friday 1 April. The plan was to record the show for a live album as a farewell gift to their fans but, in the end, the cost proved prohibitive. Motörhead played the show anyway and, according to Fast Eddie, it was one of the best they ever did. Backstage afterwards, Ted Carroll of Chiswick Records offered to bankroll a couple of days in the studio for the band to cut a single. Thoughts of quitting were put on hold as the band took their chance and instead of a single they emerged from the studio with thirteen demos, eight of which would be polished to become the debut album *Motörhead* – with a single of the same name issued in June. The single surpassed all expectations, staying in the Top 75 for seven weeks, peaking at No.51, and ensuring that the band lived on.

Motörhead returned to play the Marquee on one further occasion, a three-night residency in July 1983. Before he moved to Los Angeles in 1990, Lemmy was a regular presence at the club, hanging out at the bar and playing the fruit machine. 'He was always willing to chat to a fan, sign an autograph or pose for a snap,' recalls bar man Peter Egan. 'One of the most genuine guys you could meet.'

The first of the 'new wave' acts to step up to the Marquee were the Jam. They'd already started to establish themselves on the London scene with a run of mainly pub gigs, plus a few dates at the 100 Club. At the Marquee they were booked to support glam-rockers Bearded Lady, which was just the wrong audience for an in-your-face, three-piece from Woking wearing bomber jackets and Sta-Prest trousers. The punters were content to sit cross-legged on the floor while they waited for the main act. Frustrated at the lack of reaction, frontman Paul Weller gestured for the few Jam fans present to join the band on stage and dance in an effort to liven up the evening. Years later, Weller would remember the night in his sleevenotes to the Jam's posthumous live album, *Dig the New Breed*, referring to the confusion the band caused among the 'usual Marquee hippies'. It wasn't a dead loss though: present that night was Polydor's Chris Parry, there on a tip-off to check out the band. He offered them a recording contract and co-produced their first three albums. They would have much better gigs at the Marquee in years to come but none as critical to their career.

In February it was the turn of Ultravox! Although part of the new wave, Ultravox! were far from being a new act. They started life way back in 1973 as a wannabe Roxy Music art-pop outfit called Tiger Lily. They played the Marquee twice in 1974 as Tiger Lily, once opening for the Heavy Metal Kids, once for the Sharks. They signed to Island in 1976, which is when they became Ultravox! This is not yet the Ultravox of Midge Ure and 'Vienna'; this earlier iteration was fronted by John Foxx, wore plastic jackets and was heavily influenced by German experimental bands such as Kraftwerk and Neu! (hence Ultravox! with an exclamation mark). Island released their eponymous debut album in February 1977 (co-produced by Brian Eno, once of Roxy Music), hence the Marquee gig. Neither the album nor the associated single 'Dangerous Rhythm' troubled the charts but the band gained a solid live following and they played the Marquee a further nine times this year, including the sought-after New Year's Eve slot – although with song titles like 'Frozen Ones', 'Fear in the Western World' and 'Hiroshima Mon Amour' Ultravox! were not what you would call a party band. There would be a long break of over eight months before they returned to the club for five consecutive nights in August 1978.

March saw a club debut for the intelligently punkish Only Ones, playing support to Johnny Thunder and the Heartbreakers. They would be back in October, by which time they'd written and would be performing their one and only hit, 'Another Girl, Another Planet'. There were also first-time support slots for Bazooka Joe, who we'll come across later, and the Motors. The Motors appearance at the club, opening for the George Hatcher Band, was their first ever gig. They were formed, in early 1977, out of the remnants of Ducks Deluxe and although they were touted as new wave, they were pub rockers at heart. In April they were back at the club as headliners and by May they had been signed to Virgin. They played regularly at the Marquee throughout the rest of the year, culminating in two consecutive nights the week before Christmas.

At the end of the March, Billy Idol-fronted Generation X, a band more usually associated with the Roxy (they were the first band to play the Covent Garden club), made the first of what would be eight Marquee appearances in all, all in 1977. In early July, the *NME* was calling Generation X the 'finest punk band without a recording contract' but by the time of their second Marquee gig, on 20 July, that was no longer the case and the performance that night was filmed by their new label, Chrysalis. Temperatures in the club were always stifling in summer but the addition of the extra lights required for the filming made it even worse and part way through the set bassist Tony James collapsed. The band released a first single, 'Your Generation', in September 1977, promoting it with four appearances at the Marquee that month – these would be the last dates at the club. Generally, once a band had made *Top of the Pops*, their Marquee days were behind them, and that proved to be the case with Generation X.

Tony James and Billy Idol of Generation X at the Marquee in 1977.

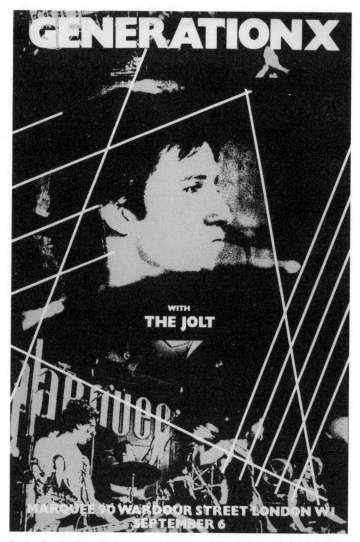

Poster for the fourth of Generation X's Marquee gigs, on 6 September 1977. The poster was designed by Barney Bubbles.

Despite the lunkheaded name, the Vibrators were a polished, highly professional outfit by the time they debuted at the Marquee in May. They went over so well they were rebooked for a three-night run at the end of July. Again, the heat was a problem, recalls drummer Eddie Edwards: 'After the first night we had to get in a couple of big industrial fans so we didn't all die on the second night.' Part way through the set, he says, condensation was dripping off the pipes in the ceiling: 'It was almost like standing in the rain.' (As a result of so many people smoking in the club, this particular rain stained clothing nicotine brown.) Nevertheless, Edwards was a fan of the club and even used to DJ there on occasion. 'The two great clubs in London in the late Seventies and early Eighties were the Marquee and Dingwalls. The Marquee used to finish at eleven and then you'd go to Dingwalls afterwards, where the band would be on at midnight. You'd stagger home about four in the morning. Great days.'

Another band the Marquee audiences were quick to take to heart were X-Ray Spex, who debuted in May playing support to the Boys. They had formed the previous year after Marianne Joan Elliott-Said saw a Sex Pistols gig on Hastings pier and put an ad in the *NME* looking for 'young punx who want to stick it together'. As lead singer Poly Styrene, Elliott-Said performed with uncool wire braces on her teeth, Day-Glo home-made stage clothes and a vocal style one reviewer who caught the band at the Marquee described as 'like a drowning woman crying for help'. The same review noted that the audience went berserk for the band and spent the whole evening pogoing like mad. The group played the Marquee seven times in total before the end of the year.

Two days after X-Ray Spex debuted, there was a one-off appearance from Wayne County and the Electric Chairs, the glam-punk outfit fronted by Jayne County – last seen at the club during the filming of David Bowie's 1980 Floorshow. Support came from the Police; bassist Sting and drummer Stewart Copeland had just come together with guitarist Henry Padovani that January and had been gigging non-stop ever since. The following month, the Police were back as headliners. Support came from the Lurkers, punks from Uxbridge. On the night, their bassist Arturo Bassick developed a problem with his gear and needed a replacement fast. 'I asked Sting if I could borrow his bass, but I'd misheard his name and I called him Stink. He thought I was taking the piss which I wasn't.' Stewart Copeland put in a word and 'Stink' reluctantly let Bassick use his gear. On the reverse of the sleeve to the Lurkers' debut single, 'Shadow', there are photographs of Bassick playing the borrowed bass. 'There must have been only about forty people at that gig,' he says. One of those forty was experienced session guitarist Andy Summers, who'd come along to check out the headliners, because they'd asked him to become the fourth member of their band. That night he joined them on stage for the encore – the first time the three future Police men played together before a live audience. What the Lurkers' drummer Pete Haynes remembers of that night is that at the bar afterwards the Police drank cartons of orange juice and seemed like the 'bright boys' at school.

The Police played their first headliner on the Friday, and the following night, Saturday, was a first headliner for Squeeze. The band had been around since 1974 and had already played a handful of support slots at the club, but for guitarist, vocalist and songwriter Chris Difford, headlining was a massive deal for the band. 'We'd made it as far as I was concerned,' says Difford. 'It was a great place to be seen, to be heard and to get written about. It seemed like miles from south London, ages away from the safety of home, almost like being in another country.' The band would make five more appearances at the club between now and December 1978, before the release of second album *Cool for Cats*, with its

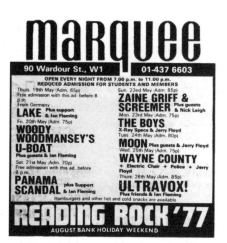

First Marquee appearance by the Police.

two huge hit singles ('Cool for Cats' and 'Up the Junction'), boosted them to bigger venues.

June also saw a first appearance at the club by the Boomtown Rats. Born from the Dublin dole queue in 1975, by the end of the following year they'd gone as far as they could at home and crossed the Irish Sea to have a go at London. The Marquee was maybe their fifth UK gig, and the second in London after a night at the Hope and Anchor. They returned again in July, August and September. 'When I walked into that wall of damp heat the place was going mad,' recalls Geldof. 'I think I got to the third or fourth song and there's a picture of me and I've got nothing on top, with sweat pouring down my face, and my pants are undone – not in a desperate attempt to be sexy, but because it was so hot – and I went down, I pegged out.' In August, the Rats released their first single, 'Lookin' After No.1' and at the Marquee Geldof begged the audience to go out and buy it. 'Make me rich,' he implored. 'When we return in a month's time, we'll be number five in the charts.' Not quite, but the song did make No.11. It was enough to ensure that the next time the Rats played London it was as headliners at the Finsbury Park Rainbow.

They never attained the commercial success of some of their contemporaries, but Chelsea were one of the most influential of all punk bands, not least because frontman Gene October was instrumental in launching the Roxy. William Broad and Tony James were early band members, although they left after only three gigs to form Generation X (William Broad becoming Billy Idol). Chelsea also had strong links with the Marquee: guitarist Dave Martin had a girlfriend who worked in the box office and the bass player shared a flat with Nigel Hutchings. They first played the club in June 1977, eventually racking up just shy of fifty appearances. 'The great thing about punk,' says Chelsea's James Stevenson, 'was you didn't have to be a technical wizard to be in a band. If you could play a few power chords you were in. And everybody wanted to play the Marquee.' Also debuting in June were ground-breaking Aussie punks the Saints, making the first of seven appearances, one of which was filmed for a cameo in ITV's cheesy *Return of the Saint* show, in an episode, screened in November 1978, that also featured scenes at the bar and on the street outside the club.

That July, independent label Stiff Records booked the Marquee over four consecutive nights for the Damned. Back in October of the previous year, Stiff had put out the Damned's 'New Rose', considered the UK's first punk single. They followed it up in February 1977 with their first album, *Damned Damned Damned*, which included a new single, 'Neat Neat Neat'. The Damned opened for T-Rex on their final UK tour, and then became the first British punk band to tour the US. They were firmly established as front-pagers in the weekly music press. The first night of the residency went down a storm. There was singer Dave Vanian looking, in the words of the *NME*'s Mick Farren, like something that had slipped out of Dr Caligari's cabinet, and bassist Captain Sensible, a show unto himself, in crumpled nurse's uniform, dog collar and monkey boots. Unfortunately, the second night was plagued by sound issues, while the third and fourth never happened. The record company had put up a huge poster obscuring the Marquee logo behind the stage. Jack Barrie demanded it be taken down, which led to a heated argument that ended with the Damned walking out.

The band that was supposed to support the Damned on the last night of their residency was the Adverts. They went on to do a handful of Marquee headliners of their own. They were formed in 1976 by Tim and Gaye Advert from Devon. After relocating to London, they recruited guitarist Howard Pickup and drummer Laurie Driver. Very quickly the image of the band began to zero in on Gaye's distinctive look of heavy black mascara, jeans, leather jacket and T-shirt. 'I hated that at the time,' she admits. 'I didn't want to be picked on for being female. I just wanted to play bass and suddenly I was getting treated completely differently from everyone else. It did cause a bit of friction in the band.'

Four nights booked, two nights played.

Gaye was one of a number of women in punk. 'Punk enabled a lot of women to be musicians because it was much more inclusive,' she says. Women were a part of punk from the beginning – as musicians, promoters, provocateurs and fans. 'They were being themselves,' says Pauline Murray of Penetration. 'And they were writing their own lyrics and expressing themselves as people.'

Formed in late 1976 in County Durham, Penetration began as a hobby. 'We'd get together once a week in the local church hall and play covers like Jonathan Richman's "Road Runner" and stuff by the New York Dolls,' recalls Murray. They played some support slots in the north of England, eventually hiring a furniture van to come down to London to play the Roxy, supporting Generation X. Given that the band's management's office was just across the street from the Marquee, it was inevitable that they'd end up playing there. Murray remembers being unnerved at how small the stage was and how close the audience were. She also recalls there being an almighty bust-up in the dressing room between the drummer and the bass player that developed into a fight. 'Just then, Simon Draper from Virgin records walked in,' says Murray. 'Virgin were thinking of signing us up to do an album and I thought, well that's it, we ain't getting a deal now.' (They did.)

One of the bands Penetration supported in the North were the Buzzcocks, who made their own Marquee debut that August. They had first played London the previous August as part of Malcolm McLaren's 'Midnight Special' at the Screen on the Green in Islington, when, along with the Clash, they supported the Sex Pistols. By the time they appeared at the Marquee, the band had already released the four-song *Spiral Scratch* EP on their own label and guitarist Pete Shelley had stepped up to become the principal singer-songwriter, following the departure of Howard Devoto. Twelve days after their Marquee gig, the Buzzcocks signed with major label United Artists. They were back at the Marquee in October and November, by which time they'd released their first major label single, 'Orgasm Addict', soon to be followed by a run of other fine singles that would see the Buzzcocks become one of punk's most successful bands.

Opening for the Buzzcocks on their first Marquee date were moody gloomsters Wire, on what was their third support slot at the club. Wire were alumni of the Roxy and Vortex, but for bassist Graham Lewis the Marquee was a place of pilgrimage. He'd been a regular at the club since moving to London in 1972. 'There was a sense of occasion when you went there. When Wire got to play it, it really meant something.' The gig he remembers most is one where he was part of the audience in May 1978 to see US rock band Pere Ubu, with cult German singer Nico supporting. 'The crowd, basically, bottled her off,' recalls Lewis. 'Then Pere Ubu came on, hit the first note and the audience just rolled over. It's extraordinary when you get that emotion in a room, whether it's for or against, as long as it's there, it can be changed.'

ADAM AND THE ANTS

Reading 1977 | John Martyn | The Tom Robinson Band | Bernie Tormé | Japan | Adam and the Ants | Sham 69 | XTC

Despite the stream of punk, post-punk and new wave bands currently appearing at the Marquee around this time, Reading '77, held 26–28 August, was notably light on fresh sounds. Headliners included Uriah Heep, Eddie and the Hot Rods, and Golden Earring on Friday; Graham Parker and the Rumour, John Miles and Thin Lizzy on Saturday; and the Sensational Alex Harvey Band, Hawkwind and the Doobie Brothers on Sunday. Saturday also had US act Aerosmith, marking only their second visit to the UK. The sole new wave bands on the bill were Ultravox! and Wayne County and the Electric Chairs, the latter pelted with cans and mud to such an extent they scarpered after five songs and never returned – suggesting maybe booker Jack Barrie was right to stick with the tried and tested formula of rock.

For the second year running, torrential rain had left the festival site in poor condition. The festival actually started under clear skies on Friday afternoon but come evening, as Eddie and the Hot Rods took to the stage, the clouds burst. John Peel's attempts to gee up the soaked audience between sets fell flat: 'Come on you miserable sods, you're supposed to be enjoying yourselves,' he goaded. In its write-up the following week, the *NME* condemned the festival for featuring a whole bunch of bands who were 'rarely anything above average'.

September 1977 saw the only visits to Wardour Street by singer-songwriter John Martyn. The two nights were part of a series of low-key club dates in which Martyn was trying out some new material ahead of a full British tour promoting his forthcoming ninth studio album, *One World*. The first fifty people through the door each night were given a free copy of Martyn's self-released *Live at Leeds* album. Chris Brazier was there for *Melody Maker*, and was won over by a set split between one-man Pink Floyd guitar effects and gentle love songs – 'late-night music for when you're wasted or wistful or both.'

Three nights later saw the first of a handful of gigs at the club by the Tom Robinson Band. The *NME* called them the 'most powerful band since the Pistols'. No chains, no razor blades, no snarling, just bucket-loads of righteous anger at the inequalities of the world. So worked up were they that Robinson (bass and vocals) and guitarist Danny Kustow broke four strings between them at one of the Marquee gigs. Sets at this time included 'Up Against the Wall', 'We Ain't Going to Take It', 'Glad to Be Gay' and future bouncy hit single '2-4-6-8 Motorway', with its rabble-rousing terrace chant chorus. Audiences at TRB gigs left the club with political leaflets and flyers, and free badges and T-shirts with the band's clenched fist logo.

In mid September, the Boomtown Rats were back, supported by fellow Irishman Bernie Tormé, who had previously appeared at the Marquee with heavy rockers Scrapyard. 'Those gigs with the Rats were just mayhem,' he recalls. 'They had twelve or thirteen hundred people in. Girls were fainting and being pulled out of the audience to the back of the stage and then out through the bar.' According to Nigel Hutchings the Marquee did regularly cram them in on their most popular nights, because that's just what you did back then. 'And I'm sure the guys on the back door were letting loads of their mates in, too.' The club mostly got away with it. 'The local fire officer did come in one night and we had to go before a GLC committee and got fined something like £2,000 for overdoing it. After that we had to rein it in a bit. But health and safety wasn't an overriding factor back then.'

Despite learning his trade from Irish heroes such as Rory Gallagher and Gary Moore, Tormé embraced new wave, touring with Generation X, and playing the Roxy and the Vortex. But he had his reservations: 'Guitar solos not allowed? I didn't dig that one.' He didn't go for the spitting, either. 'Phil Spalding, our bass player, used to spit back and then move around like Billy the dancing bucket to avoid the incoming. I couldn't move around, I was stuck at a microphone, most of the time in a snowstorm of slime. Spitting never happened to me at the Marquee, though.' (Chris Difford differs, remembering one occasion at the Marquee when Squeeze wore plastic raincoats to protect their jackets from the gob.)

'Playing the Marquee was a really big thing for me,' says Tormé. 'For any musician it was essential to have it on your CV, it was crucial to your credibility and for building an audience. The thing about the Marquee was that it was a music club, not a pub with a band. They actually treated the bands like human beings, which was not my experience on the circuit of pub rock venues at the time, where they mostly treated you like complete shit.' After opening for the Rats twice, Tormé landed his own headline slot in November. He'd go on to play 90 Wardour Street close to forty times, the last occasion being in October 1986.

Back in September 1977, three nights after the Boomtown Rats and Bernie Tormé, there was a one-and-only Marquee appearance for Japan. Formed in 1974, they'd recently signed a management deal with Simon Napier-Bell and started gigging seriously. The Marquee gig, followed appearances at Camden's Music Machine, Fulham's Greyhound and the Rock Garden in Covent Garden. At this point they were an alternative glam rock outfit in the mould of Lou Reed and the New York Dolls, and would have been playing material from debut album *Adolescent Sex*, which they would record later in the year.

When the Buzzcocks returned to the Marquee on Tuesday 4 October, the support act that night was another club debutant, Adam and the Ants. Far from novices, they were already veterans of the punk scene. Stuart Goddard joined his first band, Bazooka Joe, in 1975. Their show at St Martins School of Art in November 1975 made a big impression, not because of Bazooka Joe, but because of the support band making their debut that evening, the Sex Pistols. Blown away by what he saw that night, Goddard immediately quit Bazooka Joe and formed his own punk band, the B-Sides. They failed to get anywhere, so Goddard tried again, with another band he named Adam and the Ants, with Goddard as Adam Ant. The official debut of the Ants was in May 1977 at the ICA. Shortly after, Malcolm McLaren protégé Jordan became manager of the band. 'Anybody that could get you a gig was qualified as a manager in those days,' Adam told an interviewer in 1996.

In 1977, Adam was far from the foppish dandy highway man he'd later become. Instead, his fantasies were of S&M, and his dressing up ran to leather bondage masks and other fetish gear. One audience member recalls Jordan cutting the word 'Fuck' into Adam's back as he performed (not at the Marquee) and the blood pouring down his body. Another young fan recalled in *The Guardian* how physical it was just being in the audience: 'I used to come home covered in cuts and bruises, and my mum worried I had been mugged or run over. I used to say, "No, no, I've just been dancing and having fun".' The Ants and their hardcore audience were back for two headliners in November, followed by another in December, then a Thursday night residency in January 1978. They'd continue to play the club regularly throughout the rest of the year culminating in two consecutive nights in November 1978. The *NME*'s Deanne Pearson was present at one of those nights and she wrote that the reason the Ants were still playing the Marquee was that they were 'not good enough to graduate'. Adam must have got the message because this was the last time he played

the club. He put his nights in small, sweaty clubs in Soho behind him and recruited a new set of ants with a new, far more chart-friendly image. Still, asked by broadcaster Robert Elms in 2014 what was his most hated building in London was, the Antman replied, 'The building that replaced the Marquee club.'

As 1977 wound up, the notable club debuts kept coming. In October it was Sham 69.

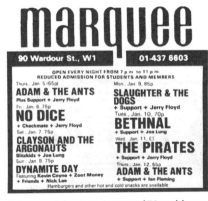

Adam and the Ants January '78 residency.

Frontman Jimmy Pursey was being hailed by the music press at this time as a true punk spirit, free of artifice. Unfortunately, what anybody who saw Sham 69 at the Marquee will remember is the violence. A bunch of skinheads packed the area in front of the stage, chanting 'Boot boys! Boot boys!' Halfway through the band's first number fighting erupted. Pursey cut the music to scream, 'What do you think this is, a football match? If you're going to fight we ain't playing.' But the trouble continued. It carried on outside afterwards, as the skins loitered on Wardour Street looking for punks to attack. Sham 69 were not asked back.

In November, it was the turn of XTC. The band's core, Andy Partridge and Colin Moulding of Swindon, had come together in the early 1970s, but they'd settled on a new four-piece line-up in December 1976. Since then, they'd signed to Virgin and released a three-track EP, called *3D EP*. At the time of their Marquee debut, critics were calling them 'musically inexpert' but capable of 'short attacks on rhythmic senses', and were comparing the band to US acts like Talking Heads and Television. Frontman Partridge had a quirky way with an audience – 'Hello, we're XTC, you're the audience and this is "Radios in Motion"' – and sets featured covers of Dylan's 'All Along the Watchtower' and the theme to *Fireball XL5*. XTC played just two more gigs at the Marquee, on 30–31 May 1978, by which time the band had released a first album, *White Music*. Partridge says that they weren't paid for one of these gigs and in retaliation the band walked out at the end of the night with one of the club's Leslie speakers. Trouble was it wouldn't fit in their van. By morning, after they'd sobered up and felt a surge of guilt, they decided to return it to the club. Creeping around the back of the Marquee at six o'clock in the morning, along with the milkman, they deposited the stolen speaker by the exit door and legged it.

DIRE STRAITS

The Police | Squeeze | Ultravox! | The Jam | The Rezillos | Tubeway Army | Dire Straits | Wilko Johnson | The Tourists | The Ian Gillan Band | Tom Petty | The Rubinoos | Reading Rock 1978 | Zaine Griff | The Skids | The Undertones

The energy and innovation of 1977 rolled over into 1978. There was Adam and the Ants' January residency and a return date for the Police, their first London date since the previous summer. Since then, they'd dropped original guitarist Henry Padovani and this was only the third UK gig with the new line-up of Sting, Stewart Copeland and Andy Summers. Also returning for a date in January were Squeeze, while Ultravox! were back for a three-night run in mid February. Toward the end of the month, the Jam were in residence for two nights as part of a four-date mini London Blitz to promote forthcoming single 'News of the World'. Ed Silvester was one of a small group of Epping punks wondering What now? since the Sex Pistols had gone to America and imploded a few weeks before. 'It really did feel like the end of something special for us,' says Silvester. In search of the next thing, they made their way to Wardour Street, joining the queue to see the Woking mods. 'Finally, after what felt like ages, we were in,' he recalls. Support came from Scottish punksters the Jolt. As the roadies busied themselves resetting the stage, the excitement and expectation built. Just after nine the Jam crashed onto the stage. Silvester's gang pogoed their way to the front. 'We could feel the sweat of the band and the energy. We could see the future – this band were going to be huge.'

The following night was the turn of the Rezillos, a punky, cartoony, fun-time outfit who started out performing high-energy covers of Fifties and Sixties songs – although when their first album came out in July 1978, *Can't Stand the Rezillos*, it was the self-penned single 'Top of the Pops' that landed them on the show of the same name. The band's guitarist, Jo Callis (who would later join the Human League), first encountered the Marquee in the mid Seventies during an art-school trip from Edinburgh. 'On our first night in town I remember going along to the Marquee with a small posse of my classmates. I think we must have walked by the door pretty much by chance as we were mooching aimlessly around Soho. We saw the iconic sign, looked at each other and decided we must step inside.' Later, playing the club, the experience was, he recalls, always the same: 'It was close up and personal, muggy and humid. Like a deep-sea diver, once your breathing had acclimatised, you launched into your set.' The Rezillos would be back in June and, again, for a two-nighter in November.

New to the Marquee in February 1978 were Tubeway Army. Formed the previous summer, they launched themselves with half a dozen gigs at the Roxy and Vortex, followed by appearances at Dingwalls, the Hope and Anchor, the Rock Garden and then two gigs at the Marquee, opening for the Lurkers. The same month they released a first single, 'That's Too Bad'. Fronted by Gary Webb, who at this point was going by the name Valerian, the band sounded like a lightweight Stranglers, with plonky punky bass and buzzing guitar. They returned in late April, again with the Lurkers, but not long after quit playing live, freaked out by the violence of their audiences. Webb decided Tubeway Army would be a studio-only band;

when their self-titled debut album appeared that November, the guitars had largely been replaced by synthesisers and the singer had adopted the name Gary Numan. Six months later Tubeway Army released the single 'Are "Friends" Electric?' and scored a No.1 hit.

When Dire Straits made their first appearance at the Marquee, on Tuesday 14 March 1978, they were a backroom bar band, living a life of greasy-spoon cafes and council flats, peddling low-key urban blues. They were by-products of the pub-rock scene, and their only appearance on vinyl to date was a single track on a Hope and Anchor compilation, alongside the Wilko Johnson Band, the Stranglers, the Only Ones and XTC. They

First Marquee appearance for Dire Straits.

had come together in 1977; early gigs were in southeast London, followed by a string of appearances at Dingwalls, the Rock Garden and the Hope and Anchor. In January 1978, they managed to get themselves onto a fifteen-date UK tour supporting Talking Heads, which they immediately followed up on by going into west London's Basing Street Studio to record an album. The next gig was the Marquee, the first in a run of four Tuesdays. It was almost unheard of for a

band to land a residency without being auditioned via a support slot, but Dire Straits were managed by a friend of the club, Ed Bicknell. 'With no record out there, no one had heard of us, so people dropped in more out of curiosity and because it was the Marquee than from an avid desire to see us,' recalls bassist John Illsley. But the band got great press. At this point in their career – pre platinum discs, pre headbands, pre collaborations with Sting – the music press loved Dire Straits. John Orme in *Melody Maker* called them 'one of the freshest new bands for years', and the paper made them one of its 'tips for the top in '78'.

'Those Marquee shows sent out a message: this band is happening,' says Bicknell. 'And when you got a residency at the Marquee it was a stamp of approval.' And then it was straight into a first headline UK tour, promoting a first single, 'Sultans of Swing', and a debut album. The tour included two more Marquee dates in the first week of July. The band had played to decent crowds during their residency in spring but this time the place was rammed. Illsley remembers that the club had to open up the doors at the back and use the loading bay as an overspill. He also remembers it being incredibly hot. 'The sweat was pouring off us, down our faces and arms and over our instruments'. Mark Knopfler had to put on a headband to stop the sweat running into his eyes; it did the trick, and he'd continue to wear a headband from then on. Illsley claims that Sid Vicious was in the audience on one of the two nights, 'totally off his face'. Keith Moon also came crashing into the dressing room afterwards, mumbled, 'Fucking brilliant! Fucking marvellous gig!' and then collapsed.

May saw the return of Wilko Johnson to the Marquee, now fronting his own band, rattling out high-energy rhythm and blues that sounded very much like the sort of thing he was doing in Dr Feelgood before his mysterious departure from the band the previous year. Before the month was out, there was a debut for the Tourists. They were led by guitarists Peet Coombes and Dave Stewart, both previously of folk/rock band Longdancer (who played the Marquee back in 1973 and '74), and fronted by singer Annie Lennox. They would play eight dates in all at the Marquee.

The last time singer Ian Gillan appeared at the Marquee it was back in 1966 and he was fronting pop outfit Episode Six. Twelve years later, and a stint with Deep Purple behind him, he was back at the helm of the Ian Gillan Band. They played jazz fusion to the general indifference of the mass public and three nights at the Marquee in June 1978 would be the last time this particular band would perform together, bar an appearance at this year's Reading. The singer would be back, though, for two nights in September and three in December, fronting a new set of musicians performing as Gillan. For the gig on 27 December, former Purple bandmate Ritchie Blackmore joined Gillan on stage for a jam. Reportedly Ritchie asked Gillan to join his band Rainbow and Gillan asked Blackmore to join Gillan. Neither took up the other's offer.

Dire Straits in the Marquee's
notorious dressing room in 1978.

Later that month there was a minor American invasion. Top-hatted Floridan Tom Petty was over in the UK to play the Midsummer's Night Dream gig at Knebworth (headlined by Genesis) in front of 60,000. He also squeezed in a night at the Marquee. He was promoting second album *You're Gonna Get It!* and, according to *Record Mirror*, the gig was pure rock'n'roll and as 'loud as hell'. Three nights later, on Friday 30th, San Francisco power-pop outfit the Rubinoos played the first date in a four-night residency. They were booked for the unusually extended run probably on the strength of hit single 'I Think We're Alone Now'. They delivered a covers-heavy set, including the Archies' 'Sugar Sugar', 'Please Please Me' and 'Telstar', and a writer from *Melody Maker* spotted Jonathan Richman in the audience singing along.

At Reading this year, alongside festival heavyweights like Status Quo and Lindisfarne, were Ultravox!, Squeeze, the Jam, Penetration, the Tom Robinson Band and Sham 69. From America there were Foreigner and Patti Smith. James Stevenson, there with Chelsea, remembers watching Foreigner play and thinking, this is why I'm a punk. Most of the new wave acts were on Friday and from the start a section of the audience treated the stage as a giant coconut shy. Every band that took to the stage was greeted with a beer-can barrage. The guitarist of the New Hearts tried to head a flying can, not realising it was full, and he had to be led off stage, blood pouring down his face. At one point, John Peel announced that if any more cans were thrown, he would start playing Bee Gees records. Jimmy Pursey of Sham 69 responded by screaming at the crowd, 'If you don't like it, you can fuck off!' Instead of fucking off, a bunch of skinheads clambered up the scaffolding onto the stage and brought the set to a standstill. Harold sent his hired Beasts on to restore order, while Pursey broke down in tears.

Seasoned pros the Pirates played a storming set of hardcore rock'n'roll that halted the barrage and was heralded by some as the highlight of the weekend. The evening's headliners were the Jam and as they played there were more stage invasions and a rostrum used by cameramen collapsed plunging dozens to the ground, although miraculously no one seemed to get seriously hurt. Before performing one of the band's most loved songs, Paul Weller offered a unifying message: 'I don't care how long ya hair is, how short it is, this is music, this is what you gotta dance to, enjoy yourselves. This is "In The City". The day's performances were filmed and released on video under two different titles, *The Kids Are United* and *Kids Like Me and You*.

There was less trouble on Saturday and Sunday, with fewer, if any, skins and punks around for a line-up of reassuringly safe programming: Lindisfarne delivering 'Meet Me on the Corner' and the theme to *Z-Cars*; Quo banging out 'Rockin' All Over the World' and 'Caroline'. One of the oddest appearances was by cowboy-hat wearing Paul Inder – Lemmy's son – who was just eleven at the time and whose set included a song called 'I Don't Want to Go to Bed'. The weekend finale was delivered by Patti Smith, who struggled with sound issues but ended on a high note with 'Because the Night', 'Gloria' and an encore of the Who's 'My Generation'.

Meanwhile, the Marquee was continuing its halcyon run. In the space of ten days in September you could have seen Adam and the Ants (twice), the Police, the Tourists, Squeeze and a debut appearance by Mark Smith's the Fall. Turn up on the wrong night, though, and you could have been watching Jolt, the Starjets, the Dodgers, Sore Throat, Dead Fingers Talk and Zaine Griff. The latter might actually have been worth a punt: Griff was a New Zealand singer-songwriter who moved to England in the 1970s and studied mime with Lindsay Kemp, along with Kate Bush. He was an early New Romantic and played the Marquee more than a dozen times. 'I was living in Great Pulteney Street in Soho so we used my apartment as our dressing room,' he recalls. 'We would waltz over to Wardour Street and enter the Marquee with the audience, through the main entrance and into the backstage room, which smelt of sweat from the previous night.' Griff's band included future film composer Hans Zimmer on keyboards.

By the time the Skids first visited London, in the spring of 1978, there was already a buzz building around the band, thanks largely to the keen support of the Stranglers' Jean-Jacques Burnel. Founded by guitarist Stuart Adamson, the Skids first played as a trio until Adamson ran into 'the only other punk in Dunfermline', sixteen-year-old Richard Jobson and recruited him as the band's front man. Following gigs earlier in the year at the Nashville and Hope and Anchor, they made their Marquee debut on 1 November.

What might have been the gigs of the year were left until late in 1978. The Rezillos were already Marquee favourites and for their two dates on 12–13 November support came from the Undertones. They'd come together in 1976 in Derry and got the attention of John Peel, who funded their first studio recordings, the *Teenage Kicks* EP, and then enthusiastically plugged the title track on his show. The band made an appearance on *Top of the Pops* playing the EP's title track on 26 October and two weeks later went out as the support act on the Rezillos tour. They delivered breakneck sets of two-minute musical assaults and took not just the Marquee but England by storm. They were back at the club the following February and March, and then for a four-night run in August as part of their Plug the LP tour. By this time, the Undertones were acknowledged as the brightest, classiest pop band around. The following month they were off to America, supporting the Clash, and the next time they were back in London it was as headliners at the Rainbow.

THE MOD REVIVAL

UK Subs | The Cure | Joy Division | Wreckless Eric | Joe Jackson | The Pretenders | John Cooper Clarke | 999 | The Cramps | The Knack | Secret Affair | The Chords | The Purple Hearts | The Lambrettas | The Merton Parkas | The Jam | The Human League | Simple Minds | Toyah | The Vapors | Reading 1979

January 1979 saw the club looking both backward and forward. There were dates for the Troggs (last at the Marquee in July 1966) and Rory Gallagher (who'd made his Marquee debut with Taste in 1968), and a headline debut for the new old, in the form of the UK Subs. One of the earliest of punk bands, they turned out to be also one of the most enduring. Singer Charlie Harper had been playing in blues bands since the mid 1960s and was a punter at the Marquee back then, attending gigs by the likes of Muddy Waters and Alexis Korner. By 1979, most punk bands had either split or turned new wave, so punk fans clung to the Subs as one of the last of a dying breed. With the Roxy and Vortex gone, the Marquee became a London base. They appeared again in March and then for three consecutive nights in November, followed by a four-nighter in 1980. The Subs played a 25th-anniversary gig at the Marquee in 2002 and, at the time of writing, they're still going.

The future was represented by the Cure. During 1978, they'd graduated from gigging around their hometown of Crawley to the London pub scene, and played a short UK tour as support to Generation X. They'd opened for Ultravox! at the Marquee just before Christmas, but 27 January 1979 was their first headliner. In his memoirs, drummer Lol Tolhurst described walking into the club for the very first time: 'Once inside we were confronted with the sheer awfulness of the facilities. The walls were as damp as a cellar and at the far end of the room was a famously vile bathroom where the glamour of rock and roll went to die. It felt like you could catch hepatitis just by breathing in the air. Despite the depressing accommodations we were agog with excitement.

The Cure, with Joy Division, March 1979.

Nothing could dampen our enthusiasm. We were playing at the Marquee.'

In March, the Cure were handed a Sunday residency. They got to choose their own support acts and on the first night the handpicked openers were Joy Division, who Cure frontman Robert Smith had heard on the John Peel show. A Joy Division setlist survives from that night, scribbled on the back of a page from a synthesizer manual: tracks played included 'Digital' and 'Glass' from the *Factory Sample* EP that had been released in December 1978, 'Transmission', which was originally recorded in 1978 for the band's aborted first album, and 'She's Lost Control' and 'Shadowplay' from the forthcoming *Unknown Pleasures* album, which the band would go into the studio to record the following month. This was the only occasion Joy Division played the Marquee.

The Cure's own sets at this time drew heavily on their own debut album, *Three Imaginary Boys*, which they were in the process of recording, and included '10.15 Saturday Night' and 'Fire in Cairo', as well as stand-alone singles 'Killing an Arab' and 'Boys Don't Cry'. Smith remembers the first Sunday as one of the best gigs they did that year, even if it was played to a half empty room. But word spread and successive Sundays saw audiences grow, until the final show was a sell-out. Tolhurst recalls taking a break from the soundcheck and wandering into the street for a cigarette. Lighting up, he saw the club's bouncer put out a 'House Full' sign. 'I stared at the sign in amazement. In a few weeks we went from being unknowns to this. We'd done it.'

In February, Wreckless Eric made the first of three appearances at the club – 'Whole Wide World' was almost certainly played – and Joe Jackson dropped in for one night as part of his Look Sharp tour. Newly arrived on the scene, he was being compared to new wave acts like Elvis Costello and Graham Parker. He fronted a tight three-piece band, promoting their debut album (after which the tour was named), and the set would have included singles 'Is She Really Going Out with Him?', 'One More Time' and 'Sunday Papers'.

At the beginning of April, the Pretenders made their debut at the club with a two-night headliner. Originally from Akron, Ohio, Chrissie Hynde worked for a time as a journalist for *NME* and in Malcolm McLaren's punk boutique. It was the do-it-yourself attitude of punk that inspired her to form a band that emerged out of a post-punk world to score a succession of hit records starting with a cover of the Kinks' 'Stop Your Sobbing', produced by Nick Lowe. The Pretenders continued to appear regularly at the club throughout 1979 and it was at one of these gigs that producer Chris Thomas saw them and was so impressed that he agreed to produce their debut self-titled album, which went on to top the British charts.

The night after the Pretenders, the stage was taken by Salford punk poet John Cooper Clarke. He'd be back for three consecutive nights in August 1981. In May, the status of the Marquee as the place punk went to die was further cemented by a three-night run of gigs by 999. Formed in 1976 – after auditions for members saw Chrissie Hynde and Tony James (Generation X) both turned down – the band established themselves on the London scene the following year, becoming regulars at the Hope and Anchor. They released their first two albums in 1978. They made a home base of the Marquee in 1979, following up those initial three nights with a five-night stint in October. Reviewing the gigs, *Melody Maker* asked whether anyone in 999 hadn't noticed that the whole snarling, shouty, head-banging, spit-soaked thing was embarrassingly old hat. Although, in the interests of impartiality, the reviewer did feel obligated to point out that the band's dedicated followers went wild and demanded encores – a phenomenon that surpassed all understanding, wrote the reviewer.

June saw a one-off appearance by US voodoo rockabilly outfit the Cramps. Preceded by just a couple of import singles and a reputation for B-movie weirdness, the band were over playing support to the Police on the final leg of their Outlandos d'Amour tour and on nights off were doing their own club dates. Later that week, there were two nights for Canadian hard rockers Max Webster, who were in the UK after opening for friends and fellow Canadian rockers Rush on the European leg of their Hemispheres tour. They were followed by two nights for Jamaican-born dub poet Linton Kwesi Johnson. He read poetry to pre-recorded backing tracks and was accompanied by four dancers. Three nights after that was a second club appearance by US band the Knack, who, just this month, would release their one-and-only hit, 'My Sharona'.

Also in June, the Marquee was host for a special Mod Weekend. The cover of a recent issue of the *NME* had featured a photo of mods on scooters, linked to a feature on a scene that had been growing over the past few months, the mod revival. The ambassadors for the movement were the Jam – their *All Mod Cons* album was a rallying call for wearers of sharp suits and fish-tailed parkas. By early 1979, a wave of acolyte bands began to break through and regular mod nights were taking place across the UK, but notably in London, at venues such as Waterloo's Wellington pub and Canning Town's Bridge House. The Marquee hosted its first mod revival band in May, who were Secret Affair. They fused rock riffs with Tamla Motown and their debut single 'Time for Action' became something of a mod anthem. Secret Affair were not part of the Mod Weekend, although they would be back at the club the following month for a run of three Sunday nights. Instead, it was the Chords who headlined both the Friday and Sunday nights. John Walters, producer of John Peel's radio show, was there and liked the band enough to book them for a Radio 1 session. They ended up being signed by Polydor. The middle night of the festival was headlined by the Purple Hearts. Both the Chords and Purple Hearts would go on to play the Marquee many more times throughout 1979. They'd be joined at the club by fellow mod revivalists the Lambrettas, from Brighton, who made their Marquee debut in 1979 (and would have a hit single the following year with 'Poison Ivy') and the Merton Parkas, who played the club a dozen times, starting in July, and whose keyboardist Mick Talbot would later team up with Paul Weller in the Style Council.

The band that launched the mod revival, the Jam, would also return to the Marquee later this year, on Friday 2 November, in a one-off secret gig, in which they were billed as John's Boys – after John Weller, Paul's dad and the band's manager. Hundreds were turned away, including some who remained determined to get in by any means possible. Journalist Garry Bushell, then working for *Sounds*, recalls walking up Wardour Street to the gig and seeing a skinhead rummaging in a skip full of debris, pulling out a scaffolding pole and launching a full-frontal attack on the club, attempting to smash through the door. The bouncers stepped aside as he charged then pounced, gave him a pummelling and tossed him out.

The support band that night were the Nipple Erectors, featuring a young Shane MacGowan. The Jam played new material from their forthcoming album, most of which was being heard for the first time. The final number was, appropriately, 'A Bomb in Wardour Street'. 'It was fantastic, one of the best gigs I saw the Jam ever play,' says Garry Bushell. 'The Marquee was the perfect place to see them because you had that low stage and that great rapport with the audience.' A couple of years later Bushell managed a band called the Blood and got them a booking at the Marquee: 'They decided that they had to make an impact so they got a blow-up doll from a sex shop round the corner and stuffed it with butcher's offal. Then they took a chainsaw to it on stage and the whole of the front row was sprayed. They never played there again.'

Back to June, and the pick'n'mix jamboree continued with two consecutive nights by the Human League. The Sheffield three-piece took to the stage with no guitars or drums, just keyboards, pre-recorded backing tracks and back-projected slides. Songs were announced by text on a screen and included 'Being Boiled' and 'Circus of Death', as well as covers of the Righteous Brothers' 'You've Lost That Loving Feeling', and an encore of Gary Glitter's 'Rock and Roll' and the Iggy Pop/David Bowie song 'Nightclubbing'. When Charles Shaar Murray of the *NME* saw them three months previously, in March, he declared, 'For all practical purposes, we may as well own up that we are now living in the Eighties.'

Another soon-to-be-influential Eighties band started life as Glasgow punks Johnny and the Self-Abusers. By the close of 1977 they'd embraced a new rockier sound and singer Jim Kerr suggested a change of name to Simple Minds. They played their first gig at the Marquee in July 1979, as part of a tour to promote their debut album, and would return several times that year, including back-to-back sold-out dates in December. In August, it was the turn of Toyah, making the first of a handful of Marquee appearances. At this point she was running dual careers as a singer and actress: in 1979 she had roles in Derek Jarman's *Jubilee* and *The Tempest*, and in *Quadrophenia*. The Marquee date coincided with the release of her EP *Sheep Farming in Barnet*. She'd be back again in October and the following January, and four years later in a special concert marking the end of her 1983 Rebel Run tour. She also made use of Marquee Studios to record her 1981 album, *Anthem*, which contained her biggest hit, 'I Wanna Be Free'. August also saw a first support slot for Guildford-based new wave band the Vapors, who were discovered by the Jam's bassist Bruce Foxton. They made ten appearances at the club, and in this time had a UK Top 3 hit with 'Turning Japanese'. They endeared themselves to fans at 90 Wardour Street with a track from their 1981 album, *Magnets*, entitled 'Live at the Marquee'.

Few of the bands that found success at the Marquee this year were invited to play Reading, with the exception of the Cure. They were part of a Friday line-up that was largely given over to minor new wave acts (Punishment of Luxury, Doll by Doll, the Tourists), none of whom, the Cure excepted, fared too well with a crowd eagerly awaiting Motörhead, who arrived backstage in a military vehicle. The *Melody Maker*'s reviewer called Motörhead the worst band he'd ever seen, but they got one of the best audience responses of the entire weekend. Closing Friday night were the Police. The band performed favourites from their debut album ('Can't Stand Losing You', 'Roxanne', 'So Lonely') along with new songs 'Walking on the Moon' and 'Message in a Bottle'. 'It's a moment of triumph,' recalled Andy Summers in his autobiography. 'And as I descend the steps to the backstage area Lemmy is standing there, and he leans forward and whispers into my ear, "Who smells of roses, then?"'

After a couple of forgettable early acts, Saturday came to life with a set by heavy rockers Gillan, now with Bernie Tormé on guitar, followed by appearances from, among others, Steve Hackett, Cheap Trick and the Scorpions (replacing Thin Lizzy, who had pulled out). Sunday had Peter Gabriel, with ex bandmate Phil Collins on drums and sharing vocals on an encore of Genesis track 'The Lamb Lies Down on Broadway', followed by Whitesnake. The festival closed a little underwhelmingly with Nils Lofgren, who was an unsatisfactory (as far as the festival audience was concerned) last minute replacement for the Ramones.

Back at the Marquee, there were some behind-the-scenes changes. Uli Pritz had decided to leave. He had been headhunted by Virgin to manage a new live music club called the Venue (it proved short-lived and Pritz returned to catering). He recalls some of the high points from his time on Wardour Street as selling 1,100 tickets for Chris Farlowe – 'with another 300 on the guest list' – the Saturday night when Czech-American Jan Hammer was headlining and Jeff Beck joined him on stage, and any gigs by his particular favourites Rory Gallagher, and Vinegar Joe. There was also the occasion Keith Moon turned up pulling a dead fish behind him on a dog lead: 'He asked me to check it into the cloakroom for him. It was a large salmon or something. He never collected it.'

Pritz's obvious replacement as manager was Nigel Hutchings. Having been assistant manager for something like five years, Hutchings knew the system. He now had responsibility for booking the bands. 'When I took over, the Marquee was a well-oiled machine and very attuned to what was going on in live music, recognising what was bubbling under and potentially what was coming up next.' His routine involved coming in around midday to do some office work, then letting the bands in, telling them what's what if they hadn't been there before, sorting the roadies out, and if they were doing any recording or filming, getting that fixed up. Because of the neighbouring offices, the council wouldn't permit any soundchecking until 6pm, an hour before opening. Generally, the headline act took up most of that hour. 'It would be about a minute to seven before the support act got to do their bit, and then we'd open the doors,' says Hutchings. 'So quite often the support act never had a soundcheck, which really pissed a lot of them off.' For the rest of the evening, Hutchings would be on the floor in case any problems arose. When the club closed at 11pm, the band took around an hour and a half to get their equipment out, and then often sauntered across the road to the St Moritz, a basement club beneath a Swiss restaurant of the same name, which, since opening in the mid 1970s, was the venue for post-gig partying.

Hutchings' promotion meant there was now a vacancy for an assistant manager. Jack Barrie already had an eye on who that might be. In partnership with Charisma-label boss Tony Stratton Smith, Barrie owned a couple of racehorses and both men were often to be found down at the Berkshire racing town of Lambourn making a day of it. Here they came into contact with an apprentice jockey named Ian Telfer, better known as Bush. He lived in the local hotel, working behind the bar in lieu of rent. When the owner went missing for three weeks at a race meeting in Ireland, Bush ended up running the place. Barrie thought he'd be perfect for the Marquee.

THE NEW WAVE OF BRITISH HEAVY METAL

Iron Maiden I Magnum I Samson I Def Leppard I Saxon I Tygers of Pan Tang I Girlschool I Angel Witch I Reading 1980

One of the more unexpected consequences of punk was the resurgence of a music that flourished in the early 1970s: heavy rock. The biggest amplifiers, the longest solos, the wailingist vocals. With punk spent and absorbed into the music industry, it left a vacuum to be filled by post-punk, new wave, the mod revival and a reinvigorated heavy rock. Established bands like Black Sabbath and Judas Priest began attracting new young fans, and new bands (or bands that had been around a while but were 'newly discovered') began attracting press. A lot of the bands originated in the Midlands and North of England, in industrial towns where the spirit of rock never went away; on their visits down to London they made base-camp at the Marquee, which, as a consequence, became the home of what the press were calling the New Wave of British Heavy Metal.

The first NWOBHM band to headline a show at the club were Iron Maiden, in October 1979, with support from fellow metallers Praying Mantis. It was a gig the band had been trying to land for some time.

Iron Maiden's debut, October 1979.

The brother-in-law of Maiden founder and bassist Steve Harris used to work for a carpet firm located behind the Marquee and he knew Jack Barrie, but Barrie wasn't keen. Meanwhile, the band were struggling to get gigs outside their native East End of London. They decided to record a demo, which they presented to a DJ named Neal Kay, who was then running a heavy metal club in Kingsbury, in northwest London, called the Bandwagon Soundhouse. Impressed, Kay began playing the tape at his club and, eventually, one of the tracks, 'Prowler', reached No.1 in the Soundhouse charts, which were published in *Sounds* magazine. On the back of this, the band landed themselves a manager, who, in turn, finally got them a coveted gig at the Marquee. They brought their fans from the Soundhouse with them and packed out the club. Also present were executives from EMI, and a few months later Maiden were in the studio recording their debut album.

The band were back at the Marquee in December and then again in April 1980 for a two-nighter, which kicked off their 1980 UK tour. They returned in July, this time playing three nights in a row; fans were queuing from lunchtime to get in and hundreds had to be turned away. 'Those nights really were something else,' recalls guitarist Dennis Stratton, who had recently joined the band after meeting with Steve Harris in the Ship. There was a last performance in December 1985, although not as Iron Maiden but as the Entire Population of Hackney, a spin off band featuring members of Maiden (Adrian Smith and Nicko McBrain), FM and Urchin. The set was mostly covers but the band were joined for encores by the rest of Maiden (Bruce Dickinson, Dave Murray and Steve Harris), and together they played fan favourite '2 Minutes to Midnight'. The performance was later released as an album, *Live in London*. Another Marquee gig, from 4 July 1980, provided material for a Japan-only four-track EP, *Live!! +one*, which features the earliest live recordings of Iron Maiden. Live footage from that same night, including interviews with some very well-spoken fans queuing on Wardour Street, featured in an episode of London Weekend Television youth culture doc *20th Century Box*, presented by Danny Baker, and first screened in 1981.

Two more NWOBHM acts made their Marquee debuts on successive nights in December 1979. Birmingham's Magnum recorded their gig on 15 December, which was released as a live album on Jet Records called *Marauder*, preceded by a four-track EP called *Live at the Marquee*, featuring material from the same show. Magnum would go on to play the club over twenty times. The following night, it was the turn of Samson, then a four-piece with Paul Samson on guitar, Chris Aylmer on bass, Barry 'Thunderstick' Purkis, formerly of Iron Maiden, on drums, and Bruce Dickinson, later of Iron Maiden, on vocals. Writing in *Sounds*, Geoff Barton – the journalist who came up with the NWOBHM tag – didn't go a bundle on the band's music but loved the OTT stage effects, which included liberal use of thunderflashes, dry ice, showers of confetti and a drummer who exited the stage during a lengthy guitar solo and reappeared dressed as a haggard old schoolteacher, giving the bassist six of the best across his backside with a cane and drooling blood from his mouth onto the audience.

Sheffield's Def Leppard played two nights in a row at the Marquee in January 1980. They had just opened for AC/DC on their Highway to Hell tour, which included three nights at Hammersmith Odeon, but the Marquee gigs were Leppard's first proper London headliners. Reviewing the gigs for *Sounds*, Chris Collingwood wrote that from the first song, 'It Could Be You', the Leppards showed why many considered them to be the leaders of the NWOBHM bands: the silk-and-leather flash, memorable riffs, energy and, by the end of the set, 'more topless chests than a bar on Sunset Strip'. The band returned to the Marquee in February 1983 to kick off their Pyromania tour, a gig that saw the introduction of new guitarist Phil Collen, who had previously played the Marquee with bands Lucy and Girl.

Barnsley band Saxon got their big break touring with Motörhead in late 1979. By the time they appeared at the Marquee, in February 1980, they were just about to release their second album, *Wheels of Steel*, which would go Top 30 and give them a Top 20 single. When Iron Maiden played the Marquee for two nights in April 1980, opening for them were another highly rated metal outfit: the Tygers of Pan Tang, from Whitley Bay in Tyne and Wear. Guitarist Robb Weir recalls arriving mid afternoon with their truck and crew, and waiting for Maiden to finish up their soundcheck: 'The club had a shiny red rubberised floor that was always sticky underfoot no matter how much it was mopped. And it always smelled of beer and cigarette smoke. It was one of my favourite places to play.' Both nights were sold out, with the guest lists full to the brim with record company executives and agents. 'After our soundcheck we crammed into the tiny dressing room behind the stage along with Iron Maiden. One of the crew produced a huge spliff and it was passed around.' At 7.30, the Tygers band went on. One of the features of the Marquee stage was that on both sides there was a gap of about one metre between the stage end and the wall. 'I used to do a thing,' says Weir, 'where I bent over backwards as far as I could while playing my guitar solo. On the first night, I bent over too far and fell off the stage. As luck would have it, our truck driver, Pete, was standing there and caught me mid fall, otherwise I probably would've broken my neck. He pushed me back up on stage and I carried on playing.'

In June, all-girl NWOBHM band Girlschool dropped in for a date – they'd return for a two-nighter in late December. In July, it was the turn of Angel Witch, making the first of what would eventually be a dozen appearances at the club over the next two years – not helped by reviews like the one in metal mag *Kerrang!*, which read, 'Give them a chance: they're not as bad as you think'.

No surprise that the Reading Rock '80 line-up was overwhelmingly heavy, including Iron Maiden, Praying Mantis, Magnum, Samson, Def Leppard, Tygers of Pan Tang and Angel Witch. The only new wave band were the Hellions, the group formed by ex-Damned guitarist Brain James. They lasted for only a handful of songs before their version of the Damned's 'New Rose' provoked such a deluge of cans that the band left the stage. Some innovators among the audience took to flattening the cans, creating jagged edges, and tossing them like Frisbees. The unwary could get concussed, cut, or both. Stewards wore crash helmets and the audience at the front spent more time scanning for incoming missiles than watching the stage. Only a handful of acts, notably UFO, Gillan, Rory Gallagher and Whitesnake, managed to distract the crowd enough to escape the dangerous barrage. *Melody Maker* headlined its coverage, 'The weekend that heavy metal turned into a hard rain and Reading ran with blood.' Other papers took to referring to Reading as the Cans Festival.

Ozzy Osbourne had been billed to play on the Sunday but he pulled out at short notice. His replacements were Slade, marking their return from the wilderness. According to drummer Don Powell, the band had more or less broken up: 'We hadn't worked together for ages. I believe [guitarist] Dave Hill didn't particularly want to go, but our manager Chas Chandler persuaded him to do it – at least go out on a high, as he put it. We had a few days' rehearsal and arrived at the gig with no passes. We had to walk into the festival with the crowd as no one knew we were on.' Their arrival on the festival stage was greeted with a hail of cans but Noddy Holder was too much of a trooper to let it phase him. The band ripped through a greatest hits package, even rolling out 'Merry Christmas Everybody' despite it being mid August. 'We literally had nothing to lose,' says Powell. 'We just went on and played all our hits.' A 65,000-strong crowd roared its approval. The performance was recorded by the BBC and forty-five minutes of the set was broadcast on Tommy Vance's *Friday Rock Show*. Slade purchased the tapes off the Beeb and released a three-track *Alive at Reading* EP, which gave the band their first chart success since 1977. 'We were on our way back,' recalls Don Powell. 'Thanks, Ozzy.'

THE EIGHTIES

Long Tall Shorty I Classix Nouveaux I Dexys Midnight Runners
I Original Mirrors I Martha and the Muffins I Nine Below Zero I
The Q-Tips I Hazel O'Connor I Athletico Spizz '80 I Tenpole Tudor
I Joan Jett and the Blackhearts I The League of Gentlemen

Despite the noise, metal was far from the only flavour of music on offer at the club as the new decade began. The mod revival was still ongoing: Long Tall Shorty were one of the earliest mod revival bands, formed in August 1978, and they finally made it to the Marquee in January 1980, when they opened for fellow mod revivalists the Teenbeats. Their first headliner followed just over two weeks later. They'd sometimes do six shows a week in the London area but, according to singer Tony Morrison, the only place Long Tall Shorty were guaranteed a big crowd was the Marquee. 'We could play somewhere like the Rock Garden on Friday and sixty people would come,' he recalls. 'But play the Marquee on Tuesday and it's sold out. That pretty much happened every month for two years.' When he wasn't performing, Morrison would come along to the Marquee as a punter, or pop in to watch other bands soundcheck. One time it was Ginger Baker and Morrison was stood off to the side, hanging out, when suddenly a drumstick went flying past his head: 'Oy, you!' shouted Baker. 'What are you doing in my soundcheck? Out!' (The former Cream drummer was back at the Marquee leading Ginger Baker's Energy, a short-lived five-piece that lasted from summer 1979 to summer 1980.) 'The Marquee was as much a part of my life as going to school was,' says Morrison.

Classix Nouveaux came together out of the break-up of X-Ray Spex. Their first gig was in August 1979 at the Music Machine (which would later become the Camden Palace) and their first appearance at the Marquee was four months later, in early January 1980. They performed with two shop dummies placed either side of the stage and singer Sal Solo in a silver astronaut suit. They played the club just twice more; Solo recalls that their support was Flock of Seagulls. He remembers the Marquee as 'really nothing to write home about – the dressing rooms resembled public toilets – but with a history that was unique and unparalleled.' Also in the first week of January was a one-and-only Marquee date by Dexys Midnight Runners. Both Kevin Rowland (vocals) and Kevin Archer (vocals, guitar) had played the Marquee before, as part of short-lived punk outfit the Killjoys. Two months after their gig here with Dexys, the band would release their single 'Geno' (about former Marquee regular Geno Washington), which would reach No.1, four minutes of pop perfection that ensured that Dexys' next London outing would be headlining at the Dominion on Tottenham Court Road.

In mid January, new wave band Original Mirrors made a third appearance at the club. They were led by Ian Broudie, later of Britpop favourites the Lightning Seeds, who relished playing the club that had hosted gigs by so many classic Sixties bands: 'What was weird was that I met Pete Townshend,' says Broudie. 'He came to the dressing room after the gig. We exchanged numbers and were in touch for many years after that. It seems unreal to have gone to the Marquee and then met someone so synonymous with the place as Townshend.'

In February, Canadian band Martha and the Muffins came seeking fame and fortune. There were actually two Marthas, Martha Johnson and Martha Ladly, both of whom sang and played keyboards. They were promoting bright and breezy new album *Metro Music*, and its lead single 'Echo Beach'. Reviews of the group's live performances were lukewarm at best but the single did rather well.

On entering the Marquee, the corridor inside was hung with old programmes and posters advertising the greats from the past. 'It was like walking down a hall of fame,' says Dennis Greaves of Nine Below Zero. As a kid he'd heard stories from his uncles about the great nights they'd spent at the Marquee, watching the likes of the Action, John Mayall and Alexis Korner. In March 1980, he got to play the club himself. 'You felt all of that history in the walls, and when you got on stage it was almost like the spirit of everybody that had played was there with you. I've never experienced that anywhere else.' Formed three years earlier, in 1977, Nine Below Zero cut their teeth on the London pub-rock circuit. 'It's where I learnt to be gobbed at, slagged off, shouted at, sworn at and loved,' says Greaves. 'It set me up for the rest of my life. I could handle anything after that.' The band's hot and tight blues was a good fit for the Marquee, and the

Zeros appeared pretty much once a month at the club through 1980. Steve Sutherland captured the essence of the band in a review for *Melody Maker*: 'Nine Below Zero lumbered on, spilled beer down my shirt, grabbed my lapels, administered a swift kick to the groin and dragged me dazed onto the dance floor.' Recently signed to A&M, the decision was made to record a show and release it as their debut album. The result was *Live at the Marquee*. Mixing superb covers, including the likes of Willie Dixon's 'I Can't Quit You Babe', with a handful of band originals, it's probably the best live Marquee recording since the Yardbirds, sixteen years earlier.

Also debuting that March was another band who would go on to make frequent appearances at the club. The Q-Tips repertoire consisted largely of 1960s soul standards, especially Motown, with vocals by a young singer by the name of Paul Young. They grooved with precision and audiences got off on dancing the mashed potato and the watusi. At one Marquee gig Young was joined on stage by American soul singer Eddie Floyd. They toured relentlessly but none of the singles or the two albums they released sold. The band broke up in early 1982 but Young went on to have major success as a solo artist, with hit singles like 'Love of the Common People', 'Wherever I Lay My Hat' and 'Every Time You Go Away'.

Not the most auspicious of dates, but on 1 April 1980 Hazel O'Connor made her Marquee debut. She'd yet to release any music but thanks to the publicity surrounding her lead role in the upcoming movie *Breaking Glass* (which wouldn't be released until September), she'd already been doing the rounds of print interviews and chat shows. Her Marquee performance was panned by the reviewers for being just that, a 'performance' – an actress delivering a simulation of a rock star, all face paint, Bowie postures and a Lene Lovich croon. By the time she returned to the Marquee in August, nobody cared what the music press said – the *Breaking Glass* soundtrack had spawned huge hits in 'Eighth Day' and 'Will You?', both written and performed by O'Connor. Both were rolled out at the Marquee that night, along with 'D-Days', the hit single from her follow-up album, *Sons and Lovers*, which would be released in November.

The second week of April featured a three-night run by Athletico Spizz '80, a band that had played their first headliner at the club just that February. They were a punkish new wave outfit founded by Kenneth

Spiers, aka Spizz, of Solihull. The band was riding high on the success of single 'Where's Captain Kirk?', which topped the indie charts at the beginning of 1980. Unfortunately, at one early gig the guitarist was a bit overawed by the experience. 'We'd been telling him, Hendrix played here and Bowie played here,' recalls Spizz, 'and during the set he slowly sneaked behind the PA stack. He vanished. He just couldn't cope.' The Spizzers were back at the Marquee in August for a massive five-night run. Technically it was six gigs: the band had been receiving a lot of fan mail from fifteen- and sixteen-year-olds who were too young to get into clubs, so they played an alcohol-free matinee gig on the Saturday. Energy levels were always high at Spizz gigs and this being August, the Marquee was at its most unbearably hot. One night, Spizz came off stage so wet he decided to see how much water was in his T-shirt: 'I squeezed nearly a pint of sweat into a glass.' A signature quirk was the changing of the band's name every year: the band's very first Marquee appearance, opening for the Human League in 1979, had been as Spizzenergi; they returned for further dates in 1981 as the Spizzles; in 1985 billed as Spizz and the Astronaughties, then later Spizz's Big Business; in 1986 as Spizzsexual; and in 1988 as simply Spizz.

Athletico Spizz's April three-nighter ran Wednesday to Friday and was followed on Saturday by the Marquee debut of the equally bonkers Tenpole Tudor, the cartoonish-punkish band fronted by the gawky Edward Tudor-Pole – who decided to form his own punk band after seeing Generation X at the Marquee. Tudor-Pole had attended the Royal Academy of Dramatic Art and it showed. 'At one gig we started off with me in bed on stage and when the lights went up, I did this thing about waking up in the morning, yawning and stretching, and then seeing the crowd and saying, "Oh, hello. What shall we do today? Shall we play some rock n roll?" Another time we had a Baby Belling on stage and I was cooking some real bacon and eggs, and then I said to the crowd, "Who hasn't had breakfast?" The audience loved it.' On other occasions, he'd arrive on stage to the strains of the 'William Tell Overture' or reciting a bit of *Henry V*. Like Hazel O'Connor the previous month, Tudor-Pole was making the most of a starring role in a forthcoming much-hyped movie, in this case Julien Temple's Sex Pistols mockumentary, *The Great Rock'n'Roll Swindle*, which was out that

May. He featured on three of the singles released from the soundtrack. Tenpole Tudor were back at the club in September and the following June, by which time they'd hit big with their own 'Swords of a Thousand Men' single, and were just about to release its follow-up, 'Wünderbar'.

In May 1980, the club hosted a gig by ex-Runaway Joan Jett and her new band, the Blackhearts, part of a European tour supporting the release of Jett's first solo album, *Bad Reputation*, recorded with the help of Paul Cook and Steve Jones of the Sex Pistols. The two nights following Joan Jett, the stage was taken by the League of Gentlemen. This was a band that existed for seven months only, formed and led by Robert Fripp, on a sabbatical from King Crimson. Featuring ex-XTC organist Barry Andrews, bassist Sara Lee and drummer Johnny Toobad, the League was what Fripp called a 'new wave instrumental dance band'. The Marquee dates were part of a tour of small clubs and colleges. 'We are, of course, the League of Gentlemen,' said Fripp as he took a seat stage left and led the band through a set of pieces underpinned by danceable pumping bass and organ. No vocals, no '21st Century Schizoid Man' or other Crimson classics, no matter how much the audiences demanded them.

U2

U2 I The Associates I Duran Duran I Son of Stiff I Thompson Twins I Lionheart I The Psychedelic Furs I Theatre of Hate I The Belle Stars I The Stray Cats I The Rockats I The Polecats I The Meteors I The Shakin' Pyramids I Rose Tattoo I Midnight Oil I The Au Pairs I Reading 1981 I Southern Death Cult I Lords of the New Church I The Aces (The Police)

Roadies have seen many sights at the Marquee as they cart in a band's equipment and start setting up. Arriving one Monday morning the crew for U2 found Lemmy, who had done a Jeffrey Bernard and got locked in for the night, still awake and playing the Space Invaders machine. Glad of the company, he offered to help out with the gear.

It was September 1980 and U2 were booked to play four consecutive Mondays: the 8th, 15th, 22nd and 29th. They'd already appeared a couple of times at the club earlier in the year, playing a couple of support slots (to heavy metallers White Spirit and the Wendy Wu-fronted punkish Photos). Nigel Hutchings had seen them and wasn't a fan. However, there was a lot of buzz around the band and on a personal level, says Hutchings, 'they were really nice guys,' so he'd given them a series of headliners, and he was interested to see how they'd do. He distinctly remembers watching a soundcheck with his girlfriend and uttering the immortal line, 'I really can't see this lot doing anything.'

At this time, things were starting to move for U2. Their debut album, *Boy*, was about to be released and they were starting to get daytime air play on Radio 1. This buzz of excitement was reflected at the Marquee where each successive Monday the crowds got larger. One Monday, the audience wouldn't let them go until they'd played three encores. The press loved them, too – 'one of the best things to come out of Ireland since James Joyce and Guinness,' said Ian Pye, at the Marquee for *Melody Maker*. A live recording, later

The first of U2's four Mondays, Sept 1980.

issued as the fan-club album *U2: Another Time, Another Place*, made on the last night of the residency, shows that the clarion-call chiming guitars, driving bass, martial drumming and earnest vocals that would define U2 were already firmly in place. They already sounded like an arena band.

For Bono, looking back on those shows in 2015, he equated the experience to the scene in *Pulp Fiction* where John Travolta stabs an adrenaline shot into Uma Thurman's heart and, whoosh, she's up and running. Another memory was walking off the stage through the crowd on the last song and out on to the street, and flagging a taxi to take him home, 'thinking that was quite a punk thing to do'. For the Edge, that series of shows was the start of a real London-based following. 'It was the perfect place for U2 to play and the legacy of the place became a spur to get us onto the next level. By the end of the month, we were just a better band.' When *Boy* appeared, on 20 October, it was to rave reviews. 'Here is the vinyl evidence to justify every superlative that has been heaped onto the band,' wrote Lynden Barber in *Melody Maker*. The band would be back for two more back-to-back dates at the end of November.

Two nights after U2's first headliner, there was a debut for Scottish band the Associates. Billy Mackenzie (vocals) and guitarist Alan Rankine (guitars, bass and everything else) grabbed attention by releasing a cover of David Bowie's 'Boys Keep Swinging', without copyright permission, just six weeks after Bowie's own version hit the Top 10. They released their debut album in mid-August (*The Affectionate Punch* – 'A kind of masterpiece,' opined Paul Morley in the *NME*) just a few weeks before their Marquee debut. Starting in October, they were handed a Sunday night residency, with Mackenzie and Rankine joined by former-Cure bassist Michael Dempsey and drummer John Murphy; support on the first Sunday came from jangly fellow Scots Orange Juice. The run ended when they pulled out of the fourth date, which was to have been 9 November. As a replacement, Nigel Hutchings decided to take a punt on a band he'd heard on a demo tape, given to him by an agent named Rob Hallet. It was short notice, but on the Friday Hutchings called Hallet and said if the band, who were from Birmingham, could get themselves down to the Marquee that Sunday, they could have the gig. Which is how Duran Duran came to play their only date at the Marquee and only their second gig outside Birmingham.

Between the final two shows of U2's Monday residency, the Marquee hosted the Son of Stiff tour. Independent record label Stiff made its name with its Live Stiffs package tour in 1977, followed by a Be Stiff tour in 1978. This was the same idea – five artists performing on the same bill each night around the UK – but with more low-key names. Shows would end with all-hands-on-deck encores featuring twenty-odd musicians. At the Marquee, though, each artist got their own night as headliner: Wednesday night was Any Trouble; Thursday was Tenpole Tudor; Friday Birmingham reggae outfit the Equators; Saturday New York-trio Dirty Looks; and

Sunday Joe 'King' Carrasco and the Crowns, playing wild Tex-Mex garage rock. The tour led to a *Son of Stiff* 12-inch EP and a short movie.

In January 1981, when they made their Marquee debut, the Thompson Twins were seven musicians, led by singer Tom Bailey. Growing up in Halifax, west Yorkshire, Bailey knew of the Marquee from the back pages of the *NME* and *Melody Maker*, where 'there was always an advert for the Marquee gigs, featuring the legends of the time'. After a couple of years living in squats in south London, messing around on borrowed or stolen instruments, when the band eventually appeared at the club, Bailey says, it felt like they'd finally made the big time. 'I remember some of the gig. We were percussion heavy and played some long-form improvised pieces, too. I'm not sure if electronic keys had begun to creep in to the live sound by then, probably not. We had a brief fashion obsession with rags, which we tied to ourselves and the stage equipment.' They were back for half a dozen further dates in 1981, including a three-nighter in June.

On Saturday 10 January, Lionheart played their first ever gig, which was at the Marquee. They were heavy metallers, formed in late 1980 and originally featuring singer Jess Cox (formerly of Tygers of Pan Tang) and guitarist Dennis Stratton (formerly of Iron Maiden). As part of the NWOBHM scene, Lionheart went down well at the club and continued to appear at least once a month through until the end of summer. 'At one gig Gary Moore was there wanting to jam with us,' recalls Stratton. 'I said no, because once he got up you couldn't stop him, and he was so good he made us look stupid.' Later in January, there were two nights by the Psychedelic Furs, warm-ups prior to going into the studio to record their second album, *Talk Talk Talk*, which would include their hit, 'Pretty in Pink'. In February there was a one-off appearance by Theatre of Hate, a great live act until they split in 1982, with singer Kirk Brandon moving on to form Spear of Destiny and guitarist Billy Duffy joining the Cult.

Not an obvious fit for the Marquee – there were so many of them for a start and the club had such a small stage – but eight-piece all-girl band the Belle Stars made Wardour Street a London base. Not only did they play the Marquee a handful of times, starting with their debut there in March 1981, they also partly recorded their debut album at the Marquee Studios in 1982 and in 1984 they performed live at the club in front of the cameras for a Live from London video release. In 1981, two members of what later would be the UK's most successful girl group of the Eighties, Bananarama, were also Marquee regulars, only not on stage – Sara Dallin and Siobhan Fahey worked evenings in the club's cloakroom.

Alongside the ongoing mod, girl-group and heavy rock revivals, American rockabilly music was also having a moment. The band spearheading the return to the double-bass and Brylcreemed quiff were the genuinely American Stray Cats, who, when news reached them on Long Island of a revival of Teddy Boy culture in England, hightailed it over to London. The snarling, crooning, swinging, string-slapping three-piece pioneered the fusion of the 1950s Sun Studio sound with elements of punk. They first appeared at the Marquee with a handful of gigs in late 1980, promoting debut single – and surprise Top 10 hit – 'Runaway Boys'. They were followed into the Marquee by the Rockats and the Polecats, the latter playing a two-nighter in mid-April with such exuberance that the guitarist snapped his strap, one member of the rhythm section busted his bass, while the other tossed all his sticks into the audience and ended up beating the skins with his hands. Fusing rockabilly with a heavier element of punk and trash aesthetics, the Meteors, who hailed from north London, were pioneers of psychobilly. Their fans, known as the 'Crazies', indulged in a style of slam dancing known as 'wrecking' – which can't have endeared the band to Jack Barrie but, nevertheless, the Meteors played the Marquee half a dozen times. There were also a handful of appearances from Scots hepcats the Shakin' Pyramids.

Spring 1981 saw debuts for two acts over from Australia. Rose Tattoo were hard rockers from Sydney, whose reissued 1978 debut album, *Rock'n'Roll Outlaw*, started to chart in Europe in 1981. They opened a first European tour with two nights at the Marquee in April, which saw them hailed as the loudest band to play the club since Led Zeppelin. The Tats were followed, in May, by fellow Sydneysiders Midnight Oil.

The Au Pairs were a short-lived post punk band from Birmingham fronted by Lesley Woods, an outspoken feminist and champion of non-conformity and equality. They played some support slots at the club in 1980, graduating to headliners in 1981; in May that year they played a three-night run, drilling through sets of songs on the subject of bad sex, diets, washing machines and Thatcher's Britain. There was also direct action against the Marquee: on a previous appearance some female fans had complained to the DJ about the sexist music he was playing to which the DJ responded by punching one of the girls. The three nights were undertaken on condition that the offending DJ wouldn't be present.

Once again, ignoring the diversity of sounds heard on Wardour Street, this year's Reading plumped for a line-up dependent on big hair and volume: Girlschool, Budgie, Gillan, Samson and Lionheart, along with old warhorses like Wishbone Ash, the Alex Harvey Band, Chicken Shack and Atomic Rooster. The only new wave act were the Thompson Twins. Festival closers were the Kinks. Tony Morrison's band Long Tall Shorty had a huge following at the Marquee, but on the big stage at Reading things were quite different. 'Our first song was met with complete disinterest. Our next effort was greeted with a hail of stones, beer cans, even a wrapped-up Cornish pasty. The festival was a kind of heavy metal utopia and we knew we were going to get canned off regardless, because of how we looked.'

Playing on the Sunday, and last to go on before the Kinks, were Nine Below Zero. It was a great slot to play, with the sun slowly beginning to set. 'There's something always special about that twilight time at festivals,' says Dennis Greaves. 'The whole atmosphere changes.' The response from the audience was rapturous and as the band walked off there were calls for an encore. 'We turned around to go back on, but the Kinks and the crew decided that we weren't going to do an encore and all our gear was dragged off stage. I didn't mind, it was Ray Davies, he's a genius. He can do that to me.' They might have been the oldest band on the bill that weekend, but in 'Lola', 'You Really Got Me' and 'All Day and All of the Night', the Kinks had all the best songs.

Notable gigs back at the Marquee in the second half of 1981 included a one-off (opening for Chelsea) for the Ian Astbury-fronted Southern Death Cult, and two support slots (opening for the Members) for Lords of the New Church, the post-punk supergroup formed by vocalist Stiv Bators (Dead Boys), guitarist Brian James (the Damned), bassist Dave Tregunna (Sham 69) and drummer Nick Turner (Barracudas). After a few try-out gigs elsewhere, James made sure that the band played the Marquee: 'It was just a great club. It didn't matter how packed it was, the sound was pretty good. I know from when I was in the audience no matter where you stood you were going to hear it okay.' The Lords would play a further half dozen dates as headliners at the club over the next few years.

On Saturday 12 December, the headline act were unknowns the Aces – unknowns because no such band existed. The Aces were actually the Police, playing a secret warm-up before three nights at Wembley Arena, the first UK dates on their Ghost in the Machine tour. There were about 200 people invited, not enough to generate an atmosphere thought Nigel Hutchings, who pointed this out to the group's manager, Miles Copeland. 'So we went out into the street telling passers-by the Police were playing and it was only two pounds a ticket,' recalls Hutchings. 'People just didn't believe it and we hardly got anybody else in.' Carl Leighton-Pope has a similar story: 'I'd just become UFO's agent and their manager, Wilf Wright, came to me and said we want to do two nights at the Marquee. They'd sold out Hammersmith Odeon and weren't a Marquee band anymore. So I called Jack and I said it was to be a secret gig and he shouldn't tell anybody. So we show up on the night and there's no one there. The band are asking what's going on? I said, well nobody knows about it, it's a secret. Wilf looked at me and he said, "Yeah, but you say you're not supposed to say this but…" So we told a few radio stations and on the following night you couldn't get in.'

MARILLION

Marillion I Spider I Rock Goddess I Mother's Ruin I Tank I Terraplane I Y&T I Howard Jones I Twisted Sister I Reading 1982

Enid fans aside, everybody thought pub rock, punk and new wave had killed off progressive rock. But if that was the case, nobody told Mick Pointer, Steve Rothery, Doug Irvine and Brian Jelliman, who spent 1980 playing prog in pubs round their local area of Aylesbury under the name

238

Marillion, picking up a small but hardcore group of followers along the way. A few personnel changes later – replacing Irvine and Jelliman with keyboardist Mark Kelly, bassist Pete Trewavas and a six-foot-five singer with a penchant for make-up called Fish – and the band decided that they needed a foothold in London. The obvious choice was the Marquee, a bastion of rock, and also a venue with links to the band's heroes, Genesis, and their record label Charisma, whose offices were upstairs. 'I knew that the Marquee was the right place for Marillion,' says Fish.

In summer 1981, Fish made a few forays to the Marquee armed with demo tapes, but it was publicist Keith Goodwin, acting for Marillion, who managed to talk Nigel Hutchings into putting the band on as support for US glam-rock outfit Girl that October. To make sure they made a good impression, the band brought a coachload of fans from Aylesbury to cheer them on. Not only did Marillion get an encore (rare for a supporting artist), they also earned themselves a first review in the rock press, in *Sounds*, and another support slot, early

Marillion's first headliner.

in January 1982, opening for Spider. Their second appearance delivered two wins. Nigel Hutchings caught them and was so impressed that he offered the band a headliner later that same month. Equally exciting was the presence, unbeknown to the band, of Tony Wilson, producer of the BBC's Radio 1 *Friday Rock Show*. He was there to see Spider – managed by his girlfriend – but he caught Marillion and liked them enough to offer them a session on the show.

Fish recalls the first Marquee headliner as, 'a huge moment for us.' The buzz around the band grew quickly, helped by the determination of Fish. 'He came in during the day, up to my office,' recalls Hutchings, 'and hung around, and we worked out a series of dates they could do to build them up, and they promised to bring in more coachloads.' There were a dozen more gigs that year, as Marillion almost became the Marquee house band. Fish was a fixture at the club, often to be found at the bar. 'Soho was a really vibrant place at that time – you used to finish at the Marquee and go across to the St Moritz, sit there in the cellar and watch Lemmy throwing his entire life and coins into a fruit machine. It was a brilliant time. Post soundcheck we'd go to the Ship and meet up with fans. It was one of my favourite periods in Marillion's history.'

By the end of 1982, the band were at work on their debut album, *Script for a Jester's Tear*, at Marquee Studios. 'Working in the studio during the day, then playing or hanging out in the club by night – we were in our London sanctuary,' recalls Fish. During the recording EMI often checked the band's expenses. One day the label's accountant rang up the Marquee's Simon White to say that although the band were entitled to charge for taxis they weren't entitled to charge for food. 'I asked what they were referring to,' says White. 'They said there was a docket saying, "Fish". I was surprised that I had to inform them that the lead singer of the group was called Fish and the receipt was for his taxi home.'

Marillion played three consecutive nights on 28–30 December, during which they debuted the title song of their forthcoming album. When *Script* was originally released in March 1983, to everyone's surprise – the band included – it reached No.7 in the UK album chart. Its success, and that of the album's single 'Garden Party', elevated the band to venues of the order of the Hammersmith Odeon, but they returned to the Marquee on several occasions for a handful of special fan gigs: in May 1983, they appeared billled as the Skyline Drifters, and in October 1983, they were Lufthansa Air Terminal. They were back again in September 1985 for a special date during their Misplaced Childhood tour, and again in December that year for a closed *Whistle Test* recording.

The close connection Marillion had with the club manifested itself in several other ways: the cover art of 1987 single 'Incommunicado' depicts fans queuing outside the Marquee and the video for the song was shot inside the club. The band's B-side 'Cinderella Search' includes a line about the 'Marquee of promises', while the chattering voices heard at the beginning of the track 'He Knows You Know', from *Script for a Jester's Tear*, belong to Marquee secretaries.

The band Marillion supported on 3 January, Spider, were making their Marquee debut that night. Formed in Wallasey, they were tagged as part of the NWOBHM, but remained outsiders to the scene – possibly because the band were all teetotal. They were also largely pilloried by the press for their Spinal Tap-like songs with titles like 'Did Ya Like it Baby' and constant references to shagging. Whatever the critics thought, Spider built up a solid fanbase, not least at the Marquee, where they played around a dozen times in 1982 alone and would regularly fill the house. Also debuting that January were Rock Goddess, another NWOBHM outfit, this one formed in south London by sisters Jody and Julie Turner, along with bassist Tracey Lamb, when they were all still at school. In summer 1981, rock mag *Kerrang!* picked them out as a band to watch. On a scene noted for its sexism, Rock Goddess quickly became accepted as a good ear-bruising, headbanging, power-driven band rather than a novelty. They became a fixture at the Marquee, playing around twenty-four times. They were also invited to play Reading '82, and the appearance led them to landing a recording contract with A&M.

Metal was still very much the Marquee house sound in 1982. February saw a debut appearance for Mother's Ruin, soon to release their debut album and later to tour with Motörhead. Frontman Dale Nathan has never forgotten that Marquee gig: 'Near the end of our set, our lead guitarist Phil Hunt caught me with his Fender and knocked my tooth out. I managed to continue singing with blood pouring out of my mouth.' In March it was the turn of Tank, the incredibly loud band fronted by former Damned bassist Algy Ward, and Terraplane, who achieved little renown beyond Wardour Street, where they were a reliable support act throughout 1982, switching up to headliners the following year. They played the club over twenty times but they never quite took off.

Californian metal band Y&T were in the UK working on their new album, *Black Tiger*, when they decided to take a break midway through recording to do a first UK tour. 'One of the first shows, if not the first show, was at the Marquee,' recalls the band's singer and guitarist Dave Meniketti. 'It was a particularly hot week in the UK and that night had every person and surface of the club drenched in sweat. There was a follow spot at the back of the club and every time they turned it on, it was like they were

Fish posing with Marillion fans during the early-morning photoshoot for the cover of the 'Incommunicado' single.

roasting me in a fire pit. To give you an idea of how intense the heat was on stage, the rubber on my guitar stand had softened and was deforming around the neck of my spare guitar. It was beyond anything we had ever experienced. But it was also one of the most exciting shows we ever performed because of the anticipation both onstage and in the audience.'

Opening for Marillion on their two consecutive dates at the beginning of July was Marquee newbie Howard Jones. The short, spiky-haired one-man-band did not receive the best of receptions: 'I remember Howard going on in front of our audience and they were ripping him apart,' says Fish. 'And he was walking off the stage and came into the dressing room and said, "Fuck this." I said, "Get back on that fucking stage now. You can't turn your back on them. You've got to deal with this."' Jones supported Marillion on a third date in October before hiring the Marquee for a Monday night headlining residency in January of the following year. He coached in fans from his High Wycombe home base and invited record labels to come and see him perform. It proved a successful strategy as Jones landed a BBC Radio 1 session, support slots with China Crisis and OMD, and a deal with Warner Music shortly afterwards. He released his first single, 'New Song', in September 1983, a month in which he appeared twice at the Marquee. His final appearance at the club was on New Year's Eve 1983, with second single 'What Is Love?' high in the charts. In 1984, he released debut album *Human's Lib*; the following year he was performing at Live Aid.

The first week of August 1982, the club gave a debut to New Jersey metallers Twisted Sister – or, as towering frontman Dee Snider would have it, 'Twisted fuckin' Sister'. The Marquee's Myra Hickey recalls that the band was not impressed by the experience. 'They came for their soundcheck having spent the day in the hotel. They'd been watching TV and were freaked out by only having access to a couple of channels. They'd had nothing to watch except a thirty-minute programme about asparagus.' The Marquee rarely, if ever, pandered to band riders, so when Dee Snider, the band's singer, asked for some soft drinks he was told the cost would be deducted from their fee. When Snider asked for towels, he was told the same thing. He then asked to have the air-conditioning turned on, only to be told there wasn't any. The Sisters brand of raunch'n'roll went down a storm with a Marquee audience who were overjoyed at the opportunity to see a band whose reputation had preceded them. Despite some technical issues, Snider leapt around like the stage was on fire and stoked up the crowd between songs with expletive-laden gonzoid raps.

For Snider, the gigs were something he's never forgotten. 'I wish my memories were better, but the first Marquee shows scarred me for life,' he says. 'The heat was debilitating. The band and I could barely move on stage because it was so hot and humid. The audience was suffering too. They were carrying the passed-out bodies of fans out of the club. It was brutal. For years after those shows I would start to have panic attacks when it would start heating up anywhere I was.' On the plus side, Phil Carson of Atlantic Records was in the audience for one of the nights and he signed the band. 'Twisted Sister were almost totally unknown at the time and on a do or die mission to come to London to get a record company,' Carson recalls. 'I signed them on the spot.'

Three weeks later, Twisted Sister were playing to 25,000 at that year's Reading Rock. The line-up was near exclusively metal and mostly Marquee regulars, including Bernie Tormé, Budgie, Gary Moore, Praying Mantis, Spider, Tank, Terraplane and Tygers of Pan Tang. Rare relief from the squalling guitars came from Dave Edmunds and Marillion. 'If you were doing well at the Marquee you knew you were going to get the festival gig, that was the bottom line,' says Fish. 'The Reading festival was just the Marquee with the roof off.' The atmosphere this year was more benevolent than in past years. There was, for the most part, no rain and no can-throwing – cans and bottles had been banned from the site. Marillion played the Sunday afternoon. At the start of the set, Fish announced the band's new contract with EMI, and then launched into a celebratory 'Garden Party'. 'It was a big gig for us because we went out and we tore the place apart and nobody expected us to do that. There were a lot of rock fans at that festival who hadn't seen us at the Marquee, and the energy that came from our existing fans spread like a wild fire through the crowd,' recalls Fish. *Kerrang!* reported that the band's piéce de résistance, 'Forgotten Sons', resulted in one of the loudest ovations of the weekend.

The Michael Schenker Group closed the festival but the bigger hit were Saturday's headliners, Iron Maiden – who'd been so keen to appear that they'd interrupted a three-month US tour and flown back for the gig. Maiden were boosted by the presence of Bruce Dickinson, erstwhile Samson vocalist, who'd been tapped up at the previous year's festival.

In a new marketing venture for the Marquee, Reading '82 was celebrated with the release of a double album, *Reading Rock Volume One*, featuring performances from most of the artists on the bill that year. Sales presumably were not great because there was never a volume two.

SAVING WOMAD

Garden Wall (Genesis) | Anvil | Hanoi Rocks | Little Steven and the Disciples of Soul | Thomas Dolby

Peter Gabriel – last seen on stage at the Marquee in September 1972 – was (and undoubtedly still is) a visionary individual. Back at the beginning of the 1980s, one of these visions was of a world that embraced music from a myriad of global cultures. To this end, he was instrumental in forming an organisation called World of Music, Arts and Dance, or Womad, for short. One of Womad's earliest activities was to organise a festival, which took place in July 1982 at Shepton Mallet, in Somerset. The bill included Peter Gabriel, Simple Minds, Echo and the Bunnymen, and the Beat, alongside the likes of the Drummers of Burundi (East Africa), Musicians of the Nile (Egypt), Imrat Khan (India), the Tian Jin Music and Dance Ensemble (China), the global collective of Suns of Arqa, Prince Niko Mbarga (Nigeria), and the Chieftains, from Ireland.

Because of his experience with Reading, Harold was asked to help with the logistics. Some of the Marquee staff, led by Myra Hickey, were also drafted in. Harold and Barbara went out to Somerset the weekend of the festival. 'As we arrived,' recalls Harold, 'Gail Colson, who was Peter Gabriel's manager, saw me coming and said, "Oh good, you're here. You're experts on disasters aren't you?"'

It was immediately apparent what the problem was. There'd been little publicity and Shepton Mallet Showground was not the easiest place to get to. As a consequence, hardly any paying punters had turned up. 'I think most of the audience were wives or girlfriends of the artists,' recalls Barbara. It was obvious that the festival was going to lose money and probably a lot of it. To make sure that the artists could at least get paid, Harold personally lent money to Womad. Other friends also weighed in with offers of help, not least Gabriel's old band Genesis, who agreed to a one-off reunion concert with their old frontman, with all proceeds going to the festival. Harold was asked to promote the event.

A couple of years earlier, Harold had been invited to view a new outdoor concert venue in Milton Keynes. It seemed to have been created without the involvement of anyone who'd actually run a major outdoor event. The stage was sited where the sun set, so at any evening concert the sun would be shining directly into the audiences' eyes. Backstage was equipped with a single toilet. 'Presumably, they expected Sting or Freddie Mercury to line up with the punters for a pee,' says Harold. Once these and a few other issues were sorted out, the Marquee organised the first ever concerts at the Milton Keynes site, with the Police headlining Rock at the Bowl in 1980. This was followed the next year by Thin Lizzy. With its capacity of 50,000, Harold thought the Milton Keynes Bowl was the ideal location for the Genesis show. It took place in October 1982 under the banner Six of the Best and saw Gabriel reunite for one evening with the band he'd quit seven years before. Despite the fact it poured with rain the entire day, the concert was a financial success and effectively bailed out Womad. Some years later, Harold persuaded Reading council to allow Womad to use the town's festival ground and the event was held there from 1990 to 2006. Years later, speaking at the celebrations for Womad's 40th anniversary, Peter Gabriel said of Harold and Barbara, 'The advice they gave us at a very crucial time was absolutely invaluable and gave us the confidence to carry on.' Not only that, he continued, 'Barbara and Harold created the first festivals in the UK and every other festival hangs from their family tree.'

The month before their Six of the Best concert, Genesis played a gig to an audience of about one-hundredth the size of the one that would turn out at Milton Keynes. After an absence of ten years they returned to play the Marquee. The event took place on Monday 27 September

1982. The band had announced dates for their Three Sides Live tour of North America and Europe, including three nights at the Hammersmith Odeon, when Nigel Hutchings got a call saying they wanted to do a secret show at the Marquee the night before the first Hammersmith date. 'It was a real military operation to keep it quiet,' recalls Hutchings. 'Then at one o'clock on the day of the show, Terry the Pill, who was this dodgy guy who did flyposting, put up these posters all over the West End, announcing "Garden Wall, Marquee, tonight". [Garden Wall being one of two Charterhouse schoolboy bands that merged to become Genesis.] Of course, the fans sussed it straight away and a queue formed all the way up to Oxford Street.'

Unlike in years past, when, for a gig like this, the club would have packed in a thousand or more fans, they stuck to a limit of 500 tickets. Sold at a face value of £4, they were changing hands for upwards of £50 on the night. The sight that met those lucky enough to get in was of a stadium gig's worth of equipment crammed onto the small Marquee stage – two huge drumkits and a vast bank of keyboards. The band played a full two-and-a-half hour set. 'We played here, 1972, 1973 last,' Phil Collins announced after the opening two numbers. 'And we were obviously so popular then that they invited us back. We've been told that if we play well here tonight, we can come back and play every week.' In another break between tracks he noted, 'Hasn't got any bigger has it?' before attempting to dance in two square foot of space and sending part of his drumkit crashing off stage.

One of the lucky punters inside the Marquee that night was Fish: 'It was one of the most amazing gigs I ever saw at the Marquee. I couldn't actually believe I was present, just an amazing show. When they played "Supper's Ready" it was absolutely fucking mind-blowing.'

A couple of weeks before the Genesis gig, a pre-fame Big Country played their one and only Marquee date (9 September). A week before that were back-to-back debut dates for Anvil. Anvil were practically unknown outside their native Canada when they were added to the bill at 1982's Monsters of Rock festival at Donington. That appearance won them a legion of new fans, so the two headliners at the Marquee were sell-outs. It was a venue high-school friends Steve 'Lips' Kudlow and Robb Reiner had wanted to perform at ever since they began playing music together in the early Seventies. Relaxing in the dressing room after their sound check, there was a knock on the door and in walked a teenager called Sacha Gervasi, who introduced himself as England's number one Anvil fan. He and the band spent some time hanging out in London and for a time he worked for them as a roadie. Flash-forward some thirty years and Kudlow receives an email from Gervasi. 'He invited me to come visit him in Los Angeles where he had become a successful screen writer. He had this idea to make a movie about the band.' The result was *Anvil! The Story of Anvil*, an award-winning documentary that chronicled Kudlow and Reiner's dreams of cracking the big time. 'Had we not played the Marquee in the summer of '82 everything would be vastly different,' says Kudlow, 'and certainly not the happy glorious miracle I've lived.'

A month after Anvil's Marquee debut, Finnish band Hanoi Rocks began a residency. They'd played a one-off gig at the club back in November 1981, but since then the band had relocated to London in a bid to make it internationally. Pretty soon the Marquee was a second home, which they turned into a site of regular rock'n'roll mayhem. 'The Marquee is where we really started creating a scene in London,' says singer Michael Monroe. 'The coolest thing was that people from all walks of life and different genres came to the Hanoi Rocks shows – punks, Teds, heavy metal fans, skins, rastas and freaks of all kinds. We got them all and this was all happening at the Marquee.' In December 1983, the band returned for a three-night run and the shows were recorded for the band's first live album, *All Those Wasted Years*.

Little Steven and the Disciples of Soul dropped in for an unadvertised, one-off gig in mid-October. Better known as Miami Steve Van Zandt, Bruce Springsteen's righthand henchman and guitarist in the E Street Band, Little Steven managed to cram ten musicians onto the Marquee stage, including a five-piece horn section. The band were promoting their first album, *Men Without Women*.

Taking up residency in November was synth-pop guru Thomas Dolby who had just released the single 'She Blinded Me with Science.' He appeared four Mondays running, along with musicians Kevin Armstrong (guitar and keyboards) and Matthew Seligman (bass and keyboards). The shows were plagued by technical faults with the computerised backing track. During one malfunction, Dolby shrugged and deadpanned, 'The Marquee – the pinnacle of my career.'

THE PROG REVIVAL

Twelfth Night | Pallas | IQ | 25th anniversary shows | The Alarm | The The | Twisted Sister | Wrathchild | Lee Aaron | Sex Gang Children | Reading 1983

By 1983, it was obvious that Marillion weren't alone in their passion for face paint and meandering keyboard solos. Reading-based Twelfth Night actually preceded Marillion into the Marquee, playing the club in June 1981, and they opened 1981's Reading festival, but then they went AWOL for a while. They returned to Wardour Street in January 1983, where they as good as took up residency for the rest of the year. When vocalist Geoff Mann decided to step away from the band, Twelfth Night gave him an emotional send off with two nights at the Marquee in November 1983, which were recorded and released as the album *Live and Let Live*.

If Marillion were the standard bearers for the prog revival in England, then the Scottish branch of the movement was headed by Pallas. A five-piece from Aberdeen, they had songs about arks of infinity and strangers on the edge of time, and a singer who sported a mirror-covered helmet.

The previous September, members of Southampton band IQ had spent an evening on the roof of the Marquee: they'd tried and failed to get tickets for the secret Genesis gig, so they went round to Richmond Mews, climbed the back of the building and listened to the gig through a skylight. Their first appearances at the Marquee were opening for Twelfth Night, Pallas and the Enid, among others. As the support slots stacked up they took to appearing on stage wearing T-shirts reading, 'Give us a headliner'. They landed top billing in October 1983. Their music careered dextrously from Genesis-inspired instrumental passages to white reggae and Talking Heads funk. IQ would play the club close to forty times over the next four years, including on 13 July 1985, the day of Live Aid, when the Marquee had a big screen on stage relaying the events at Wembley. IQ came on just as David Bowie finished his set and frontman Peter Nicholls asked the audience, 'What did you think of the support act then?'

The Marquee became the home of the new progressive movement. In addition to the already mentioned bands, there were also regular gigs from Pendragon, Solstice and Haze, and, after he left Twelfth Night, from a solo Geoff Mann, supported on a number of occasions by Niadem's Ghost, the band formed by Peter Nicholls after he left IQ.

In 1983, the Marquee marked a milestone twenty-five years as a music venue. The celebrations spread across much of the year and mostly involved getting names once associated with the club back onto the stage. The headline event was the appearance of a reformed Yardbirds. Drummer Jim McCarty and guitarist Chris Dreja had already been pulled together by an agent to play a couple of reunion shows in Spain. 'Then he said, how do you fancy playing at the Marquee's birthday,' recalls McCarty. 'So, we used the band that had gone to Spain with us, along with Paul Samwell-Smith on bass, so we had three of the originals.' Invites were extended to Clapton, Beck and Page but none of them showed up. Instead, lead guitar duties were taken up by John Knightsbridge of Ruthless Blues; John Fidler of Medicine Head and Mark Feltham of Nine Below Zero took on the vocals. To the audience's delight, the Marquee reverberated again to 'Smokestack Lightning', 'Shapes of Things' and 'For Your Love'. 'It was a very special evening,' recalls Jim McCarty.

Inevitably, given his close connections to the club, Chris Barber made a return, sharing the stage for two nights with New Orleans pianist Dr John. The Damned's Brian James was in the crowd that night: 'At the beginning of the set, Chris Barber's jazz band were outside in the street. They walked in the front door playing, along the corridor, through the bar and then up to the stage. It was fantastic.'

Ten Years After also reformed specially to take part in the celebrations. They had broken up several years earlier, with guitarist/vocalist Alvin Lee going off to do solo projects, while bassist Leo Lyons moved into producing. After just one rehearsal, the band returned to the Marquee stage and went down a storm. 'It was great,' recalls Lyons. 'The magic was

Harold and Barbara Pendleton celebrate
twenty-five years of the Marquee.

there, the enjoyment was there – and some of the reasons why we broke up in the first place were there.' There was no return by the club's most famous alumni, the Rolling Stones, but at the end of April their old mentor Alexis Korner was back for the first time in seventeen years. For the occasion, he roped in old jamming buddies Charlie Watts and Bill Wyman, as well as Georgie Fame, Dick Heckstall-Smith and Geno Washington. Mojos were worked and tailfeathers given a good shaking.

John Mayall's Bluesbreakers, with Mick Taylor (former live guitarist with the Stones), returned for three nights in June, and former club favourites Eddie and the Hot Rods also got back together specially to play two nights in April. Drummers Ian Paice (Deep Purple), Rat Scabies (the Damned) and Mick Underwood (Gillan) appeared together for a special Paiste drum clinic in March, a showcase reprised in June with a line-up of Simon Kirke (Free), Clive Burr (Iron Maiden) and Pick Withers (Dire Straits). Girlschool played three nights in June and Motörhead three nights in July; later that month there were celebration gigs by old-stagers Rory Gallagher and Caravan.

Despite all the nostalgia, new acts were not neglected. In January 1983, Welsh outfit the Alarm made their headline debut, following a couple of support slots at the end of 1982. Jake Burns, formerly of Stiff Little Fingers, joined them for future hit single 'Sixty Eight Guns'. *Melody Maker*'s Mick Mercer was also there and declared the Alarm 'one of the ultimate live bands'. They'd make a further six appearances at the club that year, before chart success propelled them to bigger venues – although they would return for two nights in October 1985. In March, Matt Johnson, aka The The, installed himself for a four-week Thursday-night residency, accompanied by special guests, including Zeke Manyika of Orange Juice and Marc Almond. Twisted Sister were back for two nights on 5–6 March. The shows were recorded for what became the *Live at the Marquee* album. The band were full of swagger having just been signed to Atlantic, with Dee Snider ranting at a thousand words a minute between numbers, dissing the crowds that couldn't get into the shows because they turned up fashionably late and asking the audience to point out the person who just threw the bottle that hit him in the face so that he could 'kick his fuckin' ass'.

A British take on Twisted Sister, Wrathchild were one of the earliest British glam-metal bands, big on make-up, platform boots and stage pyrotechnics; they made their one and only Marquee appearance on 1 May. They were followed three nights later by another one-off date, this by Lee Aaron, a Canadian rock singer gaining acclaim in her own country but unknown in Europe – other than for the photo spread she did for soft-porn mag *Oui*. She couldn't afford to bring her own band and instead hired Manchester rockers Sam Thunder who, in just twelve hours of rehearsals, learned all the material on her first album.

Motörhead played three nights in July and there was a three-nighter from the Sex Gang Children in August. The SGC first played the Marquee the previous August, an occasion notable for the closure of the ladies' toilets because someone was in there giving birth. The SGC were part of the Batcave scene, the midweek club where the goth movement began, first at 69 Dean Street, later moving to the Subway in Leicester Square. They were a dramatic band, relying on heavy bass, tribal drumming and sudden mood shifts. At the Marquee, they would have been promoting their debut studio album, *Song and Legend*, released in 1983, and which reached the top of the UK indie chart.

That August, Reading went ahead with one of the best line-ups of the Eighties. Headliners were the Stranglers (Friday), Black Sabbath (Saturday) and Thin Lizzy (Sunday). There was also reggae (Steel Pulse), anthemic pop-rock (Big Country), nostalgia (Steve Harley and Cockney Rebel, Ten Years After, Suzi Quatro), soul (Little Steven and the Disciples of Soul), blues (Climax Blues Band, Stevie Ray Vaughan), and heavy rock and metal (Hanoi Rocks, Magnum, Mama's Boys, Anvil). There was also plenty of prog from Pendragon, Solstice, Pallas, Twelfth Night, Marillion and, inevitably, the Enid. Cockily, Marillion opened with a seventeen-minute track called 'Grendel' and held the audience rapt, proving to be one of the hits of the weekend. Black Sabbath, who followed them, flopped. At this point, they were fronted by ex-Deep Purpler Ian Gillan, who viewed Sabbath as his backing band and they responded by putting in a lumbering tedious performance. The set is best remembered for the monolithic forty-five-foot Stonehenge set that was far too big for the stage – it served as the inspiration for one of *Spinal Tap*'s funniest sequences.

At least the crowd remained indifferent to Sabbath, unlike Steel Pulse, who, on Friday, got bottled and their lead singer told the crowd that if they threw any more the band would leave. The response was a barrage of piss-filled, plastic one-litre containers. The band downed instruments and vacated the stage. Hanoi Rocks were the most bottled band of the festival but they stuck it out, dancing, dodging and goading the bottlers with laughter. 'I'm just sorry that we had no time left to do an encore,' says the Rocks' Michael Monroe, 'as that would've really been the perfect "fuck-you-very-much" icing on the cake.'

For Thin Lizzy, this was their last-ever performance. The band had announced they were quitting after Reading. They turned in a rip-roaring display that included all their finest moments from the opening 'Jailbreak', announced with fireworks and explosions, through to the encore of 'Still in Love with You'. They were met with ecstatic applause. 'We'd like to thank you from our souls,' said Lynott, and with that Lizzy were no more.

Theirs was not to be the only farewell. It also seemed Reading Rock might also be no more. Before the festival, Reading Council had announced its intention to build a leisure centre on the site. They had no alternative site to offer the festival. Harold was furious: he felt he'd done an enormous amount for the area, putting money into the local economy for the last twelve years – and all for nothing.

REM

ZZ Top I New Model Army I REM I Katrina and the Waves I Thor I Metallica I Lita Ford I Joan Jett I Huey Lewis and the News I Grand Slam I The Blow Monkeys I The Waterboys I Lloyd Cole and the Commotions I The Cardiacs I Johnny Thunders

The Marquee ads in the music press for the week beginning 13 October 1983 listed that Sunday's gig as 'Little Ol' Band from Texas'. It probably wouldn't have taken too much application of the grey cells for rock fans to figure out who the Little Ol' Band were: Houston's finest, ZZ Top, were due to embark on the seven dates of the UK leg of their Eliminator tour a few days later. The bearded-ones warmed up for appearances at both the Hammersmith Odeon and Wembley Arena with an only slightly abbreviated work out on Wardour Street, opening with 'Thunderbird' and boogying on through 'Sharp Dressed Man', 'Francine' and 'Jesus Just left for Chicago', among others, before encoring with 'Tush'.

New Model Army made their Marquee debut in November 1983. Formed in Bradford in 1980, they'd been gigging around the UK for a couple of years to little effect but in 1983 they'd released their first singles, which had been given airplay by Radio 1's John Peel. An appearance at the Marquee was another rung on the ladder, where the band's forceful take on agit-rock was greeted by a sea of naked male torsos. They made a number of further appearances at the club that year, culminating in a three-night residency in April 1985, by which time they'd been signed by EMI and were about to release breakthrough album *No Rest for the Wicked*.

The highlight that November, though, was a band of university dropouts who'd spent much of the past couple of years playing college parties for free beer. REM were making their first overseas trip, in support of debut album *Murmur* ('the most beguiling album of 1983', according to Allan Jones of *Melody Maker*). An appearance on TV music show *The Tube* ensured that the band's first two UK gigs, at Dingwalls and then three days later at the Marquee, were sell outs. Walking on stage at the Marquee, a straggly-haired Michael Stipe announced, 'We're REM. Actually, we're not, they couldn't make it so we're here in their place, playing all the hits of the day.' Anyone expecting the dream-like, diffused sounds of *Murmur* was in for a shock as the band launched into a howl of feedback and stormy drumming for opener 'Moral Kiosk'. Throughout the set, guitarist Peter Buck trampolined around the stage, while Stipe mostly hugged himself tight like he was wearing a straitjacket. There were two encores, the second including the Velvet Underground's 'Femme Fatale' and, finally, debut single 'Radio Free Europe'. Reviewing the show in the *NME*, Barney Hoskyns called REM, 'the most vital American group today.' The band would return to the Marquee for two dates in the spring of the following year, on 30 April and 1 May, introducing more songs that would feature later in the year on second album *Reckoning*, including, on the second night, '(Don't Go Back to) Rockville'. Encores included the Byrds' 'So You Want to Be a Rock'n'Roll Star', Abba's 'Does Your Mother Know' and Fleetwood Mac's 'Tusk'. These were the only two dates in London on a short European tour.

REM were followed into the Marquee by several more North American acts during 1984. Katrina and the Waves were technically an English band, but they sounded American courtesy of Kansan Katrina Leskanich on vocals and keyboards, and fellow American Vince de la Cruz on vocals and lead guitar. They played the club in February and April. Fronted by a former body-building champion and Mr World Canada, Thor were from the more ridiculous end of the heavy metal spectrum. The band were based in New York but, in 1983, their *Unchained* EP got picked up for distribution in England and they travelled to London. They headlined at the club that February, appearing as a living, breathing, all-action guitar-, bass- and drum-thumping Marvel comic. Blowing up hot water bottles, chewing through mic stands and some swashbuckling with a papier mache sword all featured as

REM's first Marquee gig, November 1983.

accompaniments to full-on thrash metal. The audience apparently loved it and Thor thundered back for two further nights in May.

Hardly any less cartoonish were West Coast thrash-metal merchants Metallica. They arrived in the UK expecting to play a series of thousand-plus-capacity venues on a joint three-band Hell on Earth tour. Except the tour had proved an epic miscalculation: the Hammersmith Odeon was typical in reporting that it had only sold fifteen advance tickets. The tour was cancelled. Instead of putting Metallica on the next flight home, the record company decided to put them up in London to do press interviews while lining up a couple of appearances at the Marquee, on 27 March and 8 April 1984 – the band's first on British soil. In the downtime, the group went out drinking with Lemmy, and bass player Cliff Burton went shopping on Oxford Street and got himself arrested for possession of drugs (the suspicious substances turned out to be treatments for Burton's allergies).Worried that they might not draw enough people to fill the Marquee, singer James Hetfield and drummer Lars Ulrich headed up to the Royal Standard pub in Walthamstow, where metal band Exciter were playing. Music journalist Malcolm Dome, who was with them that night, recalls they were walking around asking people if they'd come and see them play. In the event, Metallica drew a respectable enough crowd to their gig, including most of the staff of metal magazine *Kerrang!* Playing everything at a thousand miles an hour and at a volume that literally set the Marquee shaking 'they blew the place apart,' recalls Dome. When Metallica returned just under two weeks later, they sold the place out. In 1996, Q magazine voted that show as one of the greatest gigs ever.

Lita Ford was the former guitarist of all-girl band the Runaways: she played the club for a second time in June 1984. Her most memorable gig at the Marquee, though, would come in December 1988 when members of Bon Jovi, who she was supporting on a European tour, joined her on stage for the encore. Ford's former Runaways colleague, Joan Jett, was also at the Marquee in December 1984, playing a one-off show as part of her first European tour.

On Wednesday 3 October, it was the turn of Huey Lewis, of New York City, with his band, the News. They were following up a sold-out US tour with a foray into Europe. They played the Marquee on their first night in London. An only half-full club saw the band jam with Phil Lynott, Bryan Adams and Dave Edmunds. Thirty days later Huey Lewis and the News played to a full house at the two thousand-plus-seater Dominion on Tottenham Court Road.

Before the News, Lewis was in a band called Clover, who supported Thin Lizzy on a UK tour, and Phil Lynott became friend and mentor to the young American. Lynott's new, post-Thin Lizzy outfit, Grand Slam, also made a handful of appearances at the Marquee in 1984, starting with a two-nighter in June. The gigs were intended as a record company showcase. Opening with *Top of the Pops* theme 'Yellow Pearl', the sets mixed new songs with Lizzy classics and even threw in 'Parisienne Walkways', the song Lynott co-wrote with Gary Moore. Sadly, none of the record execs were tempted and Grand Slam remained unsigned. After a final show at the Marquee in December the money ran out and the band folded.

The Blow Monkeys opened for electro-pop quintet Crown of Thorns at the Marquee in March 1984. At this point in time, the Dr Robert-fronted band were still finding their way, juggling jazz, blues, punk and pop influences. It would be another couple of years before they found chart success with first hit single 'Digging Your Scene'. Sunday 24 June and Sunday 22 July saw two Marquee dates for the Waterboys. Founder, singer and chief songwriter of the Waterboys, Mike Scott, played a four-week Wednesday-night residency at the club back in January 1982 under the name Funhouse. By the time of the Waterboys' Marquee dates, the band had already released their second album, *A Pagan Place*; they'd appeared on the BBC's *Old Grey Whistle Test* and the night before the first of their two dates they'd been performing on the Pyramid stage at Glastonbury. The band was already on the fast track to bigger things, and by November that year they were headlining the Brixton Academy. On both their Marquee dates, the Waterboys were followed onto the Marquee stage the next night by Lloyd Cole and the Commotions. The shows were around the time 'Perfect Skin' entered the singles chart and the dates were sell-outs. Two weeks or so beforehand, Cole recalls, the band had played to six people at the Mean Fiddler. The band were in the process of writing and recording debut album *Rattlesnakes* and only had ten songs – but in addition to 'Perfect Skin', those songs included crackers like 'Are You Ready to Be Heartbroken?', 'Forest Fire' and 'Rattlesnakes'.

Opening for Lloyd Cole on the second date were the Cardiacs. This was the band's third time in a support slot at the Marquee; the following month, August, they'd play the first of twenty-eight Wardour Street headliners. Formed in Kingston upon Thames in 1977, the Cardiacs' music veered from prog to post punk, although the band themselves always maintained they were a pop group playing pop music (albeit with loads of unusual chord progressions and chord modulations). Reviewing a gig at the Marquee in September 1984, Chris Roberts in *Sounds* described them as 'fabulous, funny, ugly, interesting' and 'very loopy indeed' but also a bit 'sinister'.

Ex-New York Doll Johnny Thunders, who'd played the Marquee a couple of times before, was back in August 1984 for a mammoth five-night run. He was backed by Heartbreakers Jerry Noland and Billy Rath, with occasional vocals from Patti Palladin. Thunders' performances were notoriously erratic, too often marred by stumbling and slurring, but for this week of dates he was sharp and delivered tight sets in which he zipped smartly through classics like 'Chinese Rocks', 'Born to Lose' and 'Too Much Junkie Business'.

August would normally be festival time. Having been turfed out of its Reading home, a new site had been found in good time at Lilford Park in Northamptonshire and for some months a full programme was advertised in full-page ads in the music press, promising Hawkwind, Jethro Tull and Marillion as headliners, supported by the Boomtown Rats, Hanoi Rocks, Phil Lynott's Grand Slam and many others. Unfortunately, the local council refused the licence at the eleventh hour and the event was cancelled.

THE HIT FACTORY

Nigel Hutchings was in the office when he heard a commotion. He was used to seeing the weird and the wonderful at the Marquee, but when Liverpudlian Pete Burns, sporting long black curly hair and make-up, traipsed through with his band Dead or Alive, this was something new.

Back in 1983, producer Peter Collins and former DJ and A&R man Pete Waterman had started working at Marquee Studios, where they produced hit songs for the likes of the Belle Stars and Tracey Ullman. 'The most important thing about a studio is does it have a good sound?' says Waterman. 'And Marquee Studios had a great sound.' In the past eight years, considerable money had been invested in the Marquee's recording set up by Simon White and engineer Phil Harding. Gus Dudgeon can also claim some credit. Dudgeon had produced a run of albums for Elton John, starting with 1970's *Tumbleweed Connection* through to 1975's *Captain Fantastic and the Brown Dirt Cowboy,* and including *Goodbye Yellow Brick*

Road (1973). He had a connection with the Marquee through Chris Barber and he'd said if its studio could provide a state-of-the-art MCI mixing desk he'd bring Elton in. So White ordered one. 'Ours was the first MCI desk in the UK,' says White. Dudgeon brought in Elton as promised to record the album *Blue Moves* (1976); he also used the facilities to record a Kiki Dee album, and mix the Elton John-Kiki Dee duet 'Don't Go Breaking My Heart'. The studio became popular for mixing work, used by an array of other producers including Richard Dodd and Mike Batt, working with house engineers Phil Dunn, John Eden, Gerry Collins and Steve Holroyd. Other artists who recorded at the Marquee Studios over the years included Art Garfunkel, Barclay James Harvest, the Buzzcocks, Camel, the Clash, Joan Armatrading, Lindisfarne, Ralph McTell, Toyah, Vangelis, the Walker Brothers, the Wombles, the Monty Python team and, in 1972, some of the Chelsea football squad who sang on 'Blue is the Colour'.

At the start of 1984 the Collins/Waterman partnership ended: Collins was gravitating more towards rock and album-orientated music, while Waterman wanted to stay in the dance-pop genre. Waterman set about building a new team around him at Marquee Studios. Enter the producing double act of Mike Stock and Matt Aitken. According to Aitken, he and Stock were just the next on the conveyor belt as Waterman tried out different combinations. 'We just gelled,' says Aitken. 'There was obviously a spark between the three of us.'

The first track the trio worked on was 'The Upstroke' by sister act Agent's Aren't Aeroplanes, a Hi-NRG Frankie Goes to Hollywood meets Art of Noise dancefloor filler. It did well in the clubs, but made no impression on the charts. Its real significance was that it signalled the start of the Stock Aitken and Waterman revolution. The next project was brought to them by Proto Records, an independent label: it was a song called 'You Think You're a Man' by Divine. 'We didn't really know much about Divine,' says Aitken. 'We knew he was this gay cult figure, so we were expecting some strange exotic creature to turn up, but he arrived wearing a blazer and tie, looking like a smart Bostonian. He used to like to go to Fortnum's for tea.' The track was a modest hit. The breakthrough came with the third SAW production, Hazell Dean's 'Whatever I Do (Wherever I Go)', which became their first Top 10 hit.

That September, Dead or Alive were about to start on their second album, *Youthquake*, for Epic, a subsidiary of Columbia/CBS records. 'It turned out that the band had heard the Divine and Hazell Dean records,' says Phil Harding, 'and told their manager that they wanted whoever produced those records to produce them, because that's how they wanted to sound.' It was clear to everyone that the first single should be 'You Spin Me Round (Like a Record)'. Waterman recalls the process of producing the track was fraught. All four members of the band had strong opinions on what the song should sound like. 'They were very outspoken,' recalls Harding, 'and as soon as they heard something they didn't like, they would say so, which used to infuriate Mike and Matt.' By the end of that third day the pressure was really mounting. 'We had to play the band this mix the next morning,' recalls Waterman, 'because if we didn't play them something they liked we wouldn't get the money off CBS.' The band were sent home while Waterman and Harding stayed on to finish the mix. 'We were so tired, so knackered, that we ended up not having a clue what we were listening to,' recalls Waterman. 'Then at four o'clock in the morning the desk broke down and we had to wait for the Marquee's technical engineer to come up from Southend to fix it.' Waterman has said that it was the one and only time he did cocaine – he needed the drug to keep him awake during the thirty six-hour session.

When the band returned the next morning, Waterman and Harding set the tape playing with the volume on maximum. Waterman recalls that he and Harding looked at each other thinking, 'God this is fantastic'. The song's writer, Pete Burns, seemed to agree. 'He went nuts,' recalls Waterman. 'He just went crazy, then we knew we had something.' Released in November 1984, it took its time but 'You Spin Me Round' finally made it to No.1 in the UK seventeen weeks after its release, in March 1985.

Stock Aitken and Waterman continued to work at Marquee Studios into 1985, but it was becoming increasingly clear that the facilities were no longer fit for purpose. 'One of the problems,' says Aitken, 'was we were making records of a new type, that was quite high tech, and the Marquee studio was really equipped for old-fashioned recording.' The trio moved into their own London studios, later dubbed the Hit Factory, from where they dominated the charts for the next few years, producing songs for acts including Kylie Minogue, Rick Astley, Jason Donovan, Bananarama, and Mel and Kim. But it all started at the Marquee. 'It was the first proper studio we'd been in where we had control,' says Aitken. 'It was where it felt like we were heading in the right direction.'

GOTH

The March Violets | Fields of the Nephilim | The Stone Roses | Playn Jayn | The Bolshoi | Flesh for Lulu | Balaam and the Angel | The Bangles | The Long Ryders | 10,000 Maniacs | Lone Justice | The Icicle Works | Thrashing Doves | The Babysitters | The Cherry Bombz | The Holloway All-Stars | Wham!

The Ship was the boozer most favoured by Marquee club goers but running it a close second was the Intrepid Fox, which was down the street in the direction of Shaftesbury Avenue. Traditionally a rockers' pub, in the early 1980s it became increasingly haunted by goths, a musical subsect that by 1985 had found a home at the Marquee.

The club hosted some of the original first-wave goths, including the Cure and Sudden Death Cult, and also a single appearance by ur-goths Bauhaus, who made their only Marquee appearance on Saturday 3 November 1979, promoting their recently released single 'Bela Lugosi's Dead'. By 1985, a second wave of goth bands was skulking its way around the live-music circuit, and many of them found an appreciative audience at the Marquee. The March Violets were one of the first, playing a one-off date in September 1984. Three months later, there was a first support slot for Fields of the Nephilim, who the UK music press labelled the 'scarecrows of the Apocalypse'. For live appearances, they took to the stage in weather-beaten cowboy hats and dusters – the weathered effect enhanced by a light dusting of flour. On one occasion this proved problematic when the police detained the band on suspicion of suspect substances; on testing it was determined that the white powder was Mother's Pride Self-Raising White. The Nephilim slowly built up an avid fanbase at the Marquee for their spaghetti western metal (twanging guitar, rumbling vocals), eventually landing a first headliner in 1986, and playing a bunch of further dates in 1987.

On Saturday 19 January 1985, the black-leather-and-eyeliner headliners were Mercenary Skank, goths from Rhyl. It was their third and last date at the club, and they split up not long after. However, the support band, with whom they shared a manager, were only just getting started. This was just the fourth-ever gig for the Stone Roses, following appearances at West Hampstead's Moonlight Club, the Fulham Greyhound and the Ad-Lib (formerly the Kensington), plus a session at Manchester's Piccadilly Radio. Garry Johnson was present at the Marquee for *Sounds*: he dismissed Mercenary Skank as a poor man's Alarm, while the Roses were highly impressive, with 'handsome harmony vocals' and strong original songs like 'Misery Dictionary' and 'Tragic Roundabout'. The Roses returned to the Marquee in August, this time opening for Playn Jayn, a psychedelic rock band who played the Marquee around a dozen times. During the show, singer Ian Brown rammed his mic stand through a stage monitor and the Roses were banned from ever appearing at the club again.

In February 1985, goth-rockers the Bolshoi played their first Marquee headliner. At this point they were a three-piece, plugging their first single, 'Sob Story'. The band was fronted by guitarist/vocalist Trevor Tanner, sardonic, deadpan, camp: 'My favourite thing about playing the Marquee was to do the soundcheck – which always seemed to be in an atmosphere comprised of stale beer, hungover bouncers, soundmen, the bands and anybody else allowed in before opening time – then retire to a nearby pub where no one could find us. Later, we would go back to the Marquee to find it magically transformed into the Shangri-La of live music.' By the time of their ninth and final Marquee gig in August 1987, the Bolshoi had released three albums on the Beggars Banquet label, but poor sales would see a fourth abandoned and the band would call it a day soon after.

Flesh for Lulu made their club debut in March 1985, offering what *Melody Maker* in its review of the gig called 'Black Sabbath numbers disguised as Vincent Price soundtracks'. Danse Society brought their brooding gothic introspection to the club in August, the same month that the three Welsh brothers who made up Balaam and the Angel made a first divine visitation. They were as notable for their big shaggy woollen hair as their music. At a date in December the Balaams were joined on stage by the Cult's Billy Duffy.

It wasn't all pasty-faced gloomsters: in February, the club also played host for a night to the Bangles. The all-girl quartet, who were on a mini European promo tour, brought a little bit of sun-drenched California to Wardour Street, with a jangly set of songs drawn from their 1984 debut album *All Over the Place*, including 'Going Down to Liverpool', 'He's Got a Secret' and new single 'Hero Takes a Fall'. They were followed, in April, by fellow Paisley Underground band the Long Ryders. The date was part of the band's first European tour, also launched in support of a first album, in this case *Native Sons*, a record that had received great acclaim in the UK, where *Melody Maker* had called it 'a modern American classic'. In May, the guest Americans were 10,000 Maniacs. The New York State band were temporarily based in London recording their first major-label album, *Wishing Chair*, when they played a two-nighter at the club. Andy Kershaw was there to see them for the *NME* and report on singer Natalie Merchant's assertive and mesmerising vocals, and the band's chunkily chopped, thigh-pumping mix of seductive psychedelia, folk-rock fallout and Cajun tunes. The following month was the turn of LA-originating countryfied-rockers Lone Justice, introducing their self-titled debut album to a UK audience.

Also in May, Liverpool's Icicle Works made the first of their seven Marquee appearances. The Ian McNabb-fronted band had had a hit in 1983 with 'Love is a Wonderful Colour' but struggled to tempt record buyers with any of their follow-ups. They remained locked in the orbit of the club scene where they delighted loyal audiences with their musical meanderings and droll self-effacing stage act. When they played a two-nighter in August, opening for them were the Thrashing Doves. At this point, the Doves were being touted as the next big thing and for their own Marquee headliner the following month they pulled every A&R man in London. As a result, they were signed to A&M Records in October. They returned to headline the Marquee half a dozen more times.

There was less headbanging at the Marquee these days but there were still evenings when the amps were turned up to eleven. That was the case with the Babysitters, who debuted at the club in October 1984 but properly made the club their home in 1985/86, which was around the time they were being hailed in the press as the 'best worst band in the world', thanks to songs like 'Rock'n'Roll Chicken' – sample lyric: 'It was on my head/On my head/A rock'n'roll chicken sitting on my head...' Singer Buttz Babysitter arrived in London in 1981, a seventeen-year-old punk. Hanging round Soho, life became a ritual of a few pints at the Intrepid Fox, off to a gig at the Marquee and then finishing things off at the St Moritz. The Marquee was simply 'the place to be', says Buttz, and he began casually working there collecting glasses. In the meantime, the Babysitters formed as a glam-punk band in August 1983 with Buttz on vocals, Stik on drums, Boo on bass and Jimbo on guitar. Buttz approached Bush for a shot at the Marquee. 'It was the start of a beautiful relationship,' recalls Buttz. 'All our tours ended with two nights at the Marquee. We'd turn up battered and bruised, and relax there. It was a party every gig.'

The 'Sitters were friends with Hanoi Rocks, touring with them on several occasions. When Hanoi's drummer, Razzle, died in a car accident, the 'Sitters played a gig at the Marquee in his memory and during the encore were joined on stage by the rest of the Rocks, plus Stiv Bators (of Lords of the New Church). The band recorded a show at the club for a five-track EP (*The Babysitters Live at the Marquee*; 1986). 'It was always an intense show in Wardour Street,' says Buttz. 'I truly believe that the crowd felt a part of the show at the Marquee.'

Another band with a Hanoi Rocks connection were Cherry Bombz. After the Rocks broke up, three members, Andy McCoy, Nasty Suicide and Terry Chimes joined with Anita Chellamah, previously of Toto Coelo ('I Eat Cannibals'), to form the flashy, trashy, hairsprayed glam-metal Cherry Bombz. They debuted at the Marquee with two sold-out nights in December 1985, which they followed with another two-nighter the following March. Their last appearance, in September 1986, was recorded for a live album.

Apart from Chris Barber's return as part of the twenty-fifth anniversary celebrations in 1983, the last time the club had featured jazz on the programme was summer 1966. But in the mid 1980s, a new generation of predominantly black British musicians were re-energising the UK jazz scene. This was the impetus for the Marquee to introduce a weekly jazz night, starting in June 1985. The series kicked off on Sunday 2 June with the Holloway All-Stars, a Latin big band from north London. Subsequent Sundays featured trombonist Annie Whitehead, the John Bennett Band, saxophonist Gail Thompson and an outfit called G-Swing. The experiment lasted just six weeks. The Marquee's reputation as a rock venue kept jazz fans away.

The most secretive but ultimately the most widely seen Marquee gig of the year was Wham! On Monday 28 October, the band used the Marquee to film the video for single 'I'm Your Man'. It begins with George Michael and Andrew Ridgeley outside the club on Wardour Street desperately trying to sell tickets for the show to passers-by. A frustrated Michael gets on the phone to his manager (Simon Napier-Bell) to remonstrate with him: 'Look, we've sold eight million albums in the last six months. I don't understand why we're playing the Marquee.' The action then switches to the interior of the club, where the band perform in front of the famous Marquee logo. Nigel Hutchings recalls that George Michael used his office as a dressing room, while Andrew Ridgeley used Harold's room. The audience was made up of actors and models hired from agencies. The song became Wham!'s third UK No.1 and the video was seen by millions.

BUSH

Erasure I INXS I John Waite I Charlie Sexton I Mr Mister I The Sweet I Del Amitri I Nina Hagen I Psychic TV I The Godfathers I Underworld I Reading 1986 I We've Got a Fuzzbox and We're Going to Use It I Cutting Crew I Deacon Blue I The Quireboys I Little Angels

Wham! were not the only pop band camping it up at the Marquee that year. In December 1985, Andy Bell and Vince Clarke appeared as Erasure. Clarke had already experienced success as part of Depeche Mode and as the smaller half of Yazoo, but this was one of the earliest gigs for the new outfit and only the second gig in London, following a date at gay club

Heaven. They appeared with banks of keyboards for Clarke to hide behind and two backing singers in dinner jackets, looking as if they were on loan from the BBC. The crowd was small but enthusiastic – at least they had plenty of room to dance. The experience can't have been too bad because Erasure were back the following February, including a date at the club on their Wonderland tour.

Otherwise, early 1986 seemed to be a time when international stadium rock found a home from home on Wardour Street. Between Erasure's pair of dates there was a January visit from Sydney's INXS – the club's ads in the music press announced that advance tickets for the gig were available to Aussie passport holders only. The band were huge in their home country and this was the equivalent of U2 going to Australia and playing some backstreet pub. Promoting breakthrough album *Listen Like Thieves*, for one night only, INXS squeezed their leather pants, long hair and Antipodean AOR into the Marquee's boutique space. The following week, there was a three-night run for John Waite. These were his first gigs at the Marquee and although it was unusual for an artist playing the club for the first time to be offered more than a single night, Waite rode in on the back of 'Missing You', his 1984 power ballad which had gone Top 10 in the UK and reached No.1 on the US Billboard Hot 100. Waites had flown in from America for the gig (although originally from Lancashire, he was now based in New York), as did singer/songwriter Charlie Sexton, two weeks later, to appear on *The Tube* and make a one-off appearance at the Marquee. Two weeks later, it was the turn of Mr Mister, again, over from the States on a promotional trip, and playing their first live UK date at the Marquee, performing hits 'Kyrie' and 'Broken Wings'. A week on again and it was a date from Mental as Anything, the Australian popsters whose 'Live It Up' would reach No.3 in the UK charts later this year on the back of its inclusion on the *Crocodile Dundee* soundtrack.

Back in the early 1970s the Sweet were one of the icons of glam rock, enjoying massive worldwide chart success with singles like 'Block Buster' and 'The Ballroom Blitz'. But one of guitarist Andy Scott's regrets was that they never played the Marquee. Scott was a regular at the club and says he doesn't ever remember seeing a bad band there. He occasionally raised the issue of the Sweet doing a gig with Jack Barrie, who'd laugh and say,

'We don't have pop bands on at the Marquee.' Scott remembers thinking, 'One day...' That day finally came in February 1986, when a reformed, harder-edged version of the Sweet, with Paul Mario Day (ex-Iron Maiden) on lead vocals, were offered three nights. 'We did a handshake deal and crammed God knows how many people in every night.' At the time, the band was shooting a video featuring glamour model Linzi Drew. 'I said to her, "You don't fancy coming down the Marquee and getting your kit off?", recalls Scott, 'and she laughed and said, "Cover our expenses and I'll bring a friend". So we did and they did exactly what they promised.' An album, *Live at the Marquee 1986*, was released in 1989.

Around this time, early 1986, fine Glasgow band Del Amitri became Marquee regulars, bringing their brand of evocative indie songwriting to Soho. In March, there were two nights in the company of slightly bonkers Berliner Nina Hagen, resplendent with fountain of white hair and shimmering silver catsuit. In May, there was a one-off gig by Psychic TV, the experimental outfit fronted by Genesis P-Orridge and Alex Fergusson. The band's sound was constantly shifting and at the Marquee they played a set that was a little bit psychedelic, a little bit industrial and a little like something resembling early acid house – they included a cover of Pink Floyd's 'Interstellar Overdrive'. The performance was recorded and released in 2013 as *Live at the Marquee*. Also around this time, the Godfathers played the first of nine headliners, all in 1986/87. They were an alternative rock/new wave band from south London who channelled Sixties acts like the Who, but amped up the energy and aggression. The band looked, wrote music journalist Mat Smith, like 'they'd be happier dumping a stiff in the Surrey Docks'. They were totally at home at the Marquee – singer Peter Coyne said that the club was where, 'We made our bones as a band.'

On 30 July 1986, the Marquee hosted the first ever gig by Underworld. Founders Karl Hyde and Rick Smith had previously made eight headline appearances at the club, between January 1984 and July 1985, as part of synthpop quintet Freur. Following the release of the debut Underworld album, *Underneath the Radar*, in February 1988, Hyde and Smith were back for another couple of Marquee headliners. At this point, they were still a poppy synth band, with some funky bass, sounding not unlike

Depeche Mode. It would be another few years and several personnel changes before the band would emerge as techno pioneers with hit album *Dubnobasswithmyheadman*.

At this time, full-page ads were running in the music press with the triumphal message, 'Reading Rocks Again'. After two years away, the festival was back, and in Reading. The Marquee was still denied use of the old site – where the council had done nothing, despite insisting it was needed for a leisure centre – but Harold had come to an arrangement with the farmer who owned the land adjacent to the old site. For its return, Reading veered away from the largely metal line-ups of the early Eighties – since launching in 1980, Castle Donington's Monsters of Rock had cornered that market. Saturday night headliners Saxon were the only hard rock band. The other two headliners were Killing Joke on the Friday and Hawkwind on Sunday. There was plenty of goth (the Mission, the Bolshoi, Balaam and the Angel), some post punks (New Model Army, Lords of the New Church) and a strange miscellany – Ruby Turner, John Waite, It Bites and, of course, the Enid – all of which reflected the fact that permission to proceed with the festival came through at the last minute and chief booker Jack Barrie had just a few weeks to throw it all together. Those who attended felt it was worth it just to see Hawkwind perform with special guest Lemmy for an encore of 'Silver Machine'.

That August saw the first – and only – Marquee appearances of Birmingham all-girl quartet We've Got a Fuzzbox and We're Gonna Use It, who were booked for three consecutive nights. The following month was a debut for London-based rock band Cutting Crew. Singer Nick van Eede had played the Marquee before, back in 1982 with a band called the Drivers: 'We were a three-piece, nutty-combo like XTC on speed. Nigel Hutchings had been tipped off that we were selling out pubs all across Sussex and Kent so he booked us for a quiet Tuesday night.' Van Eede remembers that at 7.45pm Hutchings came through to the dressing room asking where the expected crowd was. 'I told him to trust me – and ten minutes later coach after coach caused chaos in Wardour Street as four hundred fans arrived!' Two weeks later, the band's single '(I Just) Died in Your Arms' hit No.4 in the UK charts and Cutting Crew moved on to bigger gigs. Scottish pop-rock band Deacon Blue, fronted by Ricky Ross, played their first gig south of the border at the Marquee that November. They previewed many of the tracks they would shortly record for their seminal debut album *Raintown*.

Nigel Hutchings had heard other rumblings, too. Rod Stewart's former manager, Billy Gaff, who had been renting offices above the Marquee for years, wanted to buy the club. Hutchings wasn't happy at the prospect. 'I'd no problem with Billy, but I didn't like the people around him. I worried what was going to happen if they all got their fingers in the pot.' Hutchings resigned. He tour-managed a few artists, including Sting and Marillion, then bought a pub. Hutchings' replacement was a simple choice. For a while, Bush had been eager to become involved in booking bands for the club. He scouted other venues for up-and-coming acts, and seemed to have an instinct for spotting talent. He was given Hutchings' job. Bar manager Paul McAvoy became assistant club manager.

As manager, Bush enthusiastically embraced the club's bedrock policy of nurturing new acts, from support slots to headliners to the festival stage. One of the beneficiaries of Bush's patronage were the Quireboys. A relatively new band, they were picking up a few gigs but not really getting anywhere. They hung out a lot at the Marquee when Hutchings was the manager. 'He wasn't exactly our biggest fan,' says Spike, the band's singer. 'He thought we were a bunch of smelly kids – which we were at the time.' They sent tapes in to the club, which were mostly ignored until out of the blue they were asked to do a support slot. 'Bush loved the band straightaway,' recalls Spike. 'And after the show he bought us all a drink and said, "You've got something special."' Bush introduced them to an agent and after becoming their manager brought them in for more shows. 'We supported so many different bands,' says Spike. 'And if somebody pulled out, Bush gave us a call and we'd be straight there.' At the time the band was known as the Queerboys, which had gotten them banned from playing universities and colleges. 'We thought it was a cool name,' says Spike, 'but even Bush said we were going to have to change it.' Audiences built steadily until Bush was ready to give the band a Friday night. 'I'll never forget it,' says Spike, 'because when we arrived there was a queue right up to the Ship. And I was like – Oh my God, this is starting to happen now.' After that Bush gave them a Saturday night. 'Basically, we were like

271

the house band,' says Spike. They were added to the bill for Reading '87 and brought back again the following year and placed higher up the bill. Bush organised a limo from the hotel to the event site: 'And he made the limo stop at the off licence on the way,' recalls Spike.

Little Angels were a rock group from Scarborough that Bush occasionally encouraged with support slots. Each gig involved something like a twenty-hour round trip, driving down in a van, doing the show, then making the long drive back up North. 'We were actually doing that on a weekly basis at one point,' says the band's keyboard player Jimmy Dickinson. 'It was worth it because that's what we had to do to get in front of the right journalists.' Eventually, the band moved to London and became Marquee regulars. 'It was an incredible scene,' recalls Dickinson. 'All the bands talked to each other, the journalists talked to each other, the big rock stars talked to the younger bands, everything was integrated and centred on the club.' Little Angels eventually landed their own headline gig and were offered a record deal outside the club one night, only to turn it down and sign for Polydor later. Bush booked Little Angels as openers for Guns N' Roses. 'I also remember we played for Faith No More and Tesla,' says Dickinson. 'It was incredible. We supported Bow Wow one night, the Japanese rock band, and when we went back to the dressing room there was James Hetfield and Lars Ulrich from Metallica. They were big fans of Bow Wow and we ended up sitting and having a beer with them.'

SPIRITUAL HOME OF ROCK

Then Jerico I The Wonder Stuff I Pop Will Eat Itself I Jonas Hellborg I Chris Isaak I The Georgia Satellites I Bryan Adams I Guns N' Roses I Terence Trent D'Arby I Squeeze I All About Eve I The Mission I Reading 1987

Then Jerico made their last of nine Marquee appearances in January 1987. Since their first support slot in late 1984 they'd been building in confidence and pomp to the point where they now sounded like potential stadium fillers. Later in the year, they released debut album *First (The Sound of Music)* and scored a Top 20 with single 'The Motive'. Opening for Then Jerico were a band playing their first gig outside of their home turf of the Stourbridge and Birmingham area: they were the Wonder Stuff. They were back again in November, this time with their mates from the Midlands, Pop Will Eat Itself. PWEI were billed as headliners, possibly because they'd just released a first album, *Box Frenzy*. For Adam Mole, who played guitar and keyboards with PWEI, playing the club was a dream: 'It was in Wardour Street, and it felt like we'd made it because it's where Mick 'n' Keef met Brian Jones, and Wardour Street was named in the Jam song, "A Bomb in Wardour Street", so it felt special.' The Wonder Stuff were back in December, playing two dates supporting yet another Brummie band, Balaam and the Angel. They finally landed their own headliner the following May, when tickets sold out within seventeen minutes of going on sale.

Hailing from considerably further afield, April saw a one-off date for storming Swedish bassist Jonas Hellborg, whose regular gig was with John McLaughlin's Mahavishnu Orchestra. Also that month, the Marquee hosted the first ever UK appearance of Chris Isaak, of Elvis stunt-double looks and twangy guitar. In May, there was a rabble-rousing sole appearance from Atlanta good ol' boys, the Georgia Satellites, also making their UK debut.

The day before the Georgia Satellites played, the Marquee said goodbye to a friend. Tony Stratton Smith, founder and owner of Charisma Records, former tenant of offices above the club and generous funder of the Marquee bar had died in March. On 6 May, a memorial service for him took place at St Martin in the Fields on Trafalgar Square, after which attendees retired to 90 Wardour Street. 'It was in the afternoon,' remembers journalist Chris Welch, 'and when we got there, it was the first time ever that I had been at the club when the windows were open. I was used to the room being completely black, just stage lights, and I had always imagined it was underground, even though it was on the ground floor. There was daylight pouring in and it created an amazing atmosphere. It felt that Tony Stratton-Smith was being put to rest where he was most at home and his spirit was leaving this earth through the windows of the Marquee.' When the guests had to leave to make way for that evening's band's soundcheck, some of them continued on to the Ship, which, as no doubt someone would have pointed out, is what Strat would have wanted.

In June, stadium-filling superstar Bryan Adams played a night at the Marquee as a warm-up for his support slot with Tina Turner at Wembley Arena. Old friend of the Marquee turned promoter Carl Leighton-Pope had rung Bush to say Adams wanted to play the club and a deal was made on the spot. Bush remembers Adams as 'very down to earth' and the gig as one of the best he ever saw at the club. The setlist that night ran to twenty-three songs and included hits 'Cuts Like a Knife', 'Hearts on Fire', 'Run to You' and 'Summer of '69'. Later that month were the three appearances by Gun N' Roses.

The far-reaching reputation of the Marquee snared another North American artist for whom huge things were predicted – not least by himself – when in early August the club hosted a one-off appearance by Terence Trent D'Arby. His debut album, *Introducing the Hardline According to…* had been released just weeks before (it would go on to sell 1.5 million copies) and the gig was the hottest ticket in town. Bob Geldof was there. John Lydon was there. Ronnie Wood was there. The latter joined D'Arby on stage for a rendition of 'Under My Thumb'. Eight days later, the reformed Squeeze dropped in to revisit the scene of past glories, showcasing tunes from new album *Babylon and On*, but sporting enough to also roll out a few certified classics, including 'Pulling Mussels from a Shell' and 'Another Nail in my Heart'. At the end of the month, there was a debut appearance for folk gothsters All About Eve, who sprung a surprise on the audience with their support band, the Mission, who were doing a secret warm-up for their appearance that coming weekend at Reading.

The Mission headlined the Friday night of Reading that year, setting the tone for a weekend heavy on gothickry and college-circuit acts (the Fall, Icicle Works, Fields of the Nephilim, the Godfathers, All About Eve, the Bolshoi). Rock was represented by Saturday night headliners Status Quo, as well as Magnum, Lee Aaron, Terraplane, the Quireboys and the Babysitters. There was a debut for Zodiac Mindwarp and the Love Reaction, who managed to get into a bottle fight with the audience. *Daily Mirror*-contest-winning-band Glory also traded missiles until the singer threw a wobbler, headed for the nearest monitor and would have thrown that too had security not dashed on stage and tackled him. The Georgia Satellites delivered what many considered the performance of the weekend. There was silliness in the form of spoof metal band Bad News, put together for Channel 4 TV series the *Comic Strip Presents…* but subsequently turned into a real-life gigging band featuring Ade Edmondson, Nigel Planer and Rik Mayall. They were joined on stage at Reading by Brian May for a cover of 'Bohemian Rhapsody'. Closing the festival on the Sunday night was Alice Cooper who staged all the theatrics from his 'Nightmare Returns' tour including the snake, the blow-up doll, the dancer in rubber underwear, the straitjacket, the giant Frankenstein and the guillotine. Nobody was following that.

LAST NIGHT ON WARDOUR STREET

Robert Plant | John Shuttleworth | Faith No More | Dumpy's Rusty Nuts | Sam Brown | Transvision Vamp | Joe Satriani | Lisa Dominique

If the stars had come out for Terence Trent D'Arby at the Marquee, then there were constellations present for Robert Plant on 3 February 1988. The last time Plant appeared at the club, back in 1971 with Zeppelin, he'd been an Olympian god. In the intervening years he'd slid some way down the mountain, but he still commanded substantial reverence. There was an odd choice of support act: John Shuttleworth, alter ego of Graham Fellows, who ten years previously scored a hit as Jilted John. As Shuttleworth, he appeared as a middle-aged man in spectacles sat before a rickety keyboard singing anecdotal ditties about life in Lancashire. 'Some of my most memorable early John Shuttleworth gigs were at the Marquee,' recalls Fellows. His act then was more vaudeville than comedy. 'It involved miming to a backing track on a cassette player hidden in the shell of a large Farfisa organ. On top of the organ were various clockwork toys like a somersaulting dog and a robot, and I'd wave a plastic snake around.

The Marquee's drunken heavy rock audiences lapped it up, though I'm not sure what Robert Plant thought of it.' Fellows remembers that 'John Shuttleworth' had some photos taken with the former Led Zep singer but Plant's PR company never sent him any copies.

Plant previewed tracks from forthcoming album *Now and Zen*, but he also played nice with the audience by throwing in covers of Zeppelin's 'In the Evening', 'Trampled Under Foot' and 'Misty Mountain Hop'. There were also covers of John Lee Hooker's 'Dimples' and, for an encore, the Doors' 'Break on Through (to the Other Side)'.

As Robert Plant played on the Wednesday, Friday and Saturday saw the debut Marquee performances by Faith No More. They were the last dates on the Californian funk-metal band's first UK tour. At this point, a mohawk-sporting Chuck Mosley was still the frontman. There was a buzz around the band – 'When Faith No More visit the UK in January move mountains to be there,' *Sounds*' Neil Perry had previously advised – and by the time they got to the Marquee, having already played Camden's Dingwalls to kick

The return of Robert Plant, February 1988.

off the tour, the place was heaving. Most of the set was drawn from the previous year's album *Introduce Yourself*, from which the single 'We Care a Lot' had just been released. Amid the Beastie Boy-style raps, stormy guitars and compressed dance beats, were random references to classic rock, including a segment of 'Stairway to Heaven' and a cover of Black Sabbath's 'War Pigs'. In May 1992, Faith No More were back at the club for the UK album release party of *Angel Dust*. A select crowd of journalists and friends was invited to be the lucky few to hear FNM, in a secret gig advertised under the pseudonym Haircuts that Kill, play songs from their album a month before its release. The gig also acted as a warm-up for the band's upcoming stadium tour with Guns N' Roses.

Otherwise, the programme in 1988 was the typical eclectic mix of musical genres and bands on the way up, on the way down and not going anywhere much at all that had always characterised the club. The new wave of prog was still much in evidence, with regular appearances from the likes of Geoff Mann, IQ, Pallas and Pendragon. There was plenty of rock from established Marquee favourites like Chrome Molly, the Quireboys, Samson, Shy, Terraplane and Wolfsbane. There was folk-rock from Paddy Goes to Holyhead, electro-cow-punk from Howard Hughes and the Western Approaches, revivalist rock'n'roll from Buddy Curtess and the Grasshoppers, Canadian alt-rock from the Dave Howard Singers, and inexhaustible post-punkery from Lords of the New Church and Chelsea.

There was also still Dumpy's Rusty Nuts, a biker rock band, playing heavy, riff-driven bar boogie. The two gigs they played in July 1988 were their fifty-first and fifty-second at the Marquee since debuting as the opening act for Spider in August 1982. 'It was always a great venue to play,' says singer and lead guitarist Graham 'Dumpy' Dunnell. 'A memorable gig was when Lemmy guested with us Christmas '86 playing not bass but a borrowed Stratocaster. At one gig I walked out into the audience playing my Gibson SG cordless when someone said that Joey Tempest from the band Europe was in the audience, so he was brought on stage and did "Johnny B Goode" with us.' The band toured extensively playing biker pub and club venues, and music festivals (they were on the bill at Reading twice), but the Marquee was their home from home and where they recorded a double live album, *Somewhere in England*, in 1984. 'A great experience,' says Dumpy. 'The audience was in great form that night.' The two gigs they played in July 1988 would be their last on Wardour Street.

In 1987, a safety inspection committee determined that the façade of the building at No.90 was threatening to crumble as a result of the constant vibrations from the Marquee stage. Added to which, the owners of the property had let Harold know that when the very favourable lease he'd signed back in 1964 came to an end, which it was about to do, they were not inclined to renew and they were instead going to sell the freehold. Harold, as the sole occupier of the whole building was offered first refusal. He passed – at the age of sixty-three, Harold had no interest in becoming a property developer. Instead, Harold sold on the freehold option, plus the goodwill and name of the Marquee club to Billy Gaff. It was a decision he never regretted. Had the lease not run out, perhaps things might have been different, though Harold believes it would have been only a matter of a few more years before he walked away: 'The people that I knew and drank with had either died or given up, so I really had nothing to go down to the club for.' A consortium was put together to manage the development of the property. The idea, says Simon White, who was involved in organising the sale, was that another property would be acquired as a temporary home for the Marquee until 90 Wardour Street was redeveloped, then the club could move back. 'I didn't believe that for one moment,' says Bush.

Last night at the Marquee, 31 July 1988.

Meanwhile, the club went on as normal, with notable appearances in June from singer Sam Brown – this was around the time she released her debut album and single of the same name, 'Stop!' – and, over the next couple of weeks, New York's Living Colour and the Wendy James-fronted Transvision Vamp, who had just released their single 'I Want Your Love'. On 18 July, American rock guitarist Joe Satriani headlined. In the midst of his first overseas tour, he was playing just four dates in the UK, one of which was the Marquee. 'Before the show I forgot my backpack at a fish and chips shop around the block. It had all my stage gear in it. I rushed back to the shop in a panic, it was still there! I took this as a good omen. That night at the Marquee was such an important and pivotal show for me!'

On Sunday 31 July, the final night at Wardour Street arrived. Bush was told not to make a big deal out of it, after all the club wasn't closing for good. The headliner that night was *Kerrang!* magazine's favourite East Yorkshire rock chick, Lisa Dominque. When the last song finished fans invaded the stage. Lemmy was there, along with Bush, who recalls, 'One guy made straight for Lisa and Lemmy hit him over the head with a microphone and the thud went straight through the sound system – BOOM!' People were ripping off bits of the place to take away as souvenirs. 'One fella took the backstage door,' recalls Bush. Fish of Marillion yanked off the Charrington sign from the beer tap on the bar.

Not long after, the builders went in. The partnership between Billy Gaff and the property development company did not last long. The outcome was the developers remained in control of 90 Wardour Street and Billy Gaff kept the rights to the Marquee. The majority of the site was redeveloped as a restaurant, while the original entrance to the club became the front door to the Soho Lofts apartments. 'I was absolutely gutted when the Marquee club in Wardour Street closed,' says Fish. 'I still walk past it and get little pangs in my stomach and think, how the fuck could they let that happen?'

105–107 CHARING CROSS ROAD

With Billy Gaff now in charge, the Marquee moved to 105–107 Charing Cross Road, which was just three streets from Wardour Street, on the eastern edge of Soho. It was a five-minute walk from the old venue to the new. The building was a former cinema, opened in 1911 as the Cambridge Circus Cinematograph and closed as the Cannon Charing Cross in January 1987. The official opening was delayed by neighbours worried about the potential noise, but after in excess of £100,000 was spent on soundproofing, the launch for the new Marquee took place on 16 August 1988. The act on the first night were Kiss. The band were in the UK to do the Monsters of Rock show at Donington and Bush was offered them by super-agent John Jackson over the phone. 'It was packed out,' recalls Bush, 'and the West End came to a standstill.'

Numerous regulars from 90 Wardour Street transferred over to the new venue, including Buddy Curtess and the Grasshoppers, Chelsea, Girlschool, Johnny Thunders, Lords of the New Church, Samson, Terraplane, Wrathchild and, inevitably, Dumpy's Rusty Nuts, all in the

marquee theclub

105-107 Charing Cross Road.

first few weeks. It was a larger venue, with a comfortable 800 capacity, a balcony for better viewing, a larger stage, better backstage facilities, including a green room and showers, and a Marquee Cafe with its own entrance on Greek Street that allowed the public access even when the club was closed. It succeeded in continuing business much as before and the Marquee on Charing Cross remained an important meeting point for the British rock scene. Notable artists that played the club during this period included Inspiral Carpets (1989), James (1989), Aerosmith (1990), the Black Crowes (1990), Lenny Kravitz (1990), Spiritualized (1990), PJ Harvey (1991), Megadeth (1991), Mötley Crüe (1991), Primus (1991), the Beastie Boys (1992), the Cranberries (1992), Dream Theater (1993) and Oasis (1994). But for those who knew the old place, Charing Cross was lacking. 'It never had the same vibe,' says Fish. 'It lost all the intimacy and the magic. It just became a franchise, like a musical McDonald's. They could put a logo up and all the old posters but it was never going to be the Marquee, never.' Brian James of the Damned and Lords of the New Church played the venue a few times: 'It wasn't the same at all. It had no feeling. It was like – forget it! The Marquee was great, don't sully its name with this kind of crap.' Harold only went once to the venue and was also not impressed: 'I felt the whole thing had lost its focus and soul, and had no leader because Billy himself was in America.'

When Harold sold, he had it written into the contract that there would be no redundancies, and all the staff who wanted to could make the move to the new venue. Bush continued as manager but he didn't take to the new premises. By the end of the year, he'd handed in his notice. Fittingly, the Quireboys played at Bush's last night at the club. Jack Barrie, who'd remained as the Marquee's director, lasted until June 1989, at which point his final bit of negotiating was for his own redundancy package.

Billy Gaff continued to run the Charing Cross venue until its closure in 1995. Today the site is home to the Montagu Pyke pub, part of the Wetherspoon chain. The rights to operate a club called the Marquee were sold to a group of investors that included Dave Stewart of the Eurythmics (who played 90 Wardour Street with the Tourists) in 2001. They opened a new music club at 16 Parkfield Street in Islington the following year but financial problems saw the new venture close within just a few months (the site is now the O2 Academy). The rights were sold on again and bought by entrepreneur Nathan Lowry. He launched his version of the Marquee in 2004 at One Leicester Square in the heart of London's West End, in the space formerly occupied by the Home nightclub. The opening night featured special guest Jimmy Page. The venture lasted around a year. Lowry relaunched in a smaller, 200-capacity venue at 14 Upper St Martins Lane in 2006 but licensing problems with Westminster Council meant this venue lasted just six months.

Harold had sold the rights to the Marquee live music club, but he retained the rights to the name and logo, and other Marquee companies, including sound-and-light business Entec. As well as supplying sound and lighting to the Marquee and Reading festivals, Entec supported tours for numerous artists over the years, including a thirty-year relationship with Keith Albarn's boy, Damon, and his bands Blur and Gorillaz. Entec also worked at festivals across the world, on TV shows such as *Top of the Pops*, *The Tube*, *Crystal Maze* and *Dr Who*, and global events including the London 2012 Olympics. Harold also retained the Reading festival, which went ahead as usual in August 1988. Headliners were Iggy Pop, the Ramones, Meatloaf, Starship, Squeeze and Hothouse Flowers. The bit everyone who attended this year remembers is when Meatloaf was hit squarely on the nose by a thrown bottle and stormed off stage. Bonnie Tyler was up next and she responded to the first missile with a foul-mouthed tirade that stopped the bottle throwing dead and she finished her set to raptuous applause. Despite the decent line-up, with stiff competition from the likes of Donington for rock and Glastonbury for indie (although there was no Glastonbury in 1988), attendances at Reading had been dropping in recent years. Harold decided to look for a partner to shoulder some of the burden, someone with good industry connections who could land top acts for the festival. The search led to Vince Power.

In 1982, Irish businessman Power opened the Mean Fiddler on the site of an old boxing gym in Harlesden. He'd previously worked on demolition crews, in shops and factories, and set up a string of junk shops before going into the music business. The Mean Fiddler struggled until Powers discovered that his cellarman, Dave Phillips, knew the music scene inside out. Under Phillips's stewardship, the club went from strength to strength and by the end of the decade it was one of the capital's most successful music venues. At first, Power was apprehensive about taking up Harold's offer, not knowing anything about running festivals, but eventually a three-year partnership deal was formed. The Mean Fiddler would do the front of house and book the acts, while Harold and Barbara would do the organising.

The revamped Reading 1989 was a big success and the choice of headliners, New Order, the Pogues, the Mission, supported by the likes of the Sugarcubes, Billy Bragg, the Men They Couldn't Hang, the Wonder Stuff, Pop Will Eat Itself and My Bloody Valentine marked a huge shift in the character of the festival. The *NME* declared, 'Some day all festivals will be made this way, everyone will love each other and there'll be no such thing as a bad pop group.' The following year, Mick Jagger and Jerry Hall turned up backstage, mingling with this year's headliners: the Cramps, Inspiral Carpets and the Pixies. Noel Gallagher, at the time the Inspiral Carpets' guitar roadie, also made his first headline appearance on stage, although no one noticed because he was half of a pantomime cow. Reading 1991 (with headliners Iggy Pop, James and the Sisters of Mercy) saw the introduction of a comedy tent, christened by Sean Hughes and Jerry Sadowitz.

Despite the success, behind the scenes it wasn't working with the Mean Fiddler organisation. 'We didn't really get on,' admits Barbara. 'It was a personality clash.' After honouring the three-year agreement, Harold and Barbara walked and decided to promote the 1992 festival alone. They got Paul McAvoy, who had worked at the Marquee, to book the acts, which he did under some intimidation because Mean Fiddler wasn't happy at all about the situation. Power tried to put on another festival in Reading at the same time. 'But in the end the police stopped it,' recalls Barbara, 'saying they couldn't have two events on at the same time. Vince was absolutely furious.' An impressive line-up was put together for Reading '92, which included Public Enemy, Nick Cave, PJ Harvey, Manic Street Preachers, the Charlatans and Smashing Pumpkins. The real coup was getting Nirvana to close the festival. It was their second Reading performance – they appeared in 1991 on the afternoon of the Friday. Since then, they'd released *Nevermind* and become arguably the biggest rock band in the world. As such, Kurt Cobain was given licence to programme the day's bill, so preceding Nirvana were the Melvins, Screaming Trees, Pavement, L7, Teenage Fanclub, Mudhoney and Nick Cave – 'no lame-ass Limey bands,' as Cobain put it. Mocking the rumours of his drug-induced poor health, Cobain was pushed onstage in a wheelchair, wearing a hospital gown. He pretended to struggle to his feet, then collapsed to the ground. After lying motionless briefly, he got up, strapped on his guitar and the band kicked into 'Breed'. The performance included almost all of *Nevermind* and ended with Cobain playing the 'Star-Spangled Banner' and the band trashing their instruments. It was their last UK performance.

Barbara quite took to the band: 'They were really nice chaps. They came backstage and popped their heads in the festival worker's bar and said, "Oh, can we come in here?" And we said, "No, this is for the staff." And they begged and begged and we said, "Alright then," and they spent all their time in there.' Nicky Wire of Manic Street Preachers also recalls that year's festival with fondness: 'In all honesty, Reading is our favourite festival. It was the first time we were really accepted by a big audience when we played in ninety-two and it made us feel like we could be a really big rock band.'

Plans were begun for the following summer's event, but it never happened. Since returning to Reading in 1986, Harold and Barbara effectively had two landlords. There was the farmer on whose land the festival took place, and also the owner of a small strip of land that ran along the river that was vital for site access. Harold and Barbara had always kept the identity of this landowner a secret. As luck would have it, Vince Power was at a function, talking to a fellow invitee when the conversation turned to music and the Reading festival. It turned out that Power was talking to the very man who owned that small riverside strip. Power immediately asked if he could rent the land off him and a deal was made. Meanwhile, Harold and Barbara were busy booking acts for next summer. It was only when they put in an application for a licence that they discovered what had happened. Without proper access, the council refused permission. Instead, it was Power who secured the licence for the festival. Disappointed and a little angry, Harold and Barbara were ultimately philosophical: they'd had a good run and were unlikely to have continued for many more years. Still, it would have been preferable to have bowed out on their own terms. Eventually, Power would sell out, but the Reading festival continues to this day as the world's oldest continuously running popular music festival.

FAREWELL, HAROLD

In December 2014, for one night only, the Marquee returned to its most celebrated site when Floridita, the restaurant and bar that now occupied 90 Wardour Street, hosted the fiftieth-anniversary celebration of the club. The evening included special guests, and an exhibition of classic photography and archive material from the club. There was live music from Marquee stalwarts Ten Years After, and from Cutting Crew. Otherwise, the only evidence of the club on the street it rocked for thirty-four years is a blue Heritage Foundation plaque, erected in 2009, that reads 'Keith Moon, 1946–1978, legendary rock drummer with "The Who", performed here at the site of the Marquee Club in the 1960s.'

Earlier in 2014, there had been another landmark party, this one in celebration of Harold's ninetieth birthday. It was held in the clubhouse at the Richmond Athletic Association Ground, site of the first NJF Jazz Festival back in 1961. Many of the same people that were at the birthday party were back at the same venue three years later for the reception that followed Harold's funeral: he died on 22 September 2017. He never stopped being a Dixieland jazz fan and at the reception Chris Barber led a New Orleans marching band in tribute.

For many of the musicians who played the Marquee and appeared at the various festivals, Harold was a supportive and encouraging personality. 'I remember him as a gentleman,' says Chris Judge Smith of Van der Graaf Generator. 'And very unlike the senior music business figures I generally came across, most of whom were either predatory sleazebags or straightforward Soho thugs. I believe Harold really cared about the music.'

As for the club Harold created, it is now celebrated as one of the world's greatest ever music venues. 'It was a place that was loved,' says Ed Bicknell, former manager of Dire Straits, Gerry Rafferty and Bryan Ferry. 'People loved to play there. It was like the music was in the walls. It just had something. And you can't create that. You can't design that. It's an organic thing.'

'The Marquee always had an edge to it,' says Graham Lewis of cult punk band Wire. 'It was because of who'd played there. Places like the Marquee take on auras, and it is people that make the places.'

'It was scruffy and dark, but you could feel the excitement that had been generated in that place even when it was empty,' says Lindisfarne's Ray Laidlaw. Michael Monroe of Hanoi Rocks saw some of the greatest shows of his life at the club. 'I'm proud to have been part of it all when it was happening and music was still great with so many cool bands around.' Sentiments echoed by CP Lee of Alberto Y Lost Trios Paranoias: 'Just knowing that you could go there if it was your night off, being known on the door and being allowed in was wonderful. It was an accolade. You were part of something that was central to culture, this great simmering vat of change.'

Perhaps guitarist Bernie Tormé summed it up best: 'The Marquee was a big venue in a small club.'

MARQUEE TIMELINE

This timeline covers the period from the launch of the original Marquee on Oxford Street to the closing of 90 Wardour Street, a span of 30 years, three months and two weeks. The number of acts who appeared at the club during that time runs to the thousands, so this timeline can only include highlights and most frequent performers.

1958
April
19   The Marquee launches with the Joe Harriott Quintet and Vic Ash Quartet playing the opening night

1959
August
Chris Barber and Johnny Dankworth make their first appearances at the club, taking up residencies on Wednesday and Thursday respectively

October
Humphrey Lyttelton is added to the club's weekly line-up occupying a new Tuesday night session

1960
August
13   Saxophonist Dick Morrissey plays his first gig; he'll play the club regularly until his last gig in 1973, as part as jazz fusionists If

September
Dudley Moore makes his debut, fronting his Trio. He will make around 70 appearances at the club between now and his last in December 1964.

1961
August
26–27   The 1st National Jazz Festival is held at Richmond, in Surrey. The line-up includes Chris Barber and Ottilie Patterson, Johnny Dankworth, Joe Harriott, Tubby Hayes and Ronnie Ross

1962
January
10   Alexis Korner and Cyril Davies combine with members of Chris Barber's band

to play a set of R&B numbers in the intervals between the jazz

April
Alexis Korner and Cyril Davies make further appearances playing R&B in the intervals between Chris Barber sets

May
3   Blues Incorporated play the first of 38 gigs, all in 1962, launching Thursday night R&B sessions

June
The club launches Monday night sessions

July
12   The Rolling Stones play their first-ever gig, the first of 9 at the Marquee
28–29   The 2nd National Jazz Festival is held at Richmond, with a line-up that includes Kenny Ball, Chris Barber and Ottilie Patterson, Ken Colyer, Johnny Dankworth, Wally Fawkes, Joe Harriott, Tubby Hayes, Humphrey Lyttelton and Ronnie Ross

December
16   First gig by the Brian Auger Trio
27   Final appearance by what is now Alexis Korner's Blues Incorporated before he defects to the Flamingo

1963
January
3   The Cyril Davies All-Stars play the first of 53 gigs; the Rolling Stones are support for the first five before they are sacked
7   Blues by Six play the first of 10 gigs, in a new Monday night R&B residency

February
7   Long John Baldry replaces the Rolling Stones as support for the Cyril Davies All-Stars; including his appearances with

287

Blues Incorporated, the All-Stars and Steampacket, Long John Baldry plays the Marquee over 200 times, the most of any artist

March
11 The Mann-Hugg Blues Brothers play the first of 17 gigs

May
The club launches Tuesday night sessions, called Live New Departures, with jazz and poetry

July
The poetry is abandoned and Tuesday nights from now on feature jazz, starting on 2 July with Dinah Kaye and Tommy Whittle

15 The Mann-Hugg Blues Brothers become the Blues Brothers for the first of 5 gigs; support is from debutants the Roosters, featuring Eric Clapton and Tom McGuinness
29 Chris Farlowe plays the first of 6 gigs

August
10–11 The 3rd National Jazz and Blues Festival is held at Richmond, with a line-up that includes Long John Baldry, Chris Barber and Ottilie Patterson, Acker Bilk, the Cyril Davis All-Stars, Joe Harriott, Tubby Hayes, Ronnie Ross and the Rolling Stones
19 Manfred Mann, formerly the Blues Brothers, play the first of 72 gigs

September
14 The Brian Auger Trinity play the first of 20 gigs

November
4 John Mayall's Bluesbreakers, supporting Manfred Mann, play the first of 47 gigs

December
24 American bluesman Sonny Boy Williamson plays the first of 8 gigs

1964
John Gee joins the Marquee as its full-time manager

January
9 Long John Baldry takes over the Thursday night residency following the death of Cyril Davies the previous week. At one of the Thursday nights this month, Rod Stewart makes his Marquee debut as Baldry's harmonica player; he

will go on to play the club with the Soul Agents, Steampacket, Shotgun Express, the Jeff Beck Group and the Faces
23 The Yardbirds, featuring Eric Clapton and supporting Long John Baldry, play the first of 45 gigs

February
3 The Cheynes, featuring Mick Fleetwood and Peter Bardens, play the first of 10 gigs

March
8 Stan Getz, the Tubby Hayes Quintet, Ronnie Scott Quartet and Betty Bennett play the final night at 165 Oxford Street
13 Sonny Boy Williamson, Long John Baldry and the Yardbirds play the grand opening at 90 Wardour Street
22 BBC2 TV begins using the Marquee as a venue for recording of its Jazz 625 programme

April
13 The Mark Leeman Five, supporting Manfred Mann, play the first of 87 gigs
30 Rod Stewart receives a first billing, 'featuring with' Long John Baldry and the Hoochie Coochie Men – although he has been part of the group since January

August
7–9 The 4th National Jazz and Blues Festivals is held at Richmond, with a line-up that includes Mose Allison, Long John Baldry, Kenny Ball, Chris Barber, the Graham Bond Organisation, Georgie Fame, Manfred Mann, the Rolling Stones, Jimmy Witherspoon and the Yardbirds
27 Alex Harvey, fronting his Soul Band and supporting Memphis Slim, plays the first of his 38 gigs

September
3 The Moody Blues play the first of 21 gigs

November
24 The Who play the first night of their Maximum R&B residency and the first of 30 gigs at the Marquee
26 Howlin' Wolf plays the first of 3 gigs

December
3 Rod Stewart and the Soul Agents play the first of 9 gigs; this is the same day Stewart joins the band

1965
Jack Barrie joins the Marquee as an assistant to John Gee

January

The first single recorded in the Marquee's studio, 'Go Now!' by the Moody Blues, hits No.1 in the UK charts

30   The Joe Harriott Quintet appear at the Marquee for the last time. Playing twice a week in the 1950s and once a week through the first years of the 1960s, Harriott racked up possibly as many as 500 appearances at the club

February

10   Wednesday becomes folk night
15   Eric Clapton makes his last appearance as a Yardbird

March

1   The Spencer Davis Group play the first of 22 gigs
5   Gary Farr and the T-Bones play the first of 67 gigs
7   The Bill Evans Trio play the first of two gigs, both this month
8   Jeff Beck makes his Marquee debut as a Yardbird

May

7   Elkie Brooks makes her only solo appearance

June

14   Solomon Burke plays the first of 2 gigs

July

5   The Animals play the first of 5 gigs
8   The Graham Bond Organisation, featuring Jack Bruce and Ginger Baker, play the first of 17 gigs
22   Steampacket, featuring Long John Baldry, Rod Stewart, Julie Driscoll and Brian Auger, play the first of 17 gigs

August

6-8   The 5th National Jazz and Blues Festival is held at Richmond, with a line-up that includes The Animals, Kenny Ball, Chris Barber, Spencer Davies, Georgie Fame, Manfred Mann, the Moody Blues, Steampacket, the Who and the Yardbirds
24   Lulu and the Luvvers play their only gig

September

David Bowie and the Lower Third begin a series of Saturday afternoon slots in partnership with Radio London, billed as the Inecto Show

15   Al Stewart plays the first of 32 gigs

October

The Beatles record their Christmas fan club message at the Marquee's studio

8   David Bowie and the Lower Third, supporting Gary Farr and the T-Bones, play the first of 4 gigs

November

2   The Who return for a one-off gig
16   Eric Clapton turns up to jam with the Spencer Davis Group

December

21   The Who return for a one-off gig
27   Bluesology, featuring Reg Dwight (Elton John), supporting Ronnie Jones and the Blue Jays, play the first of 19 gigs

1966

January

30   First Spontaneous Underground event

February

7   Stevie Wonder (aged fifteen) plays his only headliner
11   David Bowie and the Buzz play the first of 4 gigs
13   Georgie Fame plays the first of 7 gigs

March

13   The Pink Floyd play the first of 14 gigs, as part of the third Spontaneous Underground event
22   The Small Faces play the first of 2 gigs

April

1   The Move play the first of 27 gigs
10   David Bowie and the Buzz play the first of 10 Sunday afternoon 'Bowie Showboats'
11   John Mayall's Bluesbreakers return to the club after a break of 18 months; it's the first time at the Marquee with Eric Clapton in the band
18   The Lovin' Spoonful play their only gig
25   The Herd, featuring Peter Frampton, play the first of 41 gigs

May

3   Eric Clapton joins his old band the Yardbirds on stage and jams with Jeff Beck
9   John Lee Hooker plays the first of 2 gigs (the second is in June 1967)

June

20   Shotgun Express, featuring Rod Stewart, Beryl Marsden, Peter Bardens, Peter Green and Mick Fleetwood, play their only Marquee gig
21   Jimmy Page plays his first gig with the Yardbirds – he's on bass, with Jeff Beck on guitar. It's the last time the group will

play the club until they reform for the Marquee's 25th birthday in 1983

July

10 Simon and Garfunkel play their only gig

12 The Creation play the first of 5 gigs

13 Sandy Denny plays a solo gig supporting the Spinners

25 John Mayall's Bluesbreakers play their first Marquee gig with new guitarist Peter Green

29–31 The 6th National Jazz and Blues Festival is held at Windsor, with a line-up that includes Kenny Baker, Chris Barber, Cream, Spencer Davies, Georgie Fame and the Blue Flames, Chris Farlowe, Spencer Davis, the Move, Small Faces and the Who

August

16 Cream play the first of 6 gigs

26 The Syn play the first of 35 gigs

November

5 The Crazy World of Arthur Brown open for the Herd for the first of their 8 gigs

21 The Iveys support the Brian Auger Trinity for the first of their 13 gigs, which come to an end when they sign to the Beatles' Apple label and become Badfinger

1967

January

19 Marmalade support Pink Floyd for the first of their 42 gigs

24 Jimi Hendrix plays the first of 2 gigs

February

19 The Bonzo Dog Doo-Dah Band play the first of 6 gigs

21 Cat Stevens plays his only gig

March

11 1-2-3 play the first of 7 gigs

21 Family open for Cream for the first of their 23 gigs

April

11 The Jeff Beck Group play the first of 4 gigs

May

Jack Barrie takes over the management of members-only club La Chasse, which becomes the unofficial Marquee bar

26 Terry Reid plays the first of 23 gigs

June

12 Procol Harum play the first of 2 gigs

20 Ten Years After open for John Lee Hooker for the first of their 29 gigs

August

11–13 The 7th National Jazz and Blues Festival is held at Windsor, with a line-up that includes Jeff Beck, the Crazy World of Arthur Brown, Cream, Donovan, Fleetwood Mac, Marmalade, John Mayall's Bluesbreakers, the Move, the Nice, the Small Faces, Ten Years After and Tomorrow

15 Peter Green's Fleetwood Mac play the first of 6 gigs

October

1 The Nice play the first of 32 gigs

November

14 Traffic play the first of 4 gigs

1968

January

The start of 'students-only' Wednesday nights

29 Fairport Convention play the first of 7 gigs

February

8 Robert Plant and the Band of Joy, opening for Edwin Starr, play the first of 2 gigs

9 Jethro Tull play the first of 19 gigs

10 Irish band Taste, featuring Rory Gallagher, play the first of 38 gigs

March

29 Fleetwood Mac, now minus Peter Green, play the first of 3 gigs with this new line-up

April

23 The Who play a gig, presenting *Tommy*, celebrating the Marquee's tenth anniversary

May

16 Joe Cocker plays the first of 16 gigs

June

21 Free, opening for Taste, play the first of 15 gigs

August

5 Yes, opening for the Nite People, play the first of 38 gigs

9–11 The 8th National Jazz and Blues Festival takes place at Kempton Park Racecourse, Sunbury, with a line-up that includes Jeff Beck, Joe Cocker, Spencer

MARQUEE TIMELINE

Davis, Deep Purple, Fairport Convention, the Incredible String Band, Jethro Tull, Jerry Lee Lewis, John Mayall, the Nice, Al Stewart, Traffic and Tyrannosaurus Rex

14 Village, opening for Joe Cocker, play the first of 27 gigs

September
30 Canned Heat play their only gig

October
18 Led Zeppelin, advertised as the Yardbirds, play the first of 4 gigs

November
12 Muddy Waters plays the first of 2 gigs (the second is one week later)
27 Van der Graaf Generator, opening for Yes, play the first of 22 gigs

December
6 The Rolling Stones use the Marquee for rehearsals for *The Rock and Roll Circus* TV show
10 Led Zeppelin play their second gig
17 The Who perform a special Christmas party show; it is their last appearance

1969
January
Mondays become audition nights

1 Yes begin a run of 27 Wednesdays over the next seven months
3 Earth make the first of 4 appearances, before becoming Black Sabbath

March
28 Led Zeppelin play their third gig
29 American West Coast band Country Joe and the Fish play their only gig

May
16 Steppenwolf make their only appearance; support comes from King Crimson playing the first of 17 gigs

June
14 Audience play the first of 23 gigs
15 David Bowie makes a low-key return to the Marquee, sharing a bill with folkies James Taylor and the Strawbs, featuring Rick Wakeman

July
8 Soft Machine play the first of 3 gigs

August
9–11 The 9th National Jazz and Blues Festival is held at Plumpton, with a line-up that

includes the Bonzo Dog Band, Family, King Crimson, the Nice, Pink Floyd, Soft Machine, the Strawbs, Van Der Graaf Generator, the Who and Yes

11 Renaissance play the first of 16 gigs

September
9 Deep Purple are advertised but don't play

October
4 Writing on the Wall play the first of 42 gigs

November
14 Black Sabbath play the first of 5 gigs
24 Hawkwind play the first of 2 gigs

1970
January
John Gee retires and is replaced by Jack Barrie

February
The club gets an alcohol licence and opens a bar

3 David Bowie plays and after the gig meets Mick Ronson for the first time at La Chasse
4 Genesis play the first of 11 gigs

March
27 Slade, opening for the Crazy World of Arthur Brown, play the first of 13 gigs

April
The Marquee introduces Saturday night disco sessions and Sunday Night Specials programmed by Tony Stratton Smith

17 Humble Pie, featuring Steve Marriott and Peter Frampton, play the first of 5 gigs
25 Status Quo play the first of 11 gigs

May
8 Wishbone Ash, opening for Slade, play the first of 14 gigs
19 Uriah Heep play the first of 5 gigs
31 Brethren play the first of 3 gigs, before they change their name to Lindisfarne

June
5 Elton John plays his only date as a solo artist

July
3 Pink Fairies play the first of 19 gigs
6 Medicine Head play the first of 25 gigs
9 Stackridge play the first of 18 gigs
14 Supertramp play the first of 5 gigs

291

15	Gentle Giant play the first of 3 gigs
31	US garage rockers MC5 make their only appearance

August

6–9	The 10th National Jazz, Blues & Pop Festival is held at Plumpton, with a line-up that includes Black Sabbath, Caravan, Deep Purple, Family, Peter Green, Cat Stevens, the Strawbs, Van der Graaf Generator, Wishbone Ash and Yes
11	Eric Clapton's Derek and the Dominos play their only gig

September

20	Lindisfarne play the first of 6 gigs
25	The Faces play the first of 4 gigs
30	Mott the Hoople play the first of 2 gigs

October

4	Phil Collins makes his first Marquee appearance with Genesis
29	Barclay James Harvest play the first of 2 gigs

December

9	Genesis play a private party for the Charisma label

1971

January

The club's stripy 'circus' decoration is replaced by all-over black and the classic Marquee logo is added to the back wall of the stage.

February

22	UFO play the first of 46 gigs

March

14	Brazilian singer-songwriter Gilberto Gil plays the first of 7 gigs
23	Led Zeppelin play a fourth and final gig
26	The Rolling Stones film a TV special promoting new album *Sticky Fingers*

April

9	Thin Lizzy, opening for Status Quo, play the first of 8 gigs

May

18	Rory Gallagher plays the first of 11 solo gigs

June

25–27	The 11th National Jazz, Blues and Pop Festival moves to Reading, with a line-up that includes Arthur Brown, Rory Gallagher, Genesis, Lindisfarne, Renaissance, Van der Graaf Generator, Vinegar Joe and Wishbone Ash

July

19	Fela Kuti plays his only show, with support from Ginger Baker

August

1	David Bowie plays with Mick Ronson, previewing songs from the forthcoming *Hunky Dory* album
9–10	King Crimson play two nights supported by Vivian Stanshall

September

21	Nazareth play the first of 11 gigs
22	Legendary rock'n'roller Gene Vincent plays his only gig
30	Vinegar Joe, featuring Elkie Brooks and Robert Palmer, play the first of 16 gigs

1972

February

28	Gary Moore plays the first of 14 solo gigs

April

27	Camel play the first of 12 gigs

May

28	David Essex plays his only gig
31	Roxy Music, supporting UFO, play their only gig

June

20	Krautrock band Amon Duul II play their only gig

August

11–13	The 12th Jazz, Blues and Pop Festival takes place at Reading, with a line-up that includes Curved Air, the Electric Light Orchestra, Shuggie Otis, the Faces, Focus, Genesis, Magma, Status Quo, Ten Years After, Vinegar Joe and Wizzard
24	The Pretty Things play the first of 5 gigs; the other 4 gigs are by the reformed 1980s version of the band

October

The club introduces Sunday night jam sessions

5	Judas Priest play the first of 11 gigs
25	The Average White Band play the first of 8 gigs

November

28	Greenslade, opening for Status Quo, play the first of 10 gigs

December

7	American art-pop outfit Sparks begin 4 consecutive Thursdays
20/21?	Queen make their Marquee debut, either

as one of two bands at a party for RCA on the 20th or opening for Sparks on the 21st – no one is quite sure which

1973
February
10–11   King Crimson, with a. new line-up featuring Bill Bruford, John Wetton and David Cross, preview forthcoming album *Lark's Tongues in Aspic*

April
The club celebrates it 15th anniversary

9   Queen play their first and only headline gig soon after signing with EMI

May
21   Welsh metal band Budgie play the first of 24 headliners

June
12   Gong play the first of 4 gigs
28   Thin Lizzy play their first headliner

July
11   Leo Sayer plays his only gig, opening for the Robin Trower Band
23   Queen, opening for Mahatma, make their last appearance at the club

August
18   Glam rockers Heavy Metal Kids play the first of 16 gigs
22   Medieval rockers Gryphon play the first of 10 gigs
24–26   The 13th Jazz, Blues and Pop Festival takes place at Reading, with a line-up that includes the Faces, Rory Gallagher, Genesis, Lindisfarne, Magma, John Martyn, Stackridge and Status Quo

September
24   Dutch rockers Golden Earring (of 'Radar Love' fame) play their only gig
25   The Edgar Broughton Band play the first of 2 gigs

October
18–20   David Bowie takes over the club for three days of filming for his 1980 Floorshow

December
5   Magma play the first of 2 gigs

1974
January
14   Be-Bop Deluxe, opening for String Driven Thing, play the first of 4 gigs

23   Pub-rockers Chilli Willi and the Red Hot Peppers play the first of 6 gigs

February
14   Bearded Lady play the first of 18 gigs

May
2   Kiki Dee plays the first of 2 gigs
3–5   Rory Gallagher and His Band play three consecutive nights

June
30   Joan Armatrading makes her only appearance

August
23–25   The 14th Jazz, Blues and Pop Festival takes place at Reading, with a line-up that includes the Alex Harvey Band, Barclay James Harvest, Camel, Georgie Fame, Focus, George Melly, Pretty Things, Procol Harum, 10cc, Thin Lizzy and Traffic

October
7   Dr Feelgood play the first of 4 gigs
10   Alberto Y Lost Trios Paranoias play the first of 12 gigs

December
3–4   Ronnie Lane and Slim Chance play two nights

1975
January
10   Kilburn and the High Roads play the first of 5 gigs
17   Ducks Deluxe play the first of 5 gigs

March
10   The Kursaal Flyers play the first of 7 gigs

July
26   The Poodles (later the Fabulous Poodles) play the first of 21 gigs

August
21   Motörhead play the first of 8 gigs

22–24   The 15th Jazz, Blues and Pop Festival takes place at Reading, with a line-up that includes Alberto Y Lost Trios Paranoias, Joan Armatrading, Caravan, Climax Blues Band, Dr Feelgood, Hawkwind, Judas Priest, Kursaal Flyers, the Mahavishnu Orchestra, Supertramp, Thin Lizzy, UFO, Wishbone Ash and Yes

November
11   The Scorpions play the first of 3 gigs

December

22   Jazz fusionists Brand X, featuring Phil Collins on drums, play the first of 3 gigs

1976

February

12   The Sex Pistols, supporting Eddie and the Hot Rods, play the club and are banned from appearing again

24   Prog-rockers the Enid play the first of 39 gigs

March

8   The Stranglers, supporting the Pink Fairies, make a first appearance

April

19–21   Manfred Mann's Earth Band play 3 consecutive nights

May

11–12   AC/DC, supporting Back Street Crawler, play the first of 10 gigs

June

4   AC/DC play their first headliner

7–8   Graham Parker and the Rumour play two nights

August

27–29   Reading Rock 1976 takes place with a line-up that includes AC/DC, Brand X, Camel, Eddie and the Hot Rods, the Enid, Rory Gallagher, Gong, Manfred Mann's Earth Band, Phil Manzanera and Brian Eno, Osibisa, Van der Graaf Generator

November

7   The Stranglers play their second gig and are banned from the club

18   Motörhead play what is intended as their farewell gig

1977

January

22   The Jam play the first of 5 gigs

February

25   Ultravox! play the first of 19 gigs

March

7   The Motors play the first of 10 gigs

28   The Only Ones, opening for Johnny Thunders and the Heartbreakers, play the first of 3 gigs

31   Generation X play the first of 8 gigs

May

1   The Vibrators play the first of 18 gigs

18   Squeeze, opening for the Count Bishops, play the first of 9 gigs

23   X-Ray Spex play the first of 7 gigs

25   The Police, opening for Wayne County, play the first of 5 gigs

June

3   The Boomtown Rats play the first of 5 gigs

8   Wire, opening for John Otway and Wild Willy Barrett, play the first of 19 gigs

20   Alternative TV play their only gig

24   The Police play their first headliner

25   Squeeze play their first headliner

July

3–6   The Damned are booked for four nights but only play two after falling out with the club's management

August

4   The Buzzcocks play the first of 4 gigs

18   Bernie Tormé, opening for the Boomtown Rats, plays the first of 29 solo gigs

21–25   Eddie and the Hot Rods return for an unprecedented five consecutive nights

26–28   Reading 1977 takes place with a line-up that includes Aerosmith, the Doobie Brothers, the Enid, Golden Earring, Hawkwind, the Motors, the Sensational Alex Harvey Band, Thin Lizzy, Ultravox! and Uriah Heep

September

7–8   John Martyn makes his only appearances at the club

9   999 play the first of 12 gigs

11   The Tom Robinson Band plays the first of 3 gigs; Robinson will play a further 4 gigs at the club with Sector 27 and 2 just as Tom Robinson

17   Japan make their one and only appearance, opening for Grand Hotel

October

4   Adam and the Ants, opening for the Buzzcocks, play the first of 16 gigs

21   Sham 69 play their only gig

November

23   XTC play the first of 3 gigs

1978

January

5   Adam and the Ants begin a four-week Thursday residency

February

5   Tubeway Army play the first of 3 gigs

11–13   Ultravox! play three consecutive nights

24–25   The Jam play two nights
26   The Rezillos play the first of 4 gigs

March
14   Dire Straits begin a run of four Tuesdays; in all they will play the club 6 times

May
8–9   Pere Ubu play two nights; support on the second night comes from Nico
10–11   Wilko Johnson plays the first of 26 gigs under his own name
24   The Tourists, featuring Dave Stewart and Annie Lennox, play the first of 8 gigs

June
12–14   The Ian Gillan Band play a three-night residency
27   Tom Petty makes his only appearance

August
7–8   Steve Hillage plays two nights
19–23   Ultravox! play five consecutive nights
26–28   Reading 1978 takes place with a line-up that includes Foreigner, the Ian Gillan Band, the Jam, Lindisfarne, Sham 69, Patti Smith, Squeeze, Status Quo, the Tom Robinson Band and Ultravox!

September
8   The Fall play the first of 6 gigs

November
1   The Skids play the first of 4 gigs
12–13   The Undertones, opening for the Rezillos, play the first of 8 gigs

December
27   The Cure, opening for Ultravox!, play the first of 9 gigs

1979
February
5   Wreckless Eric plays the first of 3 gigs
9   Joe Jackson makes his only appearance

March
4   The Cure begin a run of four Sundays, with support tonight from Joy Division

April
2–3   The Pretenders play the first two of an eventual 8 gigs
4   Salford poet John Cooper Clarke plays the first of 6 gigs

May
12   Mod revivalists Secret Affair play the first of 7 gigs
25   The Knack play the first of 2 gigs

June
5   The Cramps make a one-off appearance
10–11   Dub poet Linton Kwesi Johnson plays the first two of 3 gigs
15–17   Mod Weekend headlined by the Chords and the Purple Hearts
21–22   The Human League make their only appearances at the club

July
3   Simple Minds play the first of 6 gigs
31   Mod revivalists the Merton Parkas play the first of 12 gigs

August
1–4   The Undertones play four consecutive nights
12   Toyah plays the first of 5 gigs
19   The Vapors play the first of 10 gigs
26–28   Reading Rock 1979 takes place with a line-up that includes the Cure, Peter Gabriel, Gillan, Steve Hackett, Wilko Johnson, Nils Lofgren, Motörhead, the Police, the Scorpions, the Tourists and Whitesnake

October
1–5   999 play five consecutive nights
19   Iron Maiden play the first of 9 gigs

November
2   The Jam play a secret gig under the name John's Boys; it is their last Marquee appearance
3   Bauhaus, opening for the Books, make their only Marquee appearance

December
5   Glam-metal band Girl play the first of 21 gigs
15   Magnum play the first of 20 gigs
16   Samson play the first of 19 gigs

1980
January
3   Classix Nouveaux play the first of 3 gigs
6   Dexys Midnight Runners make their only appearance
27–28   Def Leppard play the first two of 3 gigs

February
22   Martha and the Muffins play the first of 3 gigs
25   Saxon play their only gig

March
4   Nine Below Zero play the first of 12 gigs
6–8   The Cure play three consecutive nights
15   The Q-Tips play the first of 15 gigs

MARQUEE TIMELINE

April
1   Hazel O'Connor plays the first of 2 gigs
2-3   The Tygers of Pan Tang, opening for Iron Maiden, play the first of 14 gigs
12   Tenpole Tudor play the first of 10 gigs

May
27   Joan Jett plays the first of 2 gigs
28-29   Robert Fripp's League of Gentlemen play two nights

June
7   U2, opening for White Spirit, play the first of 8 gigs
9   Girlschool play the first of 6 gigs

August
4-8   Athletico Spizz '80 play five consecutive nights
26-28   Reading 1980 takes place with a line-up that includes Budgie, Def Leppard, Gillan, Girl, Iron Maiden, Magnum, Samson, Slade, Tygers of Pan Tang, UFO and Whitesnake

September
8   U2 headline the first of four Mondays
10   The Associates play the first of 5 gigs
24-28   The Son of Stiff tour pulls into the Marquee with five nights of Stiff artists

October
19   Orange Juice open for the Associates for their sole Marquee appearance

November
9   Duran Duran step in at short notice to replace the Associates for their only Marquee appearance

December
7-8   The Stray Cats play two nights, the first of 5 gigs in a rockabilly revival

1981
January
5   The Thompson Twins play the first of 7 gigs
28-29   The Psychedelic Furs play two nights, their only gigs at the club

February
19   Theatre of Hate play their only gig

March
1   The Belle Stars play the first of 4 gigs

April
5   The Meteors play the first of 6 gigs
20-21   Rose Tattoo play the first two of 3 gigs

May
31   Midnight Oil play the first of 4 gigs

June
25   Neo-prog-rockers Twelfth Night, opening for Atomic Rooster, play the first of 26 gigs

August
28-30   Reading Rock 1981 takes place with a line-up that includes Atomic Rooster, Budgie, the Enid, Gillan, Girlschool, the Kinks, Greg Lake, Nine Below Zero, Rose Tattoo, Steve Hackett, Samson, Twelfth Night and Wishbone Ash
29   A Flock of Seagulls play their only gig

October
20   Marillion, opening for Girl, play the first of 21 gigs

November
22   Hanoi Rocks play the first of 10 gigs

December
12   The Police play a secret gig under the name the Aces; it is their last Marquee appearance
14   The Southern Death cult play their only gig
28-29   Lords of the New Church play the first two of 8 gigs

1982
January
23   Rock Goddess play the first of 30 gigs
25   Marillion play their first headline gig

March
10   Terraplane play the first of 23 gigs

June
2   Y&T play the first of 2 gigs

July
1-2   Howard Jones, opening for Marillion, plays the first of 15 gigs

August
2-3   Twisted Sister play the first two of 7 gigs
9   Sex Gang Children play the first of 4 gigs
18   Dumpy's Rusty Nuts, opening for Spider, play the first of 60 gigs (including as DRN, Dumpy's Rusty Bolts and Dumpy)
27-29   Reading 1982 takes place with a line-up that includes Budgie, Randy California, Dave Edmunds, Iron Maiden, Manowar, Marillion, Michael Schenker Group, Gary Moore, Rock Goddess, Bernie Tormé, Twisted Sister and Tygers of Pan Tang

September

2–3   Anvil play the first two of 3 gigs
22   Scots prog-rockers Pallas play the first of 22 gigs
25   Prog-rockers Pendragon, opening for Marillion, play the first of 37 gigs
27   Genesis play a secret gig under the name Garden Wall

October

18   Little Steven and the Disciples of Soul play a one-off gig

November

8   Thomas Dolby plays the first of four consecutive Mondays
21   The Alarm play the first of 9 gigs

1983
February

3   IQ, opening for Twelfth Night, play the first of 37 gigs

March

3   The The play the first of 4 consecutive Thursdays

April

The Marquee celebrates 25 years

5   Osibisa play the club for a second time; the first was back in July 1970
14–15 Chris Barber returns to the Marquee for two nights after a thirteen-year break
24   Blues by Six return to the Marquee for the first time since Match 1963
27   Screaming Lord Sutch plays his second gig; the first was back in November 1972
28–29 Alexis Korner returns to the Marquee for the first time since December 1966

May

1   Wrathchild play their only gig

June

19–21 John Mayall's Bluesbreakers return to the Marquee for the first time since 1969
22–23 The Yardbirds return to the Marquee for the first time since June 1966

July

1–2   Ten Years After return to the Marquee for the first time since February 1969
5–6   Motörhead play three consecutive nights
17   The Icicle Works play the first of 7 gigs

August

26–28 Reading 1983 takes place with a line-up that includes Anvil, Big Country, Black Sabbath, the Enid, Hanoi Rocks, Steve Harley and Cockney Rebel, Little Steven and the Disciples of Soul, Magnum, Mama's Boys, Marillion, Pallas, Suzi Quatro, Sad Café, Steel Pulse, the Stranglers, Ten Years After, Thin Lizzy, Twelfth Night and Stevie Ray Vaughan

October

16   ZZ Top play their one-and-only gig

November

14   New Model Army play the first of 8 gigs
22   REM play the first of 3 gigs

December

16   Carlene Carter plays her only gig

1984
February

6   Katrina and the Waves play the first of 2 gigs
24   Reggae band Musical Youth play their only gig

March

27   Metaliica play their first of 2 gigs; the second is the following month

June

24   The Waterboys play the first of 2 gigs
25   Lloyd Cole and the Commotions play the first of 2 gigs

August

There is no Reading festival this year

20–24 Johnny Thunders and the Heartbreakers play five consecutive nights

September

10   10,000 Maniacs play the first of 3 gigs
25   The March Violets play their only gig

October

3   Huey Lewis and the News play their only gig
5   Thrashing Doves play the first of 10 gigs
7   American alternative rockers Dream Syndicate make their only appearance

December

5   Goth rockers Fields of the Nephilim play the first of 13 gigs

1985
January

19   The Stone Roses play the first of 2 gigs
28   The Screaming Blue Messiahs play the first of 8 gigs

February

2   The Bolshoi play the first of 9 gigs

20   The Bangles play their only gig

April

25   The Long Ryders play their only gig

June

Jazz briefly returns to the Marquee

3   Swedish metal guitarist Yngwie
       Malmsteen plays his only gig

6-7   Lone Justice play the first of 4 gigs

July

6   Peter Green returns to the Marquee
       fronting Kolors

August

There is no Reading festival again this year

16   It Bites play the first of 6 gigs

October

28   Wham! film the video for 'I'm Your Man'

December

14   Erasure play the first of 2 gigs

1986

January

15   INXS play their only gig

20-22 John Waite plays three consecutive
       nights, the first of 5 gigs at the club

February

11-13 The Sweet play three consecutive nights

20   Mr Mister play their only gig

27   Mental As Anything play their only gig

May

20   Psychic TV play their only gig

25   Love and Rockets play their only gig

June

4-5   John Wetton, Robin George, Carl Palmer
       and Don Airey play 2 nights

July

30   Underworld play the first of 3 gigs

August

10-12 We've Got a Fuzzbox and We're Gonna
       Use It play, their only Marquee gigs

22-24 Reading 1986 takes place with a line-up
       that includes Balaam and the Angel,
       the Bolshoi, the Cardiacs, Dr and the
       Medics, Dumpy's Rusty Nuts, the Enid,
       Hawkwind, It Bites, Killing Joke, Lords
       of the New Church, the Mission, New
       Model Army, Saxon, Thrashing Doves,

John Waite and Zodiac Mindwarp and
the Love Reaction

September

8   Cutting Crew play their only gig

November

18   Deacon Blue play the first of 4 gigs

1987

January

20   The Wonder Stuff, opening for Then
       Jerico, play the first of 5 gigs

April

21   Chris Isaak plays the first of 2 gigs

May

7   The Georgia Satellites play their only gig

June

3   Bryan Adams plays his only gig

19   Guns N' Roses play the first of 3 gigs in
       ten days

August

5   Terence Trent D'Arby plays his only gig

27   All About Eve play their only gig; support
       comes from the Mission

28-30 Reading 1987 takes place with a line-
       up that includes All About Eve, Alice
       Cooper, Dumpy's Rusty Nuts, the Enid,
       the Fall, the Georgia Satellites, the Icicle
       Works, the Mission, Spear of Destiny,
       Status Quo, the Stranglers, Zodiac
       Mindwarp and the Love Reaction

November

19-20 Pop Will Eat Itself play two nights;
       support comes from the Wonder Stuff

1988

February

3   Robert Plant plays his only solo date

5-6   Faith No More play their only two nights

June

27   Sam Brown plays her only gig

July

11   Transvision Vamp play their only gig

18   Joe Satriani plays his only gig

31   Lisa Dominique becomes the last artist
       to play 90 Wardour Street

MOST APPEARANCES

The Joe Harriott Quintet made over 500 appearances at the Marquee between 1958 and 1965. Other jazz artists also made appearances numbering in the hundreds. The list below ignores the Oxford Street jazz years to focus on gigs played at 90 Wardour Street. It is impossible to give definitive figures for the numbers of gig played by most artists because the weekly ads in the music press, which are the key reference for who played when, do not always name the support acts.

Acts that played 90 Wardour Street 20 or more times

200	Long John Baldry, as a solo performer, and with the Hoochie Coochie Men, the Cyril Davies All-Stars and Steampacket	31	The Groundhogs/John Lee's Groundhogs
		30	David Bowie/and the Lower Third/and the Buzz
99	Mann-Hugg Blues Brothers/Blues Brothers/Manfred Mann/Manfred Mann's Earth Band	30	House of Lords
		30	Rock Goddess
		30	The Who
93	The T-Bones/Gary Farr and the T-Bones	29	Bernie Tormé
87	The Mark Leeman Five	29	Spencer Davis Group/Spencer Davis Band
63	Timebox/Patto		
60	Dumpy's Rusty Nuts/Bolts/DRN/Dumpy	29	Ten Years After
53	Brian Auger, with his Trio/Trinity/Oblivion Express, solo and with Steampacket	28	Savoy Brown/Savoy Brown Blues Band
		27	The Action
		27	The Boys
53	Cyril Davies All-Stars	27	The Move
53	Jimmy James and the Vagabonds	27	Village
49	Rory Gallagher/Taste	26	Twelfth Night
48	Mahatma Kane Jeeves/Mahatma	26	Wilko Johnson
47	Chelsea	25	Budgie
47	John Mayall's Bluesbreakers	25	Clouds
46	UFO	25	Medicine Head
45	The Yardbirds	24	Babe Ruth
42	Marmalade	24	Dream Police
42	Writing on the Wall	24	Keef Hartley
41	The Herd	24	Wild Turkey
40	Neat Change	23	Audience
39	The Enid	23	East of Eden
38	Alex Harvey/Alex Harvey Soul Band/Alex Harvey Group/Sensational Alex Harvey Band	23	Eddie and the Hot Rods
		23	Family
		23	Terraplane
38	Yes	23	Terry Reid
37	IQ	22	Fumble
37	Pendragon	22	Hardin and York
36	Spirit of John Morgan	22	Pallas
36	Stray	22	Sands
35	The Settlers	22	Skid Row
35	Solstice	22	Spizzenergi/Athletico Spizz '80/etc
35	Strider	22	Van der Graaf Generator
35	The Syn	21	Girl
33	Circus	21	Marillion
32	Al Stewart	21	The Moody Blues
32	The Nice	21	Steamhammer

LIVE AT THE MARQUEE

This list does not include studio albums recorded at Marquee Studios, only recordings of live performances at 90 Wardour Street that were given an official commercial release. They are ordered chronologically by release date, which is not always the same as the year they were recorded.

1964

The Yardbirds *Five Live Yardbirds*. The live debut album by the R&B pioneers, containing some of the earliest recordings with Eric Clapton. Recorded on 20 March 1964.

1966

Alan Bown Set/Jimmy James and the Vagabonds *London Swings: Live at the Marquee Club*. Two bluesy soul bands, both club regulars, get a side each. Recorded in 1966.

1968

The Move *Something Else from the Move*. An EP of tracks performed at a gig on 27 February 1968.

1971

Keef Hartley *Little Big Band*. Live album from the jazz/blues outfit featuring an eight-piece horn section that included Barbara Thompson. Recorded in 1971.

1976

Eddie and the Hot Rods *Live at the Marquee*. Four track EP including versions of Them's 'Gloria' and the Stones' 'Satisfaction'. Recorded on 9 July 1976.

1977

Brand X *Livestock*. Recordings from the jazz fusionists' 1977 tour, with one track from the Marquee on 23 April 1977.

Gong *Live etc*. One side of this double album features four tracks recorded at the Marquee in September 1974.

Kursaal Flyers *Five Live Kursaals*. The pub rockers final album. Recorded on 3-4 May 1977.

1978

Gillan *Live at the Marquee 1978*. A recording of the performance on the night in December 1978 that Ritchie Blackmore joined Gillan on stage for the encores.

Van der Graaf *Vital: Van der Graaf Live*. A first live album from the prog outfit, recorded in January 1978.

1980

Iron Maiden *Live!! +one*. A pre-Bruce Dickinson EP initially released only in Japan of a performance on 4 July 1980.

Magnum *Marauder*. A recording of a gig on 15 December 1979. The album was preceded by an EP *Live at the Marquee*, featuring material from the same show.

Nine Below Zero *Live at the Marquee*. Self-produced EP of blazing blues-rock covers. Recorded on 16 June 1980.

1981

The Meteors *In Heaven*. The first psychobilly album, recorded on 4 July 1981.

1983

The Alarm *The Alarm*. Studio EP that includes 'For Freedom' recorded at the Marquee on 30 January 1983.

Bow Wow *Holy Expedition*. Second live album by Japanese heavy-metal outfit. Recorded on 9 May 1983.

Gary Moore *Live*. Recorded over two nights on 6-7 November 1980. A later reissue was titled *Live at the Marquee*.

1984

Dumpy's Rusty Nuts *Somewhere in England*. Double live album from the biker band that played the Marquee more times than anybody else in the 1980s.

Hanoi Rocks *All Those Wasted Years*. First live album by the Finnish rock band, recorded in December 1983.

Osibisa *Live at the Marquee*. An album by the British Afro-rock band Osibisa, recorded live on 5 April 1983.

Stray *Live at the Marquee*. The first release by Stray since their 1977 album *Hearts of Fire*. Recorded in 1983.

Twelfth Night *Live and Let Live*. Recorded on 4–5 November 1983 at the final gigs with singer Geoff Mann.

1985

Robyn Hitchcock and the Egyptians *Gotta Let This Hen Out!* Recorded at a 27 April 1985 show, shortly after the release of the Egyptians' first studio album.

The Sound *In the Hothouse*. The only live album by the south London post-punks, recorded over two nights in August 1985.

1986

The Babysitters *Live at the Marquee*. A five-track EP recorded on 18–19 September 1986.

1987

Cherry Bombz *Coming Down Slow*. The only album release by the band. Recorded on 3 September 1986.

Iron Maiden *Live in London*. A recording of the 19 December 1985 gig in which members of Maiden performed under the name the Entire Population of Hackney.

1989

The Sweet *Live at the Marquee*. A recording of a 1986 gig by the reformed band, with Paul Mario Day on vocals.

1992

Fleetwood Mac *Live at the Marquee*. A low-fidelity recording of a Peter Green-era gig from 15 August 1967.

1994

Hardin and York *Live at the Marquee*. Mini album from former Spencer Davis Group members Eddie Hardin and Pete York. Recorded in 1971.

1998

Guns N' Roses Guns N' Roses. The second EP by the band, recorded at the Marquee on 28 June 1987.

King Crimson *Live at the Marquee*. A release through the King Crimson Collectors' Club of a performance on 6 July 1969.

2000

John Mayall *Live at the Marquee*. A set recorded on 30 June 1969, when the band was being filmed for a documentary, *The Turning Point*.

2001

Girl *Live at the Marquee*. Live set by the British glam rock band that was included as a bonus disc with reissue of 1982's *Wasted Youth*. Recorded in October 1981.

2002

Atomic Rooster *Live at the Marquee 1980*. Recorded November 1980.

Camel *Mirage*. The second studio album by the prog rockers was originally released in 1974; the 2002 remaster includes three live tracks recorded in October 1974.

2003

Man *Friday 13th*. The first new release following the Welsh rocker's reunion, recorded live at the Marquee on, indeed, Friday, 13 May 1983, during the club's 25th anniversary celebrations.

2008

Marillion *Early Stages (Official Bootleg Box Set 1982-1987)*. A box set containing live recordings of Marillion with Fish. Two discs of the five-disc set are of a performance on 30 December 1982.

2013

Psychic TV *Live at Thee Marquee*. A complete show from 20 May 1986, featuring the line-up of Genesis P-Orridge, Alex Fergusson, Mouse and Matthew Best.

2015

The Rolling Stones *From the Vault: The Marquee Club Live in 1971*. The Stones' March 1971 appearance was a closed gig filmed for broadcast in America. It received a belated CD/DVD release to coincide with the deluxe reissue of *Sticky Fingers*.

U2 *Another Time, Another Place: Live at the Marquee London 1980*. A fan club release of an incomplete concert recorded on 29 September 1980.

2018

Budgie *Live at the Marquee 1974*. Recorded 11 February 1974, with members of Judas Priest guesting on the encore.

Magma *AKT XVIII – Marquee*. Live set from the French cosmic rockers recorded at the Marquee way back on 17 March 1974.

Twisted Sister *Live at the Marquee 1983*. Recording of tracks from two shows on 5–6 March 1983, released to accompany a reissue of the band's 1983 debut album, *You Can't Stop Rock'n'Roll*.

BIBLIOGRAPHY

In addition to the books below, the websites ukrockfestivals.com, punk77. co.uk and the now defunct punkygibbon.co.uk were invaluable. The Alex Wharton quotes used in this book come courtesy of brumbeat.net.

Ant, Adam *Stand and Deliver: My Autobiography* (Sidgwick & Jackson, 2006)

Bacon, Tony *London Live* (Miller Freeman Books, 1999)

Boyd, Joe *White Bicycles: Making Music in the 1960s* (Serpent's Tail, 2006)

Clapton, Eric *Eric Clapton: The Autobiography* (Century, 2007)

Collins, Phil *Not Dead Yet: Phil Collins – The Autobiography* (Century, 2016)

Farren, Mick *Give the Anarchist a Cigarette* (Jonathan Cape, 2001)

Groom, Chris *Strat! The Charismatic Life and Times of Tony Stratton Smith* (Wymer Publishing, 2021)

Haynes, Pete *God's Lonely Men: The Lurkers* (Head-Hunter, 2007)

Hayward, Keith *Tin Pan Alley: The Rise of Elton John* (Soundcheck Books, 2013)

Hedges, Dan *Yes: The Authorised Biography* (Sidgwick & Jackson, 1982)

Holder, Noddy *Who's Crazee Now?* (Ebury, 1999)

Hutchinson, John *Bowie and Hutch* (Lodge Books, 2014)

Jones, Kenney *Let The Good Times Roll: My Life in Small Faces, Faces and The Who* (Blink Publishing, 2018)

Kilmister, Lemmy *White Line Fever – Lemmy: The Autobiography* (Simon & Schuster, 2002)

Lancaster, Phil *Can't Help Thinking About Me – At the Birth of Bowie* (John Blake, 2018)

Mason, Nick *Inside Out: A Personal History of Pink Floyd* (Weidenfeld & Nicolson, 2004)

Massey, Howard *The Great British Recording Studios* (Hal Leonard Books, 2015)

Myers, Paul *It Ain't Easy: Long John Baldry and the Birth of the British Blues* (Greystone Books, 2007)

Rutherford, Mike *The Living Years* (Constable, 2014)

Schwartz, Roberta Freund *How Britain Got the Blues* (Ashgate Publishing, 2007)

Snider, Dee *Shut Up and Give Me The Mic* (Gallery Books, 2012)

Stewart, Rod *Rod: The Autobiography* (Century, 2012)

Thomas, Bruce *Rough Notes* (Rough Notes Press, 2015)

Thomson, Graeme *Cowboy Song: The Authorised Biography of Phil Lynott* (Constable, 2016)

Tolhurst, Lol *Cured: The Tale of Two Imaginary Boys* (Da Capo Press, 2016)

Wall, Mick *AC/DC: Hell Ain't a Bad Place to Be* (Orion, 2012)

INDEX

Numbers in **bold** refer to images.

PICTURE CREDITS

pp6–8 Nick Powell, used by permission of Twelfth Night; pp18–9, p280 Richard Bellia; p26, p78, p92, p93, p117 the Pendleton family; p29, p69, p101, p189, p252 Getty Images; p75 Kingsley Abbott; pp196–97, pp212–13 ©Adrian Boot; pp242–43 image kindly supplied by Dan Henderson, photographer unknown. The Marquee ads are scanned from old copies of *Melody Maker*.

maRquee

THE STORY OF THE WORLD'S GREATEST MUSIC VENUE CONTINUES

In 2023 Paradise Road will be producing a pictorial history of the Marquee drawing on the extensive archive of the Pendleton family, which includes newsletters, posters, flyers, tickets, contracts and all manner of other documents, plus many never before seen photographs. We are looking for additional material to include in the book. If you have any interesting items relating to the Marquee, please get in touch. We are also looking for unique stories and anecdotes.

Contact us at info@paradiseroad.co.uk

Paradise Road publishes non-fiction books about London. For more information on other Paradise Road titles, visit www.paradiseroad.co.uk

Thank you for reading.